MW01098188

A ROAD *to* HEALING

Daily Reflections For Divorced Catholics

By Lisa Duffy

Also by CatholicMatch Institute:

The Catholic's Guide To Being Single

Online Dating Guide: A Simple Guide For Catholics

Purposeful Dating

Top Ten Reasons You Should Get Married

The Catholic Playbook: Lenten Reflections For Singles

CatholicMatch Institute
PO Box 154
Zelienople, PA 16063
www.CatholicMatchInstitute.com
www.CatholicMatch.com

. . . .

TABLE OF CONTENTS

PREFACE

In the early 1990's, I went through a bitter, messy, unwanted divorce. It was something I never expected to happen, and it threw my life into a tailspin filled with overwhelming emotions, pain, and grand disillusionment. I searched for books or support groups to help myself, but there was little to find and nothing that would help me stay close to my faith. So I turned to the world for healing.

After wandering in the desert for a few years and inflicting even more hurt upon myself, I embraced my faith, the sacraments, and the understanding that God would bring me through the fire to the other side. He did, and I am a better person for the experience.

This book is born out of the sufferings and joys I experienced along the way. I would like to share those gifts from God with you. Most of these reflections were written as I sat in the presence of the Lord in an adoration chapel, asking God what He wanted me to write for you. I do not know your personal circumstances, but I believe God has a message for you in these little reflections. I believe He will give you the hope and strength you need along your journey of healing.

DAILY REFLECTIONS

Day 1:
Never Give Up

"What oxygen is to the lungs, such is hope for the meaning of life."

~ Emil Brunner

Never give up hope! Your life is difficult now and the suffering may seem endless, but it won't always be this way. This is only one period of your life and things WILL change for the better.

Now is the time for persevering, strengthening, and being attentive to the gentle whisper of the Holy Spirit in your heart. Hope in the Lord and be not afraid!

"For everything there is a season, and a time for every matter under heaven: a time to be born, and a time to die; / a time to plant, and a time to pluck up what is planted; / a time to kill, and a time to heal; / a time to break down, and a time to build up; / a time to weep, and a time to laugh;/ a time to mourn, and a time to dance."

~ Ecclesiastes 3:1-4

Day 2:
Why Does God Allow Divorce?

Why does God allow divorce to happen? He allows it for many reasons, but primarily because He has given us all the gift of free will. He loves us so much that He will never force us to choose one way or another. Divorce happens because someone made a terrible choice, but every time a poor choice is made, it is an opportunity for God to bring about great things, even miracles in the lives of those who are suffering. Have faith that God will bring good things out of what has happened. It's His specialty.

We know that all things work together for good for those who love God, who are called according to his purpose.

~ Romans 8:28

Day 3:
Feeling Down?

When you are lacking the motivation to do what needs to be done, step back from the task, sit down, and contemplate Christ. He is so full of love for you. He knows the stress, anxiety and pain you are handling because of your divorce. Imagine Him in the manger, a tiny baby who was God, yet at the same time human and completely reliant on others. Imagine Him as the Good Shepherd with you, a precious lamb around His neck, as He carries you home. When you rest in Him, He will refresh you. Christ makes all things new!

I will satisfy the weary, / and all who are faint I will replenish.

~ Jeremiah 31:25

Day 4:
Suffering Is Good?

Your suffering is not useless. It is not in vain if you offer it up for the good of others—peace in the world, the souls in purgatory, a sick friend, or those who are lonely and have no one to pray for them. Uniting your suffering to Christ's is one way He allows us to play a role in His redemptive work. When you hurt and feel alone, take advantage of this wonderful opportunity to unite your pain to Christ crucified, for the sake of souls. You will turn your pain into a priceless gift.

Indeed we call blessed those who showed endurance. You have heard of the endurance of Job, and you have seen the purpose of the Lord, how the Lord is compassionate and merciful.

~ James 5:11

Day 5:
The Pearl

So many people believe that realizing their dreams is defined by the quality and quantity of their earthly possessions. Dream homes are sought after following a simple rule of thumb: "Location, location, location!" How about a different rule of thumb to attain happiness? "Adoration, adoration, adoration!"

Spending time in Eucharistic adoration is the surest way to find healing and peace, something many people do not possess, even in their dream homes. The sacraments and a solid relationship with Christ will bring you true and complete happiness in this life and the next.

On finding one pearl of great value,
he went and sold all that he had and bought it.

~ Matthew 13:46

Day 6:
Perfect In The Eyes Of God

———————◇———————

Divorce can make you feel unwanted, unlovable, and ashamed of your human imperfections and failures. But God does not see you this way. He sees His beloved in all the beauty and glory of His creation. Ask God to reveal to you the gifts He's given you that you are unaware. Maybe you have hidden talents that you've never used. Ask Him to bring all this to light for you, that you may find your new purpose in life.

———————

So if anyone is in Christ, there is a new creation: everything old has passed away; see, everything has become new!

~ 2 Corinthians 5:17

Day 7:
Hidden Blessings

Remember as a child on Christmas morning searching behind the Christmas tree, hoping to find more gifts? You can do the same when you are suffering. Look behind your cross for hidden gifts—blessings you don't readily recognize. Have you come closer to Christ as a result of your divorce? Was there an abusive behavior tearing the family apart that has now ceased since your ex-spouse left? Are you now free to live your faith to the fullest, whereas you were held back from that during your marriage? There are probably many hidden gifts behind the cross that are waiting to be discovered.

Looking to Jesus the pioneer and perfecter of our faith, who for the sake of the joy that was set before him endured the cross, disregarding its shame, and has taken his seat at the right hand of the throne of God.

~ Hebrews 12:2

Day 8:
Avoid Becoming A Victim

Gratitude is crucial to the healing process. Avoid self-pity which acts as a major stumbling block to finding gratitude. Having a victim mentality is a slippery slope. Sometimes we allow righteous anger to turn into victimization. This is detrimental to the healing process and achieving peace. Victims are created when anger is fostered and cultivated. Although a natural reaction to being betrayed by a spouse, righteous anger must eventually take a back seat to mercy, forgiveness and patience.

But if you do not forgive others,
neither will your Father forgive your trespasses.

~ Matthew 6:15

Day 9:
Don't Waste Time Feeling Jealous

Another stumbling block to finding gratitude, in the midst of difficulty, is jealousy. Being jealous of others is a tremendous waste of time and energy. Each day we wake up, breathe and live is a gift from God. Why waste it all being consumed with jealousy? It is pointless, and even more so, it does nothing to help you heal and move on, or ultimately, get to heaven.

The commandments, "You shall not commit adultery;
You shall not murder; You shall not steal; You shall not covet";
and any other commandment, are summed up in this word,
"Love your neighbor as yourself."

~ Romans 13:9

Day 10:
Seeing The Good In Others

Another stumbling block to finding gratitude in the midst of diffi-culty is failing to focus on the good of others. This can be difficult to do, but try starting with someone who is already in your good graces—a child, a friend, etc. Then work your way through your circle of acquaintances, friends and family. Always look specifically for the good qualities of another. Did a neighbor bring you a meal or run an errand for you? Did a co-worker treat you kindly? Find a way to see the good in others and then try to keep that perspective constant. The Holy Spirit will show you many good things you may have been missing.

For to this end Christ died and lived again,
so that he might be Lord of both the dead and the living.

~ Romans 14:9

Day 11:
Make A Commitment To Prayer

Having a prayer routine takes effort. We need to find creative ways to fit prayer into our busy schedule. In the midst of a divorce, however, the intense pain makes praying very difficult. Often, prayer is the first thing to fall by the wayside. This is unfortunate because prayer is the one thing that helps us the most in trying times. Communication with Christ, Our Lord and Savior, is key to helping cope with the pain, emotions, disappointments and responsibilities we must face.

So I encourage you to make a simple commitment; one that should only take a few minutes out of your day. When you open your eyes in the morning, even before you get out of bed, say a brief prayer and thank God for the new day. Ask Him for strength. At noon, say a Hail Mary, asking the Blessed Mother to show you the way. Then at night, before you sleep, review your day and thank God again. You will find great comfort and renewed hope by practicing this simple, effective prayer routine.

I am the vine, you are the branches. Those who abide in me and I in them bear much fruit, because apart from me you can do nothing.

~ John 15:5

Day 12:
Managing Anger

Anger is deceiving. It's an emotion that can make you believe it's worth gripping. It's powerful, demanding, and overwhelms you in a moment's notice. While it is a God-given emotion, one that Christ, Himself, certainly felt as a human being, it is an emotion that needs to be mastered. Many people become slaves to their anger and live lives full of bitterness and anxiety because they do not master it. Becoming a slave to your emotions makes you a victim, and then it becomes difficult to live a happy and fulfilled life. Feeling angry is not bad or wrong. How you act upon that anger is what may cause you more suffering, stress, and grief.

Journaling is an excellent way to begin managing your feelings of anger. Writing out, word for word, how you feel and why you feel that way becomes not only a cathartic exercise but a prayer. Your anger will dissipate and eventually disappear if you release your grip on it. Let it flow through the pen, and then let it go.

So when you are offering your gift at the altar, if you remember that your brother or sister has something against you, leave your gift there before the altar and go; first be reconciled to your brother or sister, and then come and offer your gift.

~ Matthew 5:23-24

Day 13:
Lazarus, Come Out!

People say divorce is like death. But if you've been divorced, you understand it is much more than losing a loved one. The pain is overshadowed by shame and feelings of failure. Often frustration continues because although you've lost your spouse, he or she is still around to make you hurt. In times like these, happiness can seem an impossible dream. But this is not the case. No matter what your circumstances, if you are with Christ, you will experience true happiness again because Christ makes all things new. Think of Martha and Mary who were grieving the loss of Lazarus, "Lord, if you had been here, my brother would not have died!" (John 11:21). Jesus allowed it to happen because it was an opportunity to glorify God. He raised Lazarus from the dead! And in the way that is best for you, He will do the same in your life. Hope in Christ! Divorce is not the end!

---

*Jesus said to her, "I am the resurrection and the life.
Those who believe in me, even though they die, will live,
and everyone who lives and believes in me will never die.*

~ John 11:25-26

Day 14:
The Eighth Sacrament

The only thing that can bring true and lasting healing from the wounds of divorce is God's grace. We receive healing grace through the sacraments and other instruments the Holy Spirit chooses to use. One of those instruments is the Catholic annulment process. Many people refer to it as the eighth sacrament because of its healing nature. Although it is not a sacrament, it should be approached in the same manner, with humility and openness to God's will. By detaching ourselves from our personal desires and expectations, we allow the Holy Spirit to guide us and those involved with the annulment process. And finally, as the truth of what happened is determined, we are provided with the certainty we need to lay the past to rest and move on to a new phase of life.

And hope does not disappoint us, because God's love has been poured into our hearts through the Holy Spirit that has been given to us.

~ Romans 5:5

Day 15:
Tell Satan To Take A Hike!!

The devil knows our weaknesses. When you go through a divorce, it only creates more opportunity for him to attack us. He takes advantage of our loneliness, depression, anger and frustration. The devil does not want you to be happy. He does not want you to turn to God in your time of need, so be assured he is working hard to convince you that your situation is hopeless. He wants you to believe that living a good life is just too difficult, so there is no hope for happiness unless you follow the way of the world. The devil wants you to believe that you are an outcast in your Church. But FEAR NOT!!! As a baptized Catholic you have grace in your soul, and Satan cannot compete with that. You always have the upper hand because God has given you His grace. So don't believe in the devil's lies and empty promises! Trust in God, for He will deliver you! Have faith in what you know is right and PRAY! And tell Satan to TAKE A HIKE!!

But he turned and said to Peter, "Get behind me, Satan!
You are a stumbling block to me; for you are setting your mind not on
divine things but on human things."

~ Matthew 16:23

Day 16:
Finding Strength In The Cross

It is not surprising that Jesus fell down three times under the weight of the cross, as well as from the pain of His wounds, as He walked to Calvary. But what is incredible is the fact that He got up—THREE TIMES! His love for us motivated Him to wipe away the blood dripping into His eyes, embrace the cross, and get back on His feet. Although Jesus was suffering under the weight of the cross, He used that huge wooden cross as leverage as He got up from the ground. This is an important point to reflect upon.

Just like Christ's heavy cross, our suffering can be used as leverage, even a springboard to a new and higher level of living. Contrary to what society tells us about suffering which is that we need to avoid it at all costs, suffering is a cleansing and renewing process that changes your life for the better, if you allow it. Your cross is heavy and painful, and difficult to handle, but it can prop you up, too. Contemplate Christ on the road to Calvary—the beatings from the soldiers, the trail of blood, and the falls. His motivation was love for us!

Try to offer your suffering up for someone you love and ask Jesus to give you the grace to persevere.

But rejoice insofar as you are sharing Christ's sufferings, so that you may also be glad and shout for joy when his glory is revealed.

~ 1 Peter 4:13

16

Day 17:
God Has Not Abandoned You!

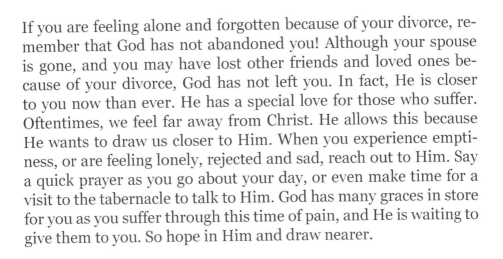

If you are feeling alone and forgotten because of your divorce, remember that God has not abandoned you! Although your spouse is gone, and you may have lost other friends and loved ones because of your divorce, God has not left you. In fact, He is closer to you now than ever. He has a special love for those who suffer. Oftentimes, we feel far away from Christ. He allows this because He wants to draw us closer to Him. When you experience emptiness, or are feeling lonely, rejected and sad, reach out to Him. Say a quick prayer as you go about your day, or even make time for a visit to the tabernacle to talk to Him. God has many graces in store for you as you suffer through this time of pain, and He is waiting to give them to you. So hope in Him and draw nearer.

Hear a just cause, O Lord; attend to my cry; /
give ear to my prayer from lips free of deceit.

~ Psalm 17:1

17

Day 18:
What Is Love?

———◇———

Love is an act of the will to desire to put another's happiness first before our own. Jesus said that we must love our enemies. This must have been very difficult for people in Jesus' time to hear and accept. It is difficult for me to hear and accept, and I have been hearing it since I was little. These teachings of Jesus were really quite revolutionary since they were contrary to what had been taught before in the Old Testament. It's clear to see that Jesus was trying to explain to people what is the actual meaning of love.

Jesus' definition of love is contrary to what society wants us to believe. Society's definition of love includes passiveness, allowance of deviant behavior, and fluffy feelings. Jesus tells us that love is none of these things. Instead, love is hard; love is difficult. Even when we have been unjustly treated, we must still wish for the good of the one who has hurt us. Even when we are understandably angry, we must still serve the needs of the one who has mistreated us. We must set aside our own feelings and seek the good of others, no matter what.

In doing so, we will be rewarded as Christ promises us. But when eternity seems so far off, and the hurt we are enduring seems to be so real and unbearable, it is difficult to persevere in love for those who hurt us. That is why prayer is so essential. Prayer is what will keep us connected to Christ, the Vine, and His grace will sustain us in our trials.

———

But I say to you, Love your enemies
and pray for those who persecute you.

~ Matthew 5:44

Day 19:
The Culture Of Divorce

Society makes it easy for divorced men and women to fall away from their faith. It's an environment that I call the "culture of divorce." People congratulate you on your divorce, or run to be the first one to set you up with the "perfect" date, etc. The entire mentality encourages the newly divorced to live it up, celebrate and engage in every type of self-serving behavior imaginable. What they don't tell you is that, down the road, you will be in worse shape than ever—more hurt, more disillusioned, and certainly farther away from your relationship with Christ, if you follow this path.

Don't be fooled by those who don't care about the fate of your soul. A new relationship will not heal you. Christ is the great Healer, and only He can give you the peace and healing you are seeking. Look to Him for what you need and He will provide it. You were made for great things and in following God's plan, you will experience more peace, more joy, and more love than the world can ever give you.

Your faith has saved you; go in peace.

~ Luke 7:50

19

Day 20:
God Is Not Looking For The Christian Who Has It All Together

Contrary to popular opinion, God is not looking for Christians that have everything under control, have perfect families, and have perfect spiritual lives. When my ex-spouse first left, I made the mistake of begging him to come to my family reunion and pretend, for my family's sake, that nothing was wrong with us. He reluctantly agreed, and we showed up as a couple. I was too ashamed and embarrassed that we were getting a divorce to let anyone in my family know; I didn't want to let them down or bring more shame upon myself. The unfortunate thing was that I had not yet realized how much my family loved me, and I never gave them the opportunity to show me. I found out months later, after the news finally broke, when they all came to love and support me. But even more regrettably was the fact that another relative's marriage was on the rocks and headed for divorce. Since I was busy pretending my marriage was fine, I missed the opportunity to talk with her on a level that we both needed to support each other.

We are not perfect. Our families are not perfect. Life is not perfect. Christ is not looking for "perfect" Christians. He wants us the way we are, with all our imperfections, so He can guide us to perfection. Let us strive to be more real, more accepting, and more loving of each other and understand that life is not perfect.

Which one of you, having a hundred sheep and losing one of them, does not leave the ninety-nine in the wilderness and go after the one that is lost until he finds it?

~ Luke 15:4

Day 21:
Letting Go

─────────◇─────────

"In my daily life, everywhere I turned, there were reminders of her...
I didn't want to let go. I took comfort in not letting go because I didn't
have to face the challenges of starting my life anew.
Even today, almost a year removed from my divorce
I think about my wife every day."

~ Grant, Voices of Hope DVD - Letting Go

Letting go of past relationships, especially a marriage, can be difficult. There is a sense of security and hope that comes with clinging to what you love, even if it no longer really exists. There is nothing wrong with this. We are human beings made of flesh and blood with hearts that were created for love. It is natural to cling to what you want. But in the end, finding a way to detach yourself from what no longer exists is better. Why? Because in detaching yourself from the person or situation, you give God permission to do His work. And in His infinite wisdom, He will always bring good things out of the pain.

──────────────

And the one who was seated on the throne said,
"See, I am making all things new." Also he said, "Write this,
for these words are trustworthy and true."

~ Revelation 21:5

Day 22:
Let Your Suffering Have Meaning

———◇———

"I never really thought that there could be a positive side to suffering, I mean, who wants to suffer? I certainly didn't and I couldn't understand why I was having to go through this."

~ Kristen, Voices of Hope DVD - The Value of Suffering

Suffering is certainly the antithesis of our societal message. The Carly Simon song, *Haven't Got Time for the Pain*, was a popular song lyric, turned pain reliever commercial jingle, turned modern perspective. In contemporary terms, with millions of Americans taking antidepressant medications, this motto's bite has some seriously sharp teeth. The truth of the matter is that people don't have time for the pain because they don't know how to suffer.

Suffering is a process which takes time to get through. You can't take a Tylenol to relieve emotional pain; you must walk through the fire so-to-speak. But the beauty of suffering is change, and the process of suffering changes you. Now you can allow it to change you for the better or for the worse. It's entirely your decision. Suffering purges, cleanses and builds character. Heroes and saints have suffered greatly, and you have the opportunity to do the same. Let your suffering have meaning by offering it up for others, for instance, the souls in purgatory, a sick friend, or your ex-spouse. There are endless opportunities for offering up suffering. But most of all, be patient. Though your divorce is painful, you can be assured that God is using this for your benefit. Your blessings will be abundant!

———

For you, O God, have tested us; / you have tried us as silver is tried.

~ Psalms 66:10

Day 23:
Nurture Your Faith

On a plane before takeoff, you are instructed that if oxygen masks become necessary, you should put your own on before you put one on your child. Well, the same holds true with faith. If your own faith isn't strong and healthy, your children will pick up on that. Why would they believe that faith is important and true if they know that you don't truly believe that? Work on growing your own faith while working on nurturing your children's faith. You'll be showing them that you know how important faith is even when you have doubts.

Rooted and built up in him and established in the faith, just as you were taught, abounding in thanksgiving.

~ Colossians 2:7

Day 24:
Forgive Yourself!

Often we can't let go of the guilt and shame of our sin, even after confessing and being resolved of those sins. Even though confession wipes the slate clean in God's eyes, we aren't always able to forgive ourselves. We are reluctant to believe we are worthy of the depth of love that elicits forgiveness. In essence, we don't believe we are worthy of love, mercy or forgiveness because we don't see ourselves through the eyes of Christ.

Brothers and sisters, gaze at the Crucifix! Do you believe that Jesus Christ died for others' souls but not yours? What can you possibly do to offend Him that He would not forgive if you repent and confess your sins? If God can forgive you, how is it that you cannot forgive yourself? Are you greater than He? Are you more complicated, or more sophisticated? Perhaps you believe you know yourself better than He knows you.

The truth is Jesus died so that you and I might catch a faint glimpse of the depth of His love and begin to understand our worthiness in His eyes. Lift Him high and look up in hope and gratitude and know that you are forgiven.

As far as the east is from the west, /
so far he removes our transgressions from us.

~ Psalms 103:12

Day 25:
I Think I Can

The way that we think and feel impacts the way that we behave. Choosing to control what we allow ourselves to think can greatly relieve emotional angst. It gives us power over our own reactions. It is a good feeling to look back and know that we have handled a treacherous life situation in a kind and compassionate manner. This is not to say that being assertive is not important. Healthy people have boundaries. Keeping the focus on our own behavior is often very hard, but it gives us the ability to choose an exemplary response to hurtfulness.

Finally, beloved, whatever is true, whatever is honorable,
whatever is just, whatever is pure, whatever is pleasing,
whatever is commendable, if there is any excellence and if there is
anything worthy of praise, think about these things.

~ Philippians 4:8

Day 26:
God's Passionate Love

Do you find it hard to celebrate love? Friends become engaged, but you just don't feel the love. Your brother and sister-in-law celebrate an anniversary, but you can't share in their joy. It's hard to feel the joy of another's love when you're not feeling worthy of being loved yourself. In order to handle these situations, try to imagine being passionately loved—the most wildly passionate love you have ever dreamed! Now realize that this is how God loves you. You are worth everything to Him, and He demonstrated that when He hung on the cross and gave you everything. You are the one He wants, and He pursues you at every moment of the day. He wants to give you the love, peace and happiness you've been waiting to receive.

Can a woman forget her nursing child, / or show no compassion for the child of her womb? / Even these may forget, / yet I will not forget you.

~ Isaiah 49:15

Day 27:
Living In Fear

---◇---

One obstacle to the happiness we desire is fear. Because our lives are completely dependent on the gift of our Creator, and since we lack perfect trust in His love, we live in constant fear of our vulnerability. This fear is so natural that we don't pay much attention to it. Nevertheless, our thoughts, feelings and actions are constantly influenced by a conscious pursuit of security. The happiness God desires for us involves a freedom from these fears. Notice how often references to fear or anxiety appear in Scripture and in the language of the Mass.

In order to free ourselves from these fears, we have to first acknowledge and accept our weaknesses, insecurities, and vulnerabilities. Then we can work toward accepting God's unique plan for each one of us. Through this acceptance, we grow closer to the Father, who longs to free us from fear and lead us to perfect happiness.

Do not fear, or be afraid; / have I not told you from of old and declared it / You are my witnesses! / Is there any god besides me? / There is no other rock; I know not one.

~ Isaiah 44:8

Day 28:
Are You Listening?

Every day, and at every moment, Christ is trying to get our attention. He is constantly trying to show His love for us and lead us along the right path. But we are distracted. We are not interested. We don't understand. We are not listening. Our faith is weak and we doubt. Is it any wonder, then, that it's during the painful times that He is able to really help us? Those times when we finally look to Him for answers? Maybe that's one great lesson of enduring pain—that through our pain, we allow Christ to come into focus, and we allow Him the opportunity to give us what we need.

But strive first for the kingdom of God and his righteousness, and all these things will be given to you as well.

~ Matthew 6:33

Day 29:
Give Your Pain To God

The anger and disillusionment we feel after a divorce may cause us to distance ourselves from God and from the Church. When we are at church, we look around at happy families and loving couples, and we feel hurt and jealous. All we seem to be able to do is focus on our pain. If this sounds familiar, give your pain to God. Come back to Him, confess your sins, and resolve to improve your life a little bit each day. You can do this through prayer and by leaving behind the things that keep you away from God. He will bless you in ways you cannot even imagine.

Come to me, all you that are weary and are carrying heavy burdens, and I will give you rest.

~ Matthew 11:28

Day 30:
Forgiveness

Forgiveness is a powerful word and in the height of anger, many people choke on it. Why? Because a crime deserves a punishment? Well, yes. But primarily because forgiveness is hard. We don't want to let the offender off the hook! We want justice! Make them pay! Some days we feel so beaten down, we just want justice; we just want someone to say, "I'm sorry." But no one does, so forgiveness becomes even harder.

When you learn how to forgive, you will begin to heal. There will be times when we don't want to forgive. That's when God's grace takes over. God will fill in what we are lacking. He loves to do this for us. He waits for the opportunity to help. We simply need to give Him the authority to take over our hearts.

Therefore, I tell you, her sins, which were many, have been forgiven;
hence she has shown great love.
But the one to whom little is forgiven, loves little.

~ Luke 7:47

Day 31:
How to Pray

"I had never experienced so much fear and pain in my life. The night my wife told me she was leaving, I dropped to my knees for the first time since I was a kid," said Craig. Craig's Catholic friends encouraged him to continue praying, but each had a different suggestion on how to pray: "One suggested I pray a novena. Another suggested I pray the rosary every day. Others suggested I pray to specific saints. My sister told me to make sure I went to adoration for an hour each week to pray."

Prayer is loving communication with God. It should be heartfelt and not contrived. The Catholic faith supplies us with a treasure of prayers, novenas and devotions. Sometimes it can be confusing to try to figure out what prayer to say. Simply find the method of prayer that feels most comfortable for you and talk to God. He is waiting to hear from you; and He is listening!

So I say to you, Ask, and it will be given you; search, and you will find; knock, and the door will be opened for you.

~ Luke 11:9

Day 32:
The Interior Castle Of Prayer

St. Teresa of Avila, one of the greatest saints of the Catholic Church, had a beautiful way of praying. She referred to it as the "interior castle" and described it as her innermost self. Inside her soul, there was a castle. And out of the many rooms in the castle, there was one particular room reserved for meeting with God. When she entered the room, she was alone with Christ and felt free to tell Him everything. She held back nothing in order to receive all that He gave her. She would go to that room often to meet with Christ, and there she would find all the strength and hope she needed to continue her work.

If you're a visual person, this is an effective form of prayer, especially during times of great distress. Simply imagine God with you, walking beside you, and listening to you. He will meet you in the castle.

Do not fear, for I am with you, / do not be afraid, for I am your God;
I will strengthen you, I will help you,
I will uphold you with my victorious right hand.

~ Isaiah 41:10

Day 33:
Channel Your Anger

Anger is a God-given emotion. It's a completely normal reaction to things or circumstances that threaten our physical, emotional or spiritual well-being. However, you don't have to allow your emotions to run your life so that you become a victim of your own emotions. As Kayla said, "Will I allow my divorce to drag me down, lose all hope, all trust, and become bitter? Or will I let my pain motivate me to move forward, to learn some lessons about life, to search for hope in my future?"

St. John Vianney was known for channeling his anger. He would take great care in the presence of whoever was frustrating him to be calm and charitable. But if you looked closely, you would see a twisted, knotted handkerchief in his hands that received all the punishment!

But I say to you, Love your enemies and pray for those who persecute you, so that you may be children of your Father in heaven; for he makes his sun rise on the evil and on the good, and sends rain on the righteous and on the unrighteous.

~ Matthew 5:44-45

Day 34:
God Has A Plan

Does God really have a plan? Was this divorce part of His plan? It seems difficult to believe that He would want such terrible pain and suffering to be part of His great design.

Sometimes, particularly in the face of disaster and distress, our beliefs are challenged. It's difficult to find a reason why God has allowed bad things to happen to us. But if you can find hope, you are able to light your path through the darkness. Hope gives you the ability to rise above the despair and confusion. With hope, you can set your feet firmly upon the path you need to walk, even though you may not understand why things are happening.

Trust in the Lord with all your heart,
and do not rely on your own insight.
In all your ways acknowledge him,
and he will make straight your paths.

~ Proverbs 3:5-6

Day 35:
Does God Want Me To Be Miserable?

Despite the agony of your situation, God does not want your life to be miserable. God is not sitting up in heaven, aloof, like some cold, distant observer who is unmoved and unloving. Quite the contrary, God is so close to you, even closer than you know.

The crosses that you bear are blessings. When you suffer—you learn, you grow, you change, you become wiser, and you become more loving. You become more like Christ. Suffering can be the door to a new life.

And not only that, but we also boast in our sufferings, knowing that suffering produces endurance, and endurance produces character, and character produces hope, and hope does not disappoint us, because God's love has been poured into our hearts through the Holy Spirit that has been given to us.

~ Romans 5:3-5

Day 36:
From Suffering Comes Good Things

We know that God brings good things out of suffering if we allow Him to enter our lives, so we receive His grace. The fact is that God has allowed this suffering to happen because He respects the gift of free will that He gave you. But it doesn't mean that He doesn't love you, or that He wants you to suffer needlessly. Rather, when bad things happen, Christ is ready to create new, good things for you. He is simply waiting for your permission to take the situation and bring good out of it. So take your broken heart to the foot of the cross and say to Christ, "Why, Lord? Help me!" He will come down from the cross, put His arms around you, and say, "I know you are suffering. I love you. And now I want to show you the way through your suffering into happiness."

Are not two sparrows sold for a penny? Yet not one of them will fall to the ground apart from your Father. And even the hairs of your head are all counted. So do not be afraid; you are of more value than many sparrows.

~ Matthew 10:29-31

Day 37:
God's Plan Can Make You Happy

There comes a time in your life when you have to take a step out in faith and really believe that God has a plan for your life. When you love God and place your trust in Him, you believe your life is not just a bunch of unrelated circumstances that happen by accident. Instead, everyone you know and everything that happens is God's hand, trying to bring you closer to Him.

God's plan will make you happy. While this may seem impossible in your situation, remember, things are not always what they seem. You are in the thick of a situation filled with anger, resentment, grief and loneliness. But if you allow God access to your life, He will take it and make something wonderful. He will make you happier than you could ever imagine!

For surely I know the plans I have for you, says the Lord, plans for your welfare and not for harm, to give you a future with hope.

~ Jeremiah 29:11

Day 38:
Seek The Church

The Catholic Church is the source of Christ's truth. While you may not always understand or agree with that truth, it is the truth, nonetheless. Since it is of God, truth has by its very nature a healing and comforting aspect to it. Although sometimes difficult, the truth will always lead you to the right place—a place of peace. If you are feeling the desire to distance yourself from the Church, you are moving away from the very thing that will bring you the abundant peace and joy you are seeking. As you reflect and discern the impact of your divorce or separation on the rest of your life, it is best to remain engaged with the Church, her Sacraments, her teaching, and her community. So go to mass, go to reconciliation, go to adoration in front of the Blessed Sacrament; seek out or start a divorce ministry, stay plugged into your faith and your Church. The Church needs you!

Cast your burden on the Lord, / and he will sustain you; / he will never permit /the righteous to be moved.

~ Psalm 55:22

Day 39:
God Makes Good Out Of Bad

Divorce can feel like a sickness that is so terrible, it makes you want to die. The pain seems never-ending. But God can take the most horrible situation and bring good out of it. In the same way He allowed Lazarus to die, He allowed your divorce to happen. And just as He raised Lazarus from the dead, He wants to raise you from your divorce. He waits for the opportunity to show you the good things He can bring about as a result of the bad. This is one way He brings us closer to Himself. He cares for you, and if you let Him, He will make you happy, despite the terrible loss you are suffering. Are you open to giving Him free reign in your life to accomplish good things?

Jesus said to her, "Did I not tell you that if you believed, you would see the glory of God?" So they took away the stone. And Jesus looked upward and said, "Father, I thank you for having heard me. I knew that you always hear me, but I have said this for the sake of the crowd standing here, so that they may believe that you sent me." When he had said this, he cried with a loud voice, "Lazarus, come out!"
The dead man came out, his hands and feet bound with strips of cloth, and his face wrapped in a cloth.
Jesus said to them, "Unbind him, and let him go."

~ John 11:40-45

Day 40:
Ask God For His Help

How much faith do you have in God at this time in your life? As you reflect on all that has happened to you in your divorce, and all that is ahead of you, what would your answer be to God's question, "Do you believe I can do this?" It is easy to say the words asking God to help you, but how much do you really believe that He will help you?

When going through a divorce, it can be particularly hard to trust again, and God knows your reservations. Yet He continually calls you to come closer to Him because He wants you to put your trust in Him, alone. Sometimes lack of trust is rooted in the fact that you just don't want to let go of the relationship with your ex-spouse. Sometimes you regret the mistakes you have made, and the pain that has resulted, therefore, you try to control everything yourself. Sometimes you are prone to complaining, whining, and bouts of self-pity. All of these indicate doubt in action. You need to ask God for His help so you will be able to forgive, heal and move on. But you also need to trust Him and believe that He will help you.

When he entered the house, the blind men came to him;
and Jesus said to them, "Do you believe that I am able to do this?"
They said to him, "Yes, Lord." Then he touched their eyes and said,
"According to your faith let it be done to you."

~ Matthew 9:28-29

Day 41:
Trust In Him

How can you increase your ability to trust in such a difficult time? First, ask God for the grace to grow in your faith and ability to trust in Him. He will give you what you need. Second, proceed in your life as if He has already taken care of the things you need.

God can heal you. God can make your life happier than you can ever imagine. Believe in His love for you and trust that He will take care of you.

Truly I tell you, if you say to this mountain, 'Be taken up and thrown into the sea,' and if you do not doubt in your heart, but believe that what you say will come to pass, it will be done for you.
So I tell you, whatever you ask for in prayer,
believe that you have received it, and it will be yours.

~ Mark 11:23-24

Day 42:
Gain Strength From The Sacraments

For a divorced person, great temptations lay around every corner. The devil has laid traps for you because he knows you have a weak spot, caused by the pain of your divorce. He uses your circumstances to make you vulnerable to these pitfalls. Christ knows the trials you will be sent (and have been sent). That's why He has given you the sacraments to strengthen you, enlighten you, and sustain you through your difficulties. He suffered, died on the cross, and went to heaven to prepare a place for us yet He is still with us, here, through the sacraments. If you consider the great gifts, just waiting for you to receive, your life would change considerably. Especially in times of personal difficulty and sorrow, you need the strength and grace that comes from the sacraments of confession and the Eucharist. Christ waits for you patiently but anxiously, for He has so much to give you. He wants to heal your heart and set it on fire with love.

Those who eat my flesh and drink my blood have eternal life, and I will raise them up on the last day.

~ John 6:54

Day 43:
Choose Faith

Believing in God's truth is a conscious decision, not a feeling or an emotion. Truth exists regardless of a feeling "in your gut" or even a negative emotion about it. For example, say you are hiking in the mountains and come across a precarious rope bridge. On it is posted a sign by the National Forestry Service stating that the bridge has been recently tested and approved completely safe. Would you be inclined to believe the authority that made that declaration? Sure you would! Why? Because you trust the authority that said it, even though you did not test it yourself. You believed it without seeing proof. If you are like most people, you would walk across the bridge, maybe a little apprehensive at first, but trusting in the Forestry Service that you will make it to the other side. This is how you should approach the Church and Her sacraments, with trust that they contain God's truth.

All things can be done for the one who believes.

~ Mark 9:23

Day 44:
This Is My Body

In the sacrament of marriage, spouses give themselves totally to each other and become one heart, one mind, and one flesh. This is a beautiful reflection of what Christ does for us in the Eucharist. He gives Himself totally to us so we can be one with Him; one heart, one mind, one flesh. What an incredible sign of love for you; even though your spouse is gone, Christ will never leave you. Unlike the imperfect love of your spouse, Christ gives you His passionate, unconditional love because His greatest desire is for you to spend eternity with Him in heaven. The gift of Himself will strengthen you for the long haul. Christ gives you the graces you need during this difficult time.

So Jesus said to them, "Very truly, I tell you, unless you eat the flesh of the Son of Man and drink his blood, you have no life in you. Those who eat my flesh and drink my blood have eternal life, and I will raise them up on the last day.

~ John 6:53-54

Day 45:
Let Love Rule Your Heart

Will it ever be possible for you to love your ex-spouse? It may not be easy to envision, but it is possible for this to happen.

Christ tells us love should be the ruler of our hearts. Love is desiring good for others. No retaliation. No desire for revenge. No desire to see things go wrong for that person. Christ is not asking you to lay down and be a doormat. No, you need to stand up for justice and do what you know is right. But in dealing with your ex-spouse, you must be charitable. And who knows? Maybe your attitude of love might change your ex-spouse as well!

Love is patient; love is kind; love is not envious or boastful or arrogant or rude. It does not insist on its own way; it is not irritable or resentful; it does not rejoice in wrongdoing, but rejoices in the truth. It bears all things, believes all things, hopes all things, endures all things.

~ 1 Corinthians 13:4-7

Day 46:
Decide To Love

Loving is simple, although it needs your decision to put it into action. When you treat your ex in a loving manner, you change the dynamic of the broken relationship. You diffuse the explosive nature of your encounters. You bring a sense of dignity and respect into the broken relationship even though there may have been damaging words and actions. However, treating your ex-spouse in a loving way does not mean you put yourself at risk in any way, whatsoever.

Love has a calming effect and speaks louder than a bullhorn. Love is all that Christ asks of you. You don't have to like your ex-spouse, and you don't have to subject yourself to his/her mistreatment; you simply need to recognize that Christ loves him/her as much as He loves you. And for that reason alone you should be able to find it within yourself to treat your ex in a fair and decent manner.

I give you a new commandment, that you love one another.
Just as I have loved you, you also should love one another.

~ John 13:34

Day 47:
Fortify Yourself

———◆———

Strengthen yourself with the sacraments and prayer. They will fortify you for the long haul. St. Thomas More spoke eloquently on this subject. He said, "If I am distracted, Holy Communion helps me to become recollected. If opportunities are offered each day to offend my God, I arm myself anew each day for the combat by the reception of the Eucharist. If I am in special need of light and prudence in order to discharge my burdensome duties, I draw nigh to my Savior and seek counsel and light from him."

———

*The Lord is my strength and my shield; / in him my heart trusts; /
so I am helped, and my heart exults, /
and with my song I give thanks to him.*

~ Psalm 28:7

Day 48:
Become Like Children

Not only does Christ show us how to deal with our children, He also shows us that we need to learn from them! In fact, we need to become just like them! What a valuable lesson for us to learn in the midst of the anger and backbiting in a divorce. The innocence, trust, honesty and humility of a child is the key. And that key is what will open the gates of heaven to you, and while you are still here struggling on earth, it is where you will find great peace. So in all that you are undertaking, practice the simple virtues you find in your children.

Let the little children come to me, and do not stop them;
for it is to such as these that the kingdom of heaven belongs.

~ Matthew 19:14

Day 49:
Heaven Can Help

Did you know that all of heaven is waiting to help you? The communion of saints, the blessed who have gone before us to heaven, can pray for us and petition God for us. All you need to do is ask them. When you become overwhelmed, pray and seek help from the saints; they are one of the greatest spiritual resources you have. Many mothers can relate to the Blessed Mother, Mary. She is the most powerful intercessor. Many fathers can relate to St. Joseph. His prayers are particularly powerful for fathers and families because he was the head of the Holy Family. Go online and search for prayers to these and other saints. There are many great prayers, litanies, and memorares to the saints.

Bless the Lord, all his hosts, / his ministers that do his will.

~ Psalm 103:21

Day 50:
Children Are A Blessing

In times of distress and worry, it is easy to forget what a gift our children are to us. Children are a sign from God that life goes on and should flourish with hope. When your family is suffering through a divorce, it is easy to lose sight of your blessings. But don't forget that even as painful as things are right now, you need to go on. Life needs to be lived and if we, as parents, remain rooted in Christ then despite all the suffering, we can show our children how to be strong and find the path to a happier life. Recall the story of Elizabeth. She was blessed with a bundle of joy, despite her history of barrenness. God gave her and Zechariah the unique joy of being parents. So, too, those who are parents are given that joy and can find hope in the gift of their children.

Now the time came for Elizabeth to give birth, and she bore a son.
Her neighbors and relatives heard that the Lord had shown
his great mercy to her, and they rejoiced with her.

~ Luke 1:57-58

Day 51:
We All Fall

We all fall. We fall to temptation. It's the human condition and no one is exempt. When Jesus fell three times as He carried the cross, He did not fall to sin, but He showed us He understood our humanity. His example was simple, yet powerful: get up again; embrace your cross; don't give up.

When you contemplate Jesus falling three times under the weight of His cross, it's hard to understand how He was able to go on. And so many times you feel as though you can't go on. Just when you think you've overcome a problem, another obstacle trips you up and you fall. Look to Jesus for strength. When you are most vulnerable, when your heart is broken, when you think your situation is hopeless, and when you want to surrender, simply pray these words, "Jesus, teach me how to do this. I cannot do it without your grace. Piece together my broken heart and spirit with the healing power of your love."

But I said, "I have labored in vain, / I have spent my strength for nothing and vanity; / yet surely my cause is with the Lord, / and my reward with my God." / And now the Lord says, / who formed me in the womb to be his servant, / to bring Jacob back to him, / and that Israel might be gathered to him, / for I am honored in the sight of the Lord, / and my God has become my strength.

~ Isaiah 49:4-5

Day 52:
The Power of the Rosary

———————◇———————

A British soldier who was serving in Iraq was out in the field one day, and his rosary beads fell off his neck, onto the ground. As he leaned over to pick them up, he noticed that he was standing directly on a landmine. With intense fear, he called to his fellow soldiers to come to his aid. After about 45 minutes, they had secured the landmine and he was safe. This soldier, named Glenn, was wearing this rosary because his parents had given it to him for protection. The rosary originally belonged to Glenn's grandfather who claimed Mary saved him in the same way during WWII when a blast killed six of his platoon members.

A divorce can certainly seem like you are standing on a landmine that is ready to explode (and then does). During this time of suffering and searching, I encourage you to rely on Mary, my mother and yours, to help you. Her sole purpose is to lead you to her Son where you can find healing. In a world of disappointments and betrayals, Mary is a woman you can count on. She will guide you and petition her Son on your behalf.

———————————

Hail Mary, full of grace, the Lord is with thee. Blessed art thou among women and blessed is the fruit of thy womb, Jesus. Holy Mary, Mother of God, pray for us sinners, now and at the hour of our death. Amen.

Day 53:
Flashback

How is suffering manifesting itself in your life? It could be in a number of ways but after divorce, memory flashbacks are a common manifestation. You may be constantly reliving the stressful, hurtful moments of your marriage as it was ending, or encounters with your ex-spouse that were quite painful. Many people report feelings that, even years later, are almost as painful as the moment they were first lived. Flashbacks entertained every time they present themselves will keep you steeped in pain and anchored in the past, unable to forgive or move forward. While your life will never be completely without pain until you die and go to heaven, holding on to pain does not make you wiser—it only perpetuates the pain. Learn to "let go and let God!"

Let your steadfast love, O Lord, be upon us, / even as we hope in you.

~ Psalm 33:22

Day 54:
The Good Samaritan

Remember the story of the Good Samaritan? It beautifully illustrates how the Samaritan compassionately cared for a broken human being despite societal prejudices of the time. During that time a Samaritan never would have considered stopping to help a non-Samaritan. And yet, the Good Samaritan cared for him without holding back. He poured oil and wine on the wounds, laid him on his own animal to be carried, took him to an inn where he could rest and heal, and paid for it all out of his own wallet.

Isn't this exactly the way Christ cares for us?

Christ will never leave you alone to die. Christ will never accidentally pass you on the same road but instead goes in search of you. He tends to all your wounds, great and small, and wants to heal them so you can be whole again. He carries you as you journey through your difficulties and brings you to a place where you can rest. He has paid the price for you through His own suffering, cross and resurrection.

But a Samaritan while traveling came near him; and when he saw him, he was moved with pity. He went to him and bandaged his wounds, having poured oil and wine on them. Then he put him on his own animal, brought him to an inn, and took care of him.

~ Luke 10: 33-34

Day 55:
Create Peace

Adjusting to life after divorce can be very difficult and painful. It may seem that you can't escape the shadow your divorce creates. It can permeate your life.

In the midst of this turmoil, identify the one thing that brings you even a moment's peace. This is different for each person. For some people it is prayer, for some it is listening to music, for others it is exercising or a long walk. Identify what it is for you and do it, every day. At first you may only have one minute of true peace but over time, the sense of peace will grow longer and longer each day. That is a sign that you are healing.

I will both lie down and sleep in peace; /
for you alone, O Lord, make me lie down in safety.

~ Psalm 4:8

Day 56:
Seek Christ First

People are vulnerable after a divorce. As a result they try to soothe their pain by jumping into another relationship. While this may validate their need to prove they are still lovable in the short-term, it is a formula for an unhealthy, unsuccessful, long-term relationship. In the first year after a divorce, your perspective, decision-making, and view of the future is not lucid or stable. The best serious relationship you should pursue is one with Christ. He is the true healer. His guidance is always perfect. Orient your life around Him and His teachings in order to open your mind and heart to the guidance of the Holy Spirit.

This is done through daily prayer and participation in the Sacraments. Turn alone time in to opportunities to really embrace Christ and your faith. Reading scripture, extended prayer time, adoration of the Blessed Sacrament, participating in Mass, and socializing with people of strong Catholic faith are all great ways to deepen your relationship with Christ. This will help sensitize you to the promptings of the Holy Spirit which will result in living a life more fully aligned with God's will. As you do that, not only will you heal, you will become a living testament to God's love and mercy and an inspiration to others. Your life will actually draw others closer to Christ. You will become a gift to all you meet.

We know that all things work together for good for those who love God, who are called according to his purpose.

~ Romans 8:28

Day 57:
Pray For Hope

Along with faith and love, hope is a theological virtue from God given freely as a gift; all you need to do is ask. When you live in hope, you can endure even the darkest of time patiently because you believe that God has a plan. He will lead you through this time of darkness to a life of peace and joy. When you live in hope, you make better decisions, are less likely to take matters into your own hands, can face challenges head-on, and are more apt to live a life of joyful anticipation of what God has in store for you, despite your current circumstances.

Abide in me as I abide in you. Just as the branch cannot bear fruit by itself unless it abides in the vine, neither can you unless you abide in me.

~ John 15:4

Day 58:
The Divine Pruner

During the winter season, you prune the branches of the tree. You cut off the dead limbs and areas where disease may have infected the tree. To the casual observer, the tree looks barren and bald— almost void of life. But when the spring comes, the tree bears beautiful blossoms in abundance, much more than if it hadn't been pruned.

You may feel that you are experiencing a wintertime in your life because of your divorce. Is God pruning your life? Do you feel like Job as you lose everything important to you: relationships, homes, and possessions? Though the winter is long, remember spring will come. This part of your life will not last forever, and the pruning that has taken place will allow you to change and grow and as a result become a better person because of the experience. As you journey through the wintertime of your life, seek to remain close to your faith and the Church so that when the springtime arrives, you will be renewed and joyful.

I am the true vine, and my Father is the vinegrower. He removes every branch in me that bears no fruit. Every branch that bears fruit he prunes to make it bear more fruit.

~ John 15:1-2

Day 59:
True Love

True love, real love, the kind we all crave is more than a wonderful feeling or powerful attraction. Love is a decision; a desire to seek the constant good of the person we love. Love is a desire to make the object of our affection happy. Now no human love is perfect, but the goal of a loving relationship is to seek each other's good and be ready to forgive each other's failings along the way.

You are experiencing a breakdown caused by imperfect love; a relationship that was not focused on seeking the good of each of the spouses. In spite of the fact that this love relationship is no longer something you can rely on, you can still experience love and its perfection through Christ, who will accept you as you are and show you this love.

[Love] does not rejoice in wrongdoing, but rejoices in the truth. It bears all things, believes all things, hopes all things, endures all things.

~ 1 Corinthians 13:6 -7

Day 60:
Christer Is The Shepherd Of Your Heart

Because Christ knows you intimately and knows the secrets of your heart, you are especially dear to Him in this time of loneliness and struggle. Jesus is the Good Shepherd so when you wander away because of self-doubt, He comes after you and calls you to Him. He waits for you to give Him the chance to show you how much you are worth to Him. Christ is not ashamed of you. He is there for you. He never forgets you. He wants you to come closer. He has seen every fight and heard all the painful words that were spoken. He knows when you fought valiantly to save your marriage, and when you grew tired of trying. He knows your heart and the hurt and disappointment. He wants you to come to Him so He can take your burden.

Peace I leave with you; my peace I give to you.
I do not give to you as the world gives.
Do not let your hearts be troubled, and do not let them be afraid.

~ John 14:27

Day 61:
You Have A Mission

God gave each of us a mission, a distinct purpose in life. Only you can fulfill the mission God gave you—no one can do it for you. God also gave you gifts and talents that will help you accomplish that mission. Divorce has such a harsh, negative effect that it is easy to lose sight of all the good things. The negativity can almost completely derail us from fulfilling our mission. If you allow the devil and all his lies to conquer your spirit and lead you to believe you are not worthy, you will not accomplish your mission. The many souls that you come in contact with will not see the wonderful person God created you to be but will instead behold a broken and uninspiring individual. Don't allow this to happen to you! If you persevere and stay close to Christ, you will be able to rise above it all and find your comfort and strength in God, our Savior.

Can a woman forget her nursing child, / or show no compassion for the child of her womb? / Even these may forget, / yet I will not forget you.

~ Isaiah 49:15

Day 62:
Light For the World

You are who you are for a reason. It is not an accident. God created each one of us for Himself.

Because your divorce places such heavy burdens on you that in your time of difficulty you may be tempted to give up hope and become discouraged. But you are precious to Him and He loves you. He loves everything about you because He created you. You can be an example of love to others through drawing on the strengths Christ has given you to help get through this difficult time.

In the same way, let your light shine before others, so that they may see your good works and give glory to your Father in heaven.

~ Matthew 5:16

Day 63:
When You Can't See The Light
At The End Of The Tunnel

More than 2,000 years ago, a young fourteen-year-old girl was visited by the Archangel Gabriel and learned of her glorious new role as the mother of God. Can you imagine what an incredible event that must have been for Mary? A momentous day, indeed, since that was her one heavenly apparition. When she had to explain to Joseph why she was pregnant and painfully endure his decision to quietly divorce her, there was no angel present to back her up. Later, when she and Joseph discovered that Jesus had been missing for three days, while she was overcome with anxiety over her lost child, there was no angel to guide her back to her Son. Mary endured the greatest sufferings a mother could endure by standing at the foot of the cross as her Son was so brutally and unjustly crucified. How did she do it? How did she get through it all? When Jesus was placed in the tomb, and there was nothing left of her family, where did she find the hope and the strength to go on living?

Mary found her strength in her unshakeable trust in God. God was her rock at all times. She trusted the plan God put in place.

This is a great time for you to look to your heavenly mother for help. Your suffering may seem as if it will never end, but follow Mary's example and trust in God's plan for you. Just as Mary lived to experience the joy of the Resurrection, after such incredible pain and suffering, so will God bless you with the peace and joy you are seeking.

My soul magnifies the Lord

~ Luke 1:46

Day 64:
Each Moment Is A Gift

———————◇———————

Viewing each moment of your life as a gift when you are going through a divorce is hard, maybe even impossible. But even so, this is a necessary exercise if you want to truly heal from the pain you are suffering through. Gratitude allows you to reflect back on the bad times and still be grateful for the relationship. When you can practice the virtue of gratitude, you know you have arrived in the healing process. When you can look back on the good days and appreciate the fact that even though you don't have that now, it was still something good. Sometimes it's even good to remember the fights you had with your ex-spouse, not to relive them, but to *learn* from them.

Relationships fail when God is lacking. You may not be able to bring God back to your marriage, but you can certainly include Him in your everyday moments, thoughts, desires, and prayers, right now! Let Him be a part of you so He can bring good things out of your situation. He loves you so much! He wants to show you happiness!

———————

Every generous act of giving, with every perfect gift, is from above,
coming down from the Father of lights,
with whom there is no variation or shadow due to change.

~ James 1:17

Day 65:
When You Have Every Reason To Be Angry

A friend of mine went through a divorce six years ago. His wife packed up the kids and moved out, and he found himself embroiled in a nasty custody battle that left him financially bankrupt. He stunned me one day as we spoke about what he was going through. Just when I expected him to pour out his bitterness over these devastating losses, he simply told me that his only goal—one that he worked toward each day—was to try to see Christ in his ex-wife.

What a miracle was taking place in this man's life—a miracle no one else could see. The world would call him "stupid," but I call him "heroic." What a beautiful example of charity and grace in the midst of suffering! Let us pray that God will grant us this gift of heroic virtue.

But I say to you, Love your enemies and pray for those who persecute you.

~ Matthew 5:44

Day 66:
Nothing Is Impossible With God

Divorce can make you feel like life has come to an end. Yes, the sun is still shining and modern life is moving forward but inside, you feel as if there is nothing good to look forward to in your future. Looking ahead you think that holidays will always hurt, being single will always be lonely, and family gatherings will always be hard. But God says, "No way!"

Let not your faith and trust in God be limited to what you are experiencing now. God is so big, so loving, and so merciful, we cannot comprehend. You may be walking through fire now but in His perfect timing, God will lead you out of the trials and into a new part of your life, where you will experience the peace and joy only He can give you. Trust Him; cling to Him. He won't let you down!

Say to the Lord, "My refuge and my fortress; /
my God, in whom I trust."

~ Psalm 91:2

Day 67:
The Hardest Part

Someone once challenged me by saying, "The harder it is, the more you know you need to do it." I've never been overjoyed to hear that statement, but I do know that it is true.

What is the hardest part about what you're going through right now? Is it forgiving? Is it letting go of the relationship you had with your ex-spouse? Is it watching your children leave with your ex-spouse, knowing you have no control over what will happen while they are gone? There are many difficult things about divorce that we don't want to accept. Because of that, we run the risk of drowning in anger and resentment.

But I extend the same challenge to you that was extended to me: "The harder it is, the more you know you need to do it." Just as exercising flabby muscles is painful, so will be doing what is difficult. But the results will be AMAZING! You will purify and strengthen your will in such a way that you will become a different person—a better, stronger person. And that, my friend, is something that God will bless you for.

For this very reason, you must make every effort to support your faith with goodness, and goodness with knowledge, and knowledge with self-control, and self-control with endurance, and endurance with godliness, and godliness with mutual affection, and mutual affection with love.

~ 2 Peter 1:5-7

Day 68:
What Is Your Motto?

In times of difficulty, such as divorce, many people reach for some-thing to use as a life preserver—something to keep them afloat or distract them from the pain. Sometimes, oftentimes, it is the wrong thing, such as spending all their time working, drinking alcohol in excess, or diving into another relationship. In order to get through the rough times with grace and sanity, the best life preserver, first put yourself in God's hands, then latch on to something that will keep you focused and motivated. Setting goals and priorities are probably the best way to do this.

Adopting a motto helps you remain focused on your goal. Find a brief statement that incorporates your goals into words and re-minds you of why you are fighting this good fight. A couple of ex-amples are St. John Paul II's "Be not afraid!" for when you are ex-periencing fear and anxiety, or St. Francis' "Make me a channel of your peace" for when you are having trouble managing anger. Mot-tos come in handy most when you find yourself overwhelmed. Say-ing your motto out loud or under your breath, like a quiet prayer, reminds you of your goal to be a better person and find peace.

So, what's your motto?

_____

And God is able to provide you with every blessing in abundance,
so that by always having enough of everything, you may share
abundantly in every good work.

~ 2 Corinthians 9:8

68

Day 69:
Modern Day Heroes

◆

Sometimes God's ways are totally incomprehensible. Since your divorce you may be wondering, *why in the world would God allow this terrible thing to happen?* To answer this, we can look to the life of St. Rita. St. Rita also puzzled over God's will. She wanted to become a nun, but her parents arranged for her to be married. She lived for years in an unhappy relationship with her husband. Even still, she remained faithful to God and her husband and endured difficult times. She not only found a way to make her home happy, she also helped cause her husband's conversion to Christ through her suffering.

During this time of suffering, try not to wrestle with wondering if your divorce was or was not part of God's will, instead try to accept the fact that moving forward, your life will be the way God wants it. Accept that God allowed this cross to befall you and look for what He wants you to learn, where He wants you to go next, and what His will is for your life, today. God gave us St. Rita as a striking example of heroic patience and humility. Let us follow her example and find what joy God has waiting for us in the future.

Blessed are those who mourn, for they will be comforted.

~ Matthew 5:4

Day 70:
Don't Let The World Beat You Down

Today, you may be feeling defeated as you read this reflection. Maybe your relationship with your children is suffering because of the divorce. Maybe you had an unpleasant encounter with your ex-spouse recently. Maybe you are struggling to make ends meet and can't see your situation getting better anytime soon. Maybe you are hurting terribly.

The Lord wants you to know He has not forgotten you. He sees your suffering and is very close to you. He is still in control and is working to bring good things for you out of these difficult times. When you are feeling defeated, remember Christ as He was flogged mercilessly by the angry soldiers; they couldn't keep Him down. He got back up. As He carried His cross to Calvary, He fell three times under the weight of the heavy burden, but He got back up. Let Christ show you how to get back up and carry on. Open yourself to the graces He has waiting for you, and never forget that He loves you and this, too, shall pass.

I will not leave you orphaned.

~ John 14:18

Day 71:
Are You Ready To Receive?

It is true that any suffering we bear—divorce, illness, death of a loved one, loss of a job—any cross is a gift from God and a blessing in disguise. Why? Why would a loving God do this? It is because of the good that He will bring out of it. No matter what bad choice someone has made, God can bring about more good than any bad that happened because of it. When we suffer, we change and although change hurts, we become better people because of it. Are you able to look at your suffering with hope and await the gifts God will bring your way?

God is not stingy in giving gifts but oftentimes, we are stingy in receiving them. We are not open to them because we are clinging to anger, resentment, or unforgiveness. Today, take a step forward in trusting God, let go of what is holding you back, and look for whatever good may be coming out of your situation.

If you then, who are evil, know how to give good gifts to your children, how much more will your Father in heaven give good things to those who ask him!

~ Matthew 7:11

Day 72:
Doing The Things You Dislike
Can Save You

When I was in the post-divorce years living in an apartment by my-self, the weekends were a very dangerous time for me. I was living in a new area, starting a new job, and didn't know many people. I spent the weekends mostly on my own. When the weather was cold, I rarely even got outside. I often slipped into a pity party, and then my weekend was a disaster. I knew I had to do something to change the dynamic of my free time.

I reflected on how many times I wished I could do something but did not have the time. Well, suddenly I had the time! Time to clean out my closets, time to sew on missing buttons, time to read a book my mother had sent me, and time to purge my personal files. All those things I had been procrastinating doing were back on my to-do list. So when the next weekend rolled around, instead of crying myself to sleep on the couch, I began marking the tasks off the list. By the time Sunday afternoon rolled around, I had the most orga-nized closets and actually felt good about myself.

There are many things we can do to help ourselves get through the suffering. Things that are right in front of us, but we don't recognize as helpful. But then when we do them, we find that we are distract-ed from our pain, or they help us process the pain in a constructive fashion. If the weekend, or some other time, is a dangerous time for you, think about ways to change that. Make a list! When you've finished all the things you don't like, fill up your list with things you do like. You will be glad you did!

A highway shall be there, / and it shall be called the Holy Way.

~ Isaiah 35:8

Day 73:
Come Back!

Have you drifted away from your faith since your divorce? Maybe you feel angry, disconnected, or simply don't understand if you are welcome? In dealing with divorce, we find ourselves starving for something to fill that horrible void. Oftentimes we look to the wrong things for comfort. But the sacraments of reconciliation and the Eucharist can give you all that you need.

Christ feeds us with His own body and blood. That is how much He loves us! There is no need to hunger for fulfillment because the nourishment in the sacrament of the Eucharist is the comfort we are seeking. A wonderful priest once said: "The greatest danger is not to starve, but to convince yourself that you are not starving." If you are drifting away, I offer this personal invitation, from me to you, to come back. I welcome you home because I know the sacraments are the very thing that will comfort and sustain you in times of trial.

Jesus said to them, "I am the bread of life. Whoever comes to me will never be hungry, and whoever believes in me will never be thirsty."

~ John 6:35

Day 74:
They Can't Take That Away From You

When you feel you have lost everything and are left empty-handed; when the winds of gossip and criticism are howling in your direction; when those you love have left you alone; there is one thing no one can take away from you, a treasure far greater than any other, the interior freedom and peace that comes from God alone.

As St. John Paul II said, "Be not afraid!" Even in this state of loss, you are wealthier than any millionaire if you are connected to Christ. By joining your heart to His, He will give you everything you need: courage, strength, patience, love, and forgiveness. He will deny you nothing if only you ask Him for it. And after you have fought the good fight, He will reward you with the eternal treasure of life with Him in heaven.

What no eye has seen, nor ear heard, / nor the human heart conceived, / what God has prepared for those who love him.

~ 1 Corinthians 2:9

Day 75:
Will I Always Feel This Way?

As time puts distance between you and your divorce, the bad days come less often, and you begin to look forward to your new place in life. But then a song, a movie, or a memory will remind you of the terrible pain you are trying to leave behind. You wonder, "Will I always feel this way? Will the pain always be there?" Well, yes and no. Yes, because the loss of a marriage is a significant event that has deeply affected you. While most of the pain will fade away with time, some things will remain with you. I don't think that is a bad thing, necessarily, because the ability to feel that pain increases your compassion for others who suffer.

Oftentimes the pain you acutely re-experience, as time goes by, has less to do with the failure of your marriage and more to do with the growing pains of your relationship with God. Allow your pain to be the catalyst that leads you closer to Christ. Don't become discouraged—your challenges equal the beauty of change which causes the purification that brings peace and joy to your life.

I lie down and sleep; / I wake again, for the Lord sustains me.

~ Psalm 3:5

Day 76:
Is Prayer Your Steering Wheel
Or Your Spare Tire?

In asking this question, Corrie ten Boom, survivor of the Holocaust, focuses us on the need to pray in times of distress. So often prayer is difficult when life is painful whether during an illness, divorce, or some other suffering. Pain brings forth many questions about life and the future. Part of the reason why it can be difficult to pray is because we do not have the answers to these questions.

Scripture tells us that no branch can bear fruit unless it is connected to the Vine. Are you well connected? The Bible also tells us that all things are possible with God. If you are working to achieve peace, healing, patience, or whatever it is you seek, be sure to commit everything to prayer and let God work for you. He desires your happiness and wants you to bear much fruit in your own life. If you have the chance today, or this week, why not go spend an hour with Him in adoration? Even just sitting in His presence and opening your heart to Him is a prayer!

*Abide in me as I abide in you. Just as the branch cannot bear fruit
by itself unless it abides in the vine,
neither can you unless you abide in me.*

~ John 15:4

Day 77:
God Loves Everyone, Even Your Ex-Spouse

Most men and women who go through a divorce harbor a great deal of resentment toward their ex-spouse, primarily due to infidelity and abandonment. This can make living a Christian life difficult at best. Prayer becomes a dry and arduous task. It is easy to become consumed with negativity, however, there are ways to release these toxic feelings.

While your anger and bitterness toward your ex-spouse (and your in-laws, the other man/woman, etc.) are most likely justified, you should remember two things: First, you cannot control your ex-spouse's words, thoughts or actions, and accepting that reality begins the detachment process. The only person you can control is yourself. Clinging to resentment will only eat away at your heart like a cancer. Second, God loves your ex-spouse as much as He loves you, and He wants you BOTH in heaven! No matter how badly your ex has behaved, God still wants his/her soul for Himself. Therefore, keep the Golden Rule. Ask God for the grace to forgive and for the knowledge of how to let go of the resentment. He will bless you abundantly for this.

For God so loved the world that he gave his one and only Son, that whoever believes in him shall not perish but have eternal life.

~ John 3:16

Day 78:
Finding God In The Simple Things

———————⬦———————

Life after divorce can seem lifeless and mundane. We struggle to find something that will restore happiness in our lives. This is often why people jump quickly into other relationships, or drink alcohol in excess, or latch on to other destructive behaviors, seeking happiness in error.

But you can find happiness without risk in the little details, the simple everyday things you have to do. Focus on one main theme: right now, you are exactly where God wants you. As you fulfill your daily responsibilities, you are cooperating with His plan. God's plan for you is never a mistake, so whatever you are doing at this moment is part of God's plan for you. Therefore, you can go through your day doing your work, folding the laundry, having lunch with a friend, or whatever it is, and focus on the fact that you are doing God's will, despite your pain. God loves this! Doing these little things will bring you greater peace because you will become aware of God's close presence in all that you do.

———————————

And whatever you do, in word or deed, do everything in the name of the Lord Jesus, giving thanks to God the Father through him.

~ Colossians 3:17

Day 79:
You Don't Have To Do It All By Yourself!

Has a spiritual advisor or friend presented the idea of forgiving your ex-spouse? Your response might have been "NO WAY!" Don't worry, this is quite normal. Forgiving someone who was supposed to love you 'till death do us part' but instead hurt you deeply is very difficult. Quite frankly, it can seem impossible. But you don't have to do it all by yourself.

Ask God for the grace to forgive. He has stockpiles of grace that He is waiting to give you, if you would only ask. If the mere thought of forgiving your ex-spouse seems to turn your stomach, then ask God for the grace to contemplate the possibility of maybe, possibly forgiving. This is a step in the right direction. Forgiveness is a process that takes time. So even if you have to start from way, way outside the circle and make your way into the point of forgiving, that is a good thing. Christ knows your suffering. He wants to help you and set you free from the burden you carry. Trust Him and He will give you what you need.

But I say to you, Love your enemies and pray for those who persecute you.

~ Matthew 5:44

Day 80:
What's Holding You Back?

---◇---

Are you itching to move forward in your healing process but feeling kind of stuck? This is a common problem with people who have experienced a devastating change in their lives but certainly one that can be overcome.

Begin by spending time in Adoration and reflect on what might be holding you back. Do you indulge in any behavior that might be a roadblock to healing, such as angry encounters with your ex-spouse, working too much or doing anything in excess, being involved in another intimate relationship, or reliving the bad memories over and over, etc.? Identify whatever it is that is preventing you from moving forward. Then determine a practical way to overcome that obstacle. For instance, if your encounters with your ex-spouse are heated and volatile, do not partake in that kind of behavior. Resolve to remain calm and collected when you speak to your ex-spouse or find a different mode of communication. If you are in a relationship without having a decree of nullity, get out of it. If you are reliving memories, and it has been longer than one year since your divorce, say a quick prayer when the flashbacks happen for the graces of detachment and healing. These are just some examples. By making the choice to help yourself, God will bless you.

No testing has overtaken you that is not common to everyone.
God is faithful, and he will not let you be tested beyond your strength,
but with the testing he will also provide the way out
so that you may be able to endure it.

~ 1 Corinthians 10:13

Day 81:
The Sacrament Of Confession
Is A Good Thing!

Has it been a while since you've been to confession? Or do you go frequently? Whatever your practice, the sacrament of confession acts as a superior form of restoring peace of mind, reconciliation, and spiritual direction, especially during a divorce. Did you know confession is not simply about taking responsibility for the things we have done wrong but also a chance to get rid of the interior crud weighing us down? By celebrating the sacrament of confession frequently, you can make real, noticeable progress toward healing through the good advice from the priest and the abundant graces the sacrament brings. Don't worry about what you have to confess— they've heard it all! You can ask questions and receive excellent advice on how to proceed with the things that are bothering you. Most importantly, your soul is washed clean, and you can walk away with a renewed interior freedom, confident in the fact that God loves you!

If it's been more than six months since your last confession, make time to go to confession. If you are particularly troubled by certain things that require more discussion than Saturday confessions allow, call your parish and make an appointment with the priest so you can have the time you need.

Repent therefore, and turn to God so that your sins may be wiped out.

~ Acts 3:19

Day 82:
The Sneakiness Of The Evil One

Whether you are kneeling down to pray, trying to forgive someone who has hurt you, running late to mass, or just trying to live a good Christian life, the Devil is there to distract you and trip you up. He does not want you to succeed. When Jesus knelt in the Garden of Gethsemane, sweating blood and in total distress, the Evil One was there, doing his best to convince Christ that He couldn't save humanity. He was whispering lies that the burden was too heavy; that no man could make this sacrifice. He tried to convince Jesus that He was a failure; His own people had rejected Him and handed Him over to be crucified.

It's Lucifer's job to create doubt and if you are trying to do what's right, He will be there, whispering in your ear. But God wants you to succeed! By virtue of your baptism, you have the graces to fight the good fight. God will never allow you to be tempted beyond your strength. He will always give you a way out of your struggle. So when you kneel down to pray, and the kids come bursting through the door to interrupt; or when you are trying to find forgiveness for someone, and the painful memories keep playing in your head like a TV rerun; when you are running late for mass, and you feel discouraged to the point that you don't want to go, remember these two important things—the devil is always whispering lies into your ear so you will fail, but God is always showering you with graces and strength so you can succeed. The choice is yours.

Little children, you are from God, and have conquered them; for the one who is in you is greater than the one who is in the world.

~ 1 John 4:4

Day 83:
Let It Be

"When I find myself in times of trouble, Mother Mary comes to me speaking words of wisdom, let it be." What consoling insight Paul McCartney offered us in that famous song. Mary certainly comes to us in our hour of need to console us as any mother would. Praying the rosary always brings a sense of peace and calm.

The real wisdom of the song is in the title: *Let It Be*. Often when we pray we are asking God to change something. But maybe our prayer should be, "Your will be done, Lord, let it be." This beautiful prayer of acceptance Our Lady modeled for us throughout her life, even when she watched her innocent and Divine Son die a criminal's death on the cross. Today, take some time to reflect on your life and ask your Mother in heaven to obtain for you the grace to say, "Your will be done, Lord, let it be."

Pray then in this way: Our Father in heaven, hallowed be your name. Your kingdom come. Your will be done, on earth as it is in heaven.

~ Matthew 6:9-10

Day 84:
Christat Makes All Things New

There is an old parable about a bamboo tree whose master comes to cut it down. The Bamboo is distressed and does not want to be cut down, but the master lovingly says, "I want to use you." They both know the cutting will be painful, but even so the master proceeds to cut down the tree. Then the master tells Bamboo that he will cut off his leaves and hollow him out. Bamboo protests and cries out in pain as the master proceeds just as he said. Then the master lays the bamboo across a field with one end in the river so the water can flow through. Bamboo realizes that despite the pain his master allows him to experience, he has become something totally new and is now able to bring life-giving water to the rest of the crops. This makes him very happy.

You may feel the pain of your divorce has been much like being cut down, sheared, and gutted. But in Christ, as He lovingly prunes you for His use, He will create you into a new creature and in your new life, you will find great joy.

Very truly, I tell you, unless a grain of wheat falls into the earth and dies, it remains just a single grain; but if it dies, it bears much fruit.

~ John 12:24

Day 85:
What Do You Want Me To Do For You?

The Gospel of Mark tells us the story of Bartimaeus, a blind beggar that sat outside the walls of Jericho begging for money. When Bartimaeus knew that Jesus was near, he called to Him loudly making quite a ruckus. Jesus told the apostles to bring Bartimaeus to Him and Jesus asked, "What do you want me to do for you?" Bartimaeus wanted to see.

What is it that you want? What are you praying for? God wants you to come to Him with all your cares, worries, concerns, hopes, dreams, and desires. It is not selfish to ask God for things that benefit you. He wants you to speak with Him about these things. What is it that your heart most desires at this point in time? Spend some quiet time with God today and tell Him what is in your heart.

Jesus said to him, "Go; your faith has made you well."
Immediately he regained his sight and followed him on the way.

~ Mark 10:52

Day 86:
You Can Do It!

———◇———

There is a great scene in the movie, *The Passion of the Christ*, where Simon of Cyrene is helping Jesus stand back up after a fall so He can carry the cross again. Simon says to Jesus, *"It's almost over. You can do it. We're almost there."* It is apparent that by this point, it must have taken every ounce of His energy, will, obedience to the Father, and love for us to stand back up and continue to Calvary.

You may be experiencing something similar. Your cross may be heavy to the point of being unbearable. But don't give up. *You can do it.* Does it seem like every day is a struggle just to keep it together? Don't get discouraged. *You can do it.* Are you looking for that light at the end of the tunnel but seeing nothing but darkness? Don't lose hope. *You're almost there.* These are the struggles that fashion you into a world-class spiritual athlete, and every moment of pain will change you into a better, stronger person, especially if you unite your cross to Christ's.

———

I have fought the good fight, I have finished the race,
I have kept the faith.

~ 2 Timothy 4:7

86

Day 87:
Enter Through The Narrow Gate

Divorce is so unjust and unfair, especially for those who kept it as a last option and ended up being forced to file. Does anyone really ever get married with the intention of getting divorced? In the aftermath it seems injustice just keeps going when you see your ex-spouse remarry, as if your marriage never existed; or when your ex-spouse speaks dishonestly to others about what really happened; or when he or she continues to receive the sacraments while not being free to do so. It can all seem so unfair.

But remember Christ's words in the Gospel of Luke where He tells us that not everyone who cries, "Lord! Lord!" will have the door to heaven opened for them. When you have to deal with the injustice of your situation, remember that Jesus told us we would need to enter through the narrow gate, and not everyone will be able to do so. Let your suffering help you go through the narrow gate. As you carry on, remember those who perpetrate the injustices against you, for they might be the ones to whom Christ says, "I do not know you" when the end comes. Consider offering up your suffering for them so that they might be humbled before the Lord, repent, and be let into eternal life. That could be a final gift of love for your ex-spouse.

When once the owner of the house has got up and shut the door,
and you begin to stand outside and to knock at the door, saying,
'Lord, open to us,' then in reply he will say to you,
'I do not know where you come from.'

~ Luke 13:25

Day 88:
The Hope Family

Thirty-five years ago, a woman lay dying in a Southern California hospital. She was never raised in a particular faith, nor did her parents instill in her any belief in God. Her long-time neighbors, the Hope family, knew this. The Hopes were Christians who had been trying to lead this woman and her family to Christ by their daily example. They now felt compelled to take this opportunity to be more vocal. They visited her the day before she died and helped her convert her heart to God before she left this earth. As a result, all her children eventually came to convert as well.

Sometimes it takes a tragedy to pave the way to meet people who will change your life, but when they appear you can almost find a reason to be thankful for the tragedy. Who has God brought in to your life since your divorce that has helped you come closer to Him? Or maybe helped you gain a different perspective on your situation? Has "the Hope family" visited you in some way? If so, thank God for that beautiful gift and if not yet, then be on the look-out. God often speaks to us directly through others, and they will share His words with you. They will bring you consolation.

Blessed are those who mourn, for they will be comforted.

~ Matthew 5:4

Day 89:
Jesus, I Trust In You!

Have you ever contemplated the Divine Mercy image of Jesus? It's a beautiful image of the resurrected Christ with a radiant face. Red and white rays shower down from His Sacred Heart and represent the blood and water that flowed from His side when the Roman soldier pierced Him. Underneath the image are the words, "Jesus, I Trust In You."

So many people in our country and around the world are suffering, this very moment, because of divorce. They have no parish community to support them, no prayers offered on their behalf, and far too often, no faith in God at all. As Catholics, we have the richness of our faith to hold us, sustain us, and help us to persevere. The Divine Mercy is an excellent example of the riches of our faith. It is there to inspire us to persevere, to fight the good fight, and to trust that God will take care of us and keep us close to Him. I encourage you to take five minutes to say the Divine Mercy Chaplet for your intentions and for those who have no faith. Entrust yourself to Jesus! Jesus, I trust in You!

My refuge and my fortress; / my God, in whom I trust.

~ Psalm 91:2

Day 90:
For This I Am Thankful

---◇---

For the gift of waking up this day, *I thank you, Lord.*
For the gift of my sight and being able to speak and hear,
I thank you, Lord.
For the gift of your glorious nature and the beautiful world
I live in, *I thank you, Lord.*
For a roof over my head, *I thank you, Lord.*
For the gift of free will and the ability to make my own choices,
I thank you, Lord.
For the gift of my faith, *I thank you, Lord.*
For the gift of knowing what it is like to love, *I thank you, Lord.*
For the gift of my children and the opportunity to be a parent
to your precious souls, *I thank you, Lord.*
For the gift of experiencing life as a child, brother or sister, parent,
aunt or uncle or cousin, grandmother or grandfather,
I thank you, Lord.
For the gift of my friends who love me, *I thank you, Lord.*
For the gift of experiencing a little of what you suffered for me
as I carry my cross, *I thank you, Lord.*

For the gift of the good things you will bring out of my suffering, *I thank you, Lord.*
For the ways you will change my heart and help me become a better person because of what's happened, *I thank you, Lord.*
For the little triumphs as well as the big ones, *I thank you, Lord.*
For forgiving me, for saving me, and for not forgetting about me, *I thank you, Lord.*
For calling me by name into existence out of all eternity and giving me a purpose in life, *I thank you, Lord.*
For loving me with the most perfect love anyone could ever experience, *I thank you, Lord.*
For the promise of eternal life with you in heaven, *I thank you, Lord. Amen.*

———————

O Lord, our Sovereign, / how majestic is your name in all the earth!

~ Psalm 8:1

Day 91:
Accepting Yourself

---◆---

Sometimes the hardest thing to do is look in the mirror. It's the one place where you cannot escape the truth. For each time you meet your own gaze, you come face-to-face with your own soul. You know who you are, what you've been through, and where you've been. No one else can fully know what your life has been like except God.

Next time you look in the mirror, ask yourself if you've accepted yourself on every level. If you haven't, what is it that you are refusing to accept? Have you accepted yourself as a divorced person? Have you accepted the fact that you cannot control the thoughts, words, or actions of those who have hurt you? Have you accepted the fact that from now on, life will be different even though it's not what you wanted? Have you accepted the role you played in your divorce?

Acceptance is the first critical step toward healing, and if you feel you need to work on this, I encourage you to do so. Acceptance will bring you internal peace. If you are able to set aside the time, and if you are within distance of an Adoration chapel, make a resolution to spend one hour in Eucharistic Adoration each week. Work on acceptance and ask God for the graces you need. This will be the start of something great for you!

And the peace of God, which surpasses all understanding, will guard your hearts and your minds in Christ Jesus.

~ Philippians 4:7

Day 92:
Rest In Me And Do Not Worry

"Lord, give me patience, now!" is a funny way of illustrating how we feel, especially in times of adversity. We want the hardship to end, the pain to subside, and the sun to shine down on us again. And we want it now! We know we need to be patient but oftentimes, we just can't seem to capitalize on this virtue. It's hard to find patience when we live in a society that constantly offers us instant gratification.

But think of Mary, your mother who loves you, and her example of patience. Her life was spent in waiting. She waited with joyful anticipation for her Son and Savior to be born. She waited with quiet patience for thirty years while Jesus prepared to begin His mission (which they both knew would be the beginning of the end). She waited with grace and dignity, hour upon agonizing hour, as He was tortured and hung on the cross to die. And after He was gone, she waited with undying faith and hope for Him to return to her and take her with Him to heaven.

Pray to Mary and ask her to help you be patient with your situation while you wait.

Now you have observed my teaching, my conduct, my aim in life, my faith, my patience, my love, my steadfastness, my persecutions, and my suffering the things that happened to me in Antioch, Iconium, and Lystra. What persecutions I endured! Yet the Lord rescued me from all of them.

~ 2 Timothy 3:10-11

Day 93:
The Elevator

People lose so much during a divorce—family, friends, belongings, reputations, health, etc. This enormous loss makes it easy to feel hopeless, especially when it seems as if your future appears to hold nothing but sadness and negativity. This is precisely the point where you can become discouraged and lose hope.

But here's the good news: Hope is born out of poverty, and these losses you've experienced are exactly what Christ taught about in the Beatitudes. Experiencing poverty is really the only way to find hope. In divorce we experience not only financial poverty but a spiritual and emotional poverty, as well. Instead of losing hope, recognize hope as your elevator back up to the top floor. Your poverty has opened the door to the elevator. And if you argue that things are just too bad, or too rotten for anything good to come along in the future, then reconsider your level of faith in who God actually is—He is the Almighty, the Creator. God can do anything. God does not give according to your merits, He gives according to your hope; according to your faith. So stand up, brush yourself off, and take the elevator of hope to the top floor where you can see the sun rise on a new day!

————————————

Blessed are the poor in spirit, for theirs is the kingdom of heaven.
Blessed are those who mourn, for they will be comforted.
Blessed are the meek, for they will inherit the earth.
Blessed are those who hunger and thirst for righteousness,
for they will be filled.
Blessed are the merciful, for they will receive mercy.
Blessed are the pure in heart, for they will see God.
Blessed are the peacemakers,
for they will be called children of God.
Blessed are those who are persecuted for righteousness' sake,
for theirs is the kingdom of heaven.

~ Matthew 5:3-10

Day 94:
God Isn't Looking For Perfect Catholics

Many people are suffering silently through their troubles because they are afraid to bring their problems out into the light so they can get help. They are afraid of being judged by others. They are ashamed to admit they do not have perfect lives, especially when others look like they have perfect lives. So often, no one knows what is going on until it is too late, and the problem cannot be helped. This happens frequently when a divorce occurs—people suffer in silence because they are ashamed of their divorce.

But Christ isn't looking for "perfect" people. You don't need to have it all together for God to love you. It may appear that the way to get God's attention and favor is by being perfect, but the truth is quite the contrary! The more broken and sinful you are, the more passionately God loves you. The Gospels tell us that Christ was repeatedly criticized for associating with the tax collectors and other known sinners. When a sinful woman washed His feet with her tears, dried them with her hair, and anointed Him with expensive perfume, Jesus was criticized for allowing the encounter. But Jesus told us that those who are not sick do not need a doctor; He comes to those who are suffering. He is the divine healer! Do not hide your suffering and problems from Him. Allow Him to heal you by giving Him access and control to all that is troubling you. He will care for you and heal you because He loves you!

Then turning toward the woman, he said to Simon, "Do you see this woman? I entered your house; you gave me no water for my feet, but she has bathed my feet with her tears and dried them with her hair.

~ Luke 7:44

Day 95:
Divine Intimacy

---◇---

When a marriage ends, so does the intimacy between spouses. Not only sexual intimacy but the deep connection between spouses; being one heart, one mind, one soul, as well as one body. This loss of intimacy on multiple levels can shake you to the core, leaving you with nothing but emptiness.

But you are not alone in suffering your loss. God is not merely close to you during this time, *He is present within you*—Father, Son, and Holy Spirit. Each time you receive Holy Communion, you are united with God, the Blessed Trinity, in the deepest and most personal way. God resides in you. This is Divine intimacy, and no other type of intimacy can be more precious, more loving, or more valuable. What a tremendous gift! I encourage you to receive Holy Communion as often as possible.

Jesus said to them, "I am the bread of life. Whoever comes to me will never be hungry, and whoever believes in me will never be thirsty."

~ John 6:35

Day 96:
Don't Let Your Pursuit of Justice Steal Your Peace

———◇———

No justice, no peace.

That slogan is meant to be unsettling. Despite the threatening tone, there is much truth in this saying. It's hard to feel at peace when you are treated unjustly. Ultimately though, a divorced person cannot find peace in a heated and unrelenting search for justice because you most likely will never get it. You cannot force your ex-spouse to return or apologize. You cannot make the judges rule in your favor. You will never be at peace if you are always on the warpath.

I struggled with this for a long time, and I found comfort in contemplating Jesus washing the feet of His disciples, even Judas, His betrayer. In the Gospel story, Christ says, "as I have done for you, you should also do." We are called to treat everyone, even those who have hurt and betrayed us, with dignity and charity.

This can be a bitter pill to swallow, but be confident Christ's command to love does not mean you must become a doormat. Definitely not. It means you should stop participating in the fight. Stop living and responding in the emotional moment and consider how all the collective moments will affect your future.

———————

So if I, your Lord and Teacher, have washed your feet,
you also ought to wash one another's feet.

~ John 13:14

Day 97:
Blessed Are You

Going through a divorce and trying to rebuild your life afterward can make you feel like a failure. It can strip you of your self-esteem and make you forget you are a person who is worthy of being loved. In the Gospel of Matthew we read the following passage: "Blessed are those who mourn, for they shall be comforted." When you mourn, you are not happy, *but you are blessed!* Blessed because God is closer to you than ever before. And blessed because God rewards those who suffer.

How does He reward us? Well, frankly, there are too many ways to count. You may be praying for a job, you may be praying for the pain to stop, you may be praying for the healing of your children, you may be praying for so many things, and God will bless your requests according to the ones that He knows will make you happy. But one of the primary ways He rewards you is in purification, your refinement as a human being. You may feel that is not a reward at all, and I know why you might feel that way. It's because you didn't want the pain in the first place. You didn't want to be divorced; you wanted to be happy. But I can attest that being tested by fire is one of the greatest rewards I have ever received. Suffering changes you in a way you would have never thought possible. Suffering makes you a different person and a better person, if you allow it. You become stronger, more virtuous, and wiser.

Blessed are those who mourn, for they will be comforted.

~ Matthew 5:4

99

Day 98:
Live Instead Of Waiting To Live

What would you think if you took your baby to church to be baptized, and the priest gave you a prophetic warning that you would suffer so much that "a sword will pierce your very soul?" That would be pretty intense, to say the least. That is exactly what happened to our Blessed Mother when she and St. Joseph presented baby Jesus to the high priest, Simeon, in the temple.

If you put yourself in Mary's shoes, it might seem reasonable to go forth from that point with an extreme sense of caution—never trusting, thinking twice or even three times before making decisions, and trying to remain in control of every aspect of life to reduce the likelihood of something bad happening. Yes, this would make sense to any parent. But Sacred Tradition and the Scriptures give us a very different description of how Mary responded, all the way to when the sword did, indeed, pierce her heart. She was kind, loving, and patient; humble, thoughtful and generous. But her most astute display of virtue was her unwavering trust in God and obedience to His will despite her suffering. Everything she did was in accordance with His Divine plan, even when she had good reason to fear the future or be skeptical. Her life, and that of those whom she loved, lay completely in the hands of God. This total donation of herself was what enabled Mary to live a life of complete freedom and joy, despite the sorrows she endured. She was truly a beacon of hope to all that knew her, and still is to us today.

Your divorce may have you believing that you cannot trust anymore; that the pain you have suffered is too much to find joy in life; that God has somehow left you to fend for yourself. But what kind of life is this? This is not living! If you are feeling this way, I encourage you to contemplate Mary's example for us. Since the world is imperfect, place your trust and hope in the only thing that is perfect. Ask your mother in heaven to obtain for you the graces she knows you need to live with generosity, charity, humility, and joy. Ask her to help you live today instead of waiting to live when everything becomes just right.

Then Simeon blessed them and said to his mother Mary, "This child is destined for the falling and the rising of many in Israel, and to be a sign that will be opposed so that the inner thoughts of many will be revealed—and a sword will pierce your own soul too."

~ Luke 2:34-35

Day 99:
Blessed Are They Who Hunger And Thirst For Righteousness

---◇---

This is an important and compelling beatitude, indeed. Those who hunger and thirst for righteousness are often the ones who suffer the most. They understand the consequences of immoral decisions that are made and have seen the depths of the terrible effects. And when it seems that justice is never served, or that the crime committed is celebrated and perpetuated, it can be easy to become bitter, mistrusting and cynical toward life. So many men and women who are divorced understand this in an acute way.

But don't let the disappointment take root. Remember that heaven is our ultimate goal, not earth. There should be happiness in our earthly life, but there will also be suffering. And the justice we seek will take place when we all stand before God and account for our lives—your sins and your good works, and everyone else's. Nothing will go unnoticed, especially your own hunger for righteousness. Our goal is to spend eternity in heaven with Jesus where there will be no more suffering, and every tear will be wiped away. Keep the faith, my friend, and hope in the promise of eternal life.

See, I am coming soon; my reward is with me,
to repay according to everyone's work.

~ Revelation 22:12

Day 100:
The Ultimate Dinner Date

Everything Jesus did during His life was for the salvation of souls—every healing He performed, every parable He told, and every visit to someone's home for dinner. He had a purpose for everything He did, and it was all for saving souls. He dined with the sinners and tax collectors, as well as His more righteous friends, Lazarus, Martha, and Mary.

I believe that every day, all day, you and I receive invitations to "dine" with Christ. Invitations to the banquet in heaven that are offered through our everyday circumstances, trials and challenges. Do you recognize these invitations from Christ?

In my opinion, to "dine" with Christ is simply to connect with Him on a personal level, whether it is during your designated prayer time, at mass, driving in the car, doing homework with the children, or meeting a client. Every moment of our day can be an opportunity to connect with Jesus, simply by thinking of Him always and making sure our spiritual "antennae" are up and alert. I invite you to open your eyes to the ways Christ is inviting you to connect with Him and accept His invitation. Know that His entire reason for inviting you is to love and refresh you.

One of the dinner guests, on hearing this, said to him, "Blessed is anyone who will eat bread in the kingdom of God!"

~ Luke 14:15

Day 101:
When It's Hard To Do The Right Thing

Do you frequently feel tempted by someone of the opposite sex even though you know being involved with that person may not be good for you? Are you having a hard time controlling your temper during encounters with your ex-spouse? Do you try to ease your pain by eating or drinking too much, shopping too much, or working too much?

It's difficult enough trying to do the right thing every day and even harder when you're suffering the terrible pain of divorce. These reactions are normal for someone trying to recover from a traumatic life event, but we all know they are not behaviors that will bring you the peace and healing you are seeking. This is precisely when you need to remember that you can't do this alone, you need the graces God is waiting to give you. When you're feeling that creeping temptation, reach out for help with a quick prayer: *Jesus, I love you, be my strength!* He will give you everything you need to persevere.

No testing has overtaken you that is not common to everyone.
God is faithful, and he will not let you be tested beyond your strength,
but with the testing he will also provide the way out
so that you may be able to endure it.

~ 1 Corinthians 10:13

Day 102:
Rely On Christ, Not On Yourself

Going through a divorce and trying to make your way afterward can be incredibly daunting. There are many times when your responsibilities, worries, and anxieties can overwhelm you like a tidal wave. But when you begin to feel overwhelmed by it all, step back, take some deep breaths, and remember that God is with you. He sees it all. He knows your every thought and your every concern.

Remember the words of St. Paul: "By the grace of God, I am who I am." You are able to do many things because God enables you. He will give you the strength to achieve your goals and accomplish your necessary responsibilities. Most importantly, He will never give you a cross that is too heavy for you to bear. Take time each morning to renew your commitment to Christ and ask for His help in getting through the day.

But you have saved us from our foes, /
and have put to confusion those who hate us.

~ Psalm 44:7

Day 103:
True Nobility

In today's society we have lost a sense of nobility as a people. In our "instant gratification" society, we have lost our understanding of what it means to work long and hard for what we have. We've forgotten the virtues of perseverance and patience. In decades past, a noble person would be described as one who never gave up the fight for what was good; someone who sacrificed himself for the good of others. Patience, perseverance, hard work, and sacrifice were the jewels in the prized crown of achievement that was received at the end.

Your divorce, as painful as it is, has given you the opportunity to exemplify true nobility to society. You have the chance to not only strengthen yourself through the practice of these important virtues, but also to be an example to those who are watching you. I had someone watching me during my struggle though I was completely unaware. Years later, she told me how observing my courage and perseverance helped her in her own personal trial. Don't let your divorce drag you down. Ask God for the graces you need to persevere and carry your cross with nobility. He will give you all you need!

Strength and dignity are her clothing,
and she laughs at the time to come.

~ Proverbs 31:25

Day 104:
Your Blueprint For Building Holiness

When going through a divorce and trying to rebuild your life afterwards, it's easy and quite typical to become consumed with details—children, court battles, and angry encounters with your ex-spouse; the whys, the how-did-it-happens, the what-ifs. It can be a veritable merry-go-round of emotions and anxieties. But God wants you to lift your face up from these details to see your life in the context of time and eternity. There is more to your life than what is happening now. And although details of this time are part and parcel of the process, they should all be a means to an end—your life in eternity. There is nothing more important than getting to heaven.

You may be suffering terribly and experiencing incredible pain. Don't worry, that is part of your life at the moment. But it's only part of your life. It will not always be this way. Even though it might seem the pain will never end, change will come, and a new phase of life will arrive. Your life is a precious gift, and the way you handle yourself now is your blueprint for building holiness. Take some time today to pray, be as open with God as possible, and thank Him for the gift of your life.

Therefore, since we are surrounded by so great a cloud of witnesses, let us also lay aside every weight and the sin that clings so closely, and let us run with perseverance the race that is set before us.

~ Hebrews 12:1

Day 105:
Why Do Good Things Happen To Bad People?

In the book, *Making Sense Out of Suffering*, Dr. Peter Kreeft makes a very poignant statement. He states that the common question posed when people experience suffering is "Why do bad things happen to good people?" But if you look at it from the opposite angle, he says, you need to ask, "Why do good things happen to bad people?" This statement puts all our pain and suffering into a completely different context, one that makes more sense in trying to tackle the question of why God allows suffering.

We are all sinners, each and every one of us. We may be good people: practicing Catholics, taxpayers, vigilant voters, etc., but we are not perfect people. We offend God daily with our sins. And yet, He continues to bless us. He continues to shower us with His graces. If you sat down to write a list of your blessings, you might never finish because the list would be nearly inexhaustible. Every second of your life, every breath you take is a gift to you from God. Take time today to share your suffering with Christ in prayer. Find consolation, comfort, and perspective in reflecting on the great blessings He has bestowed upon you.

But God proves his love for us in that while we still were sinners Christ died for us.

~ Romans 5:8

Day 106:
Learning To Pray Well

Oftentimes the first thing to go out the window when a divorce occurs is prayer time. Most of the time, this is not deliberate. It is because there is so much pain. Prayer becomes difficult, dry, and stilted. But if we stop praying, we have no life line—no connection with God, the One we need most during this terrible time.

Try to remember, prayer should be very simple, a personal conversation with God. I'm willing to bet that you pray more than you think you do over the course of a day. The questions you ask silently, the quick requests for help, and your responses to inspirations from the Holy Spirit are all ways of praying. Prayer is not an obligation to fulfill, nor an item to check off a list. Prayer is our loving connection with God. I encourage you to make time during the day for prayer in this simple way; communicating with God, the One who loves you most.

But he would withdraw to deserted places and pray.

~ Luke 5:16

Day 107:
Going To Extremes

When a divorce occurs, life becomes "extreme." You experience extreme emotions, extreme circumstances, and extreme life changes. These extremes can be exhausting and overwhelming as you try to find a place to plant your feet firmly on the ground and move forward.

But not all of the extremes you encounter will be bad. As you work to push forward, you may feel terribly alone and afraid of the future. But think for a moment about the apostles. These Jewish men were considered to be extreme because they believed Jesus was the Messiah, yet they were great men precisely because of their faith. As they huddled together in the Upper Room in fear for their lives, God rewarded their faith by pouring out the Holy Spirit upon them. They were filled with refreshment, renewal, courage, and extreme joy, which they spread to all nations.

Let your faith be the one extreme that you use to keep your head above water during this difficult time; your life preserver. Let the Holy Spirit show you how to become a great apostle by staying faithful when it's hard to pray and by believing when it's hard to believe. God will reward your faith with many blessings.

He asked them, "But who do you say that I am?"
Peter answered him, "You are the Messiah."

~ Mark 8:29

Day 108:
Forgive The Debts

In the Gospel of Matthew we find Jesus' teaching on how to forgive. There are two verses that strike me as intersecting even though they are found in different chapters. They are: "Not seven times, but, I tell you, seventy-seven times." (Matthew 18:22), and, "If anyone forces you to go one mile, go also the second mile." (Matthew 5:41). It's as if Christ is saying that simply obeying His law of forgiveness is not enough. "I want you to put your whole heart into it," He tells us. "It doesn't matter if what happened is fair—just give and give until it hurts. That's what I want from you, because that's what I give to you." Compelling thoughts, indeed.

The wicked servant in chapter eighteen did not appreciate the great favor the master granted him. He was about to be sold into slavery along with his wife and children and as a result would lose all his possessions. The same thing would happen to us if we did not have Christ's mercy and forgiveness—we would be lost! How can you show Christ that you appreciate His great gift of mercy and forgiveness? Take some time to reflect upon this and make a few resolutions in forgiveness that you can practice.

Blessed are the merciful, for they will receive mercy.

~ Matthew 5:7

Day 109:
Real Security

Security. What does that mean to you? For many people, security equals large amounts of possessions, a nice home, savings in the bank, and happy relationships. There is nothing wrong with feeling secure because you have a nice home, money in the bank, the freedom to purchase at will, and a happy family. These things make us feel safe, content, snug, and unfortunately for some of us, even smug. I was smug before my divorce happened. I believed that divorced people, especially Catholics, were failures and "bad Catholics." But when it suddenly happened to me, my perspective changed completely. It's precisely at this point, when the worst happens, and you begin seeing yourself stripped of the things you love that something very good will happen; if you allow it.

Divorce is humiliating and degrading. You might ask what can be good about having the things you love stripped away? Well, it's not good, unless it's coupled with the desire to become holy. So many times in my life, I have lost things—reputation, money, friendships, my home, and my marriage. They've all been very painful events. It wasn't until I learned to ask God to help me look at my life through His eyes, from His perspective, that I was able to see the possessions and relationships that I lost were actually separating me from Him. In most cases, I was just too attached. They held a higher place in my life than He did. I realized God was doing me a favor. He was removing an obstacle between Him and me. He was removing the beam from my eye.

It wasn't until after my divorce that I could see how absent God was in my marriage and how far my relationship with my husband was dragging me away from Him. God and the promise of life with Him in heaven became all the security I needed. No possession or human being can give me that, only God. I invite you to reflect on how God may be trying to remove obstacles between you and Him. Count on my prayers for clarity and peace.

Jesus, looking at him, loved him and said, "You lack one thing; go, sell what you own, and give the money to the poor, and you will have treasure in heaven; then come, follow me."

~ Mark 10:21

Day 110:
Feeling Overwhelmed? Turn To Christ

If you are feeling overwhelmed by all the challenges of life, you are not alone. Even the apostles felt the same way, and they had Jesus walking and talking with them every day. In Mark's Gospel account of Jesus feeding the multitude (Mark 6:34-44), the apostles were totally overwhelmed with the prospect of feeding over 5,000 people. They had no money, they were in the middle of nowhere, and it was getting dark. They did what most people would do in that situation: they panicked! You know the rest of the story. Jesus came to their rescue by taking charge of the situation and feeding everyone by multiplying the bread and fish.

The apostles were blinded by their panic and failed to see that they had Jesus—God Himself—right there with them. So instead of turning to Christ, they tried to solve the problem all on their own and basically gave up. We tend to do the same thing. When the problems that result from separation and divorce overwhelm us, we tend to try and solve them all on our own, ignoring Christ, who is standing right next to us anxious to help. All we need to do is ask Him and trust that He will help. Resolve today to turn to Christ first when the challenges and problems of life overwhelm you. Like the apostles, you will be amazed at how Christ, in His infinite love and mercy, will work in your life.

And all ate and were filled.

~ Mark 6:42

Day 111:
You Are Not Alone

You are not alone. Turn to your strongest and truest ally, the Holy Spirit. The Holy Spirit, living within you, has what you need and more. For the battles of divorce, strength. For the decisions, guidance. For the trials, patience. And for the pain, consolation.

Call on the Holy Spirit, in all things, but especially in your times of greatest need. Consider the following prayer:

O, Holy Spirit, beloved of my soul, I adore you.
Enlighten me, guide me, strengthen me, console me.
Tell me what I should do, give me your orders.
I promise to submit myself to all that You desire of me and to accept all that You permit to happen to me.
Let me only know Your will. Amen.

Do you not know that you are God's temple
and that God's Spirit dwells in you?

~ 1 Corinthians 3:16

Day 112:
Holiness Through Divorce

Divorce is a severe and heavy cross that many men, women and children bear these days. It is so difficult that I believe it is one of the primary reasons people leave the Church and lose their faith. So it's important to remember that Christ promised us He will never give us more than we can handle; that He will ease our burdens. It is true. Our trials and challenges in life are meant to purify us and make us holy. You're probably thinking, "Divorce is so painful that words cannot really describe how I feel, and there are times when I'd rather lay down and sleep for the rest of the year than face another day of hurting. Society is telling me that I should just find someone new and get over it already. The Church says I can't have sex outside of marriage, and I can't remarry without a decree of nullity. No one really understands the pain I'm in, and I can't find consolation anywhere. How the heck is my divorce supposed to make me holy?!?!"

Well, simply stated, holiness is spending your entire lifetime serving and doing good for others. For some that might seem fairly easy to do. But when there are so many reasons to be angry and resentful, the idea of holiness looks impossible. But holiness really depends primarily upon two things: self-dominion and willpower.

Self-dominion is the act of knowing yourself as completely as possible and overcoming the obstacles that stand in your way of doing good. To know yourself as completely as possible, you must constantly review yourself. Take note of your behaviors, your temperament, and how the circumstances in your life have affected and changed you. Creating a life program is a fantastic way to do this and acts as a powerful tool to help you through your entire life. Willpower is attained by forming your will in such a way that you can accept the tragedy of your divorce; trusting that God has designed a different future for you than what you expected. And responding to that unexpected future with love: love for God and a love that will pave the way for forgiveness of the ones who have hurt you.

Yet, O Lord, you are our Father;
we are the clay, and you are our potter;
we are all the work of your hand.

~ Isaiah 64:8

Day 113:
You Can Rise Above It All!

There are three enemies of your soul right now: the world and all its distractions, the devil, and yourself. The world and all its distractions wants to redefine your moral standards and make you think that doing what you know is wrong is actually just fine. The world wants you to put yourself first, in every way possible, and seek only the things that will "make you happy." The devil is constantly whispering in your ear that you can't succeed and that you aren't worthy. He echoes the voice of the world; changing your values and standards is what you must do as a result of your divorce. He wants you to believe that you have no other choice. And you—you are your own worst enemy if you try to fight all this on your own.

God's grace is far more powerful than all of these three. God is not stingy with His grace or His love. He wants to shower you with graces and blessings so you can fight the good fight. Make a resolution today to allow Christ full access over your life. Seek Him in the sacraments, in prayer, and in Eucharistic Adoration. Let Him give you all that you need so you can be all that He wants you to be.

The God who gave me vengeance /and brought down peoples under me, /who brought me out from my enemies; / you exalted me above my adversaries, / you delivered me from the violent.

~ 2 Samuel 22:48-49

Day 114:
There Is A Reason

Have you ever contemplated the fact that because God is God and the Almighty Creator of the universe, He could have easily just said to mankind, "Be redeemed"? He could have simply opened the gates of heaven to us just like that. But He did not. Instead, He chose to send His only Son into a world that hated Him and offered His Son to suffer and die for us. God is always deliberate in what He does. For example, in the Gospel of Luke when Jesus meets the disciples on the road to Emmaus, He pretends not to know what they are talking about because He wants them to tell Him. He wants them to communicate their sadness and disappointment with Him. Therefore, you too, should share your sadness and disappointment with Christ. He walks by your side, ready to listen.

Was it not necessary that the Messiah should suffer these things and then enter into his glory?

~ Luke 24:26

Day 115:
You Are A Light For The World!

Typically in a divorce situation, the worst comes out in both spouses. Insults and heated exchanges become the new mode of communication with each other. This leaves everyone involved feeling discouraged and often feeling terrible about themselves. But no matter what hurtful words have been exchanged in your divorce, do not become discouraged. It is not by accident that you are who you are. Everything about you as a person from your physical attributes to your temperament was a deliberate act of God, for He created you a unique and beautiful creature.

If you need a reminder of how much you are loved, I recommend two things to help you: receive Holy Communion and spend an hour in Eucharistic Adoration. Through the Blessed Sacrament you receive the Father, Son, and Holy Spirit within you. What an incredible gift. What an incredible consolation that the Creator of the universe chooses to make His home within your soul! Let the light of Christ shine through the darkness of the pain you feel and radiate through your entire being. Then you will become a light to all who see you.

In the same way, let your light shine before others, so that they may see your good works and give glory to your Father in heaven.

~ Matthew 5:16

Day 116:
Save Me, Lord!

Sometimes the frustration, anger and disappointment of divorce are so overwhelming you may feel you can hardly stand it! The fear of the unknown future and the implications of things continuing to turn out badly can weigh heavily upon you. We can easily see ourselves as the apostles while they were in the boat, with the storm beating down and the waves beginning to overtake the boat. But remember, Christ was there with them in the boat. Many mistake His sleeping for ignoring the apostles in their time of need but in reality, Christ was setting the example for us. *Be at peace in the midst of your storm. Do not worry. Do not fear. Have faith, have hope, be peaceful, for I am your Lord. I will take care of you.*

The apostles were astounded because although they loved Jesus and believed He was "the Christ, the Son of God," their faith was still weak. They still had to learn that their peace would only come through trusting Jesus. And so at this particular time, fear ruled their souls and dictated their behavior. But oh, how different it was when the Holy Spirit came to them at Pentecost and filled them with a holy boldness! How incredible it was to see their fear changed to inspiration and zeal!

Imagine yourself in the boat with Jesus, asleep. Imagine your fears, worries and hurts as the waves crash upon you trying to destroy your boat. Now, look at Jesus asleep and imagine—what should you do?

And he said to them, "Why are you afraid, you of little faith?"
Then he got up and rebuked the winds and the sea;
and there was a dead calm.

~ Matthew 8:26

Day 117:
The Art Of Letting Go

We all know the story of the rich young man who approached Jesus (Mark 10). He calls Jesus "Good Teacher" as he approaches Him. The rich young man wants to know how he can inherit eternal life. Jesus replies, "Why do you call me good?" By saying this, Jesus places himself on the same level as the young man; Jesus wants this young man to know that he can approach Him with trust and ease. In the same way, Jesus wants you to approach Him with trust and ease.

Then Jesus asks the young man to follow the commandments. Because of Jesus' divine nature, He already knows the young man obeys the commandments. So why would He say that? Because He wanted the young man to recognize himself as a good person. And that is the same with you. Christ wants you to understand that you are good. Despite all that has happened to you in your divorce, He sees and loves this goodness in you.

Then Jesus tells the rich young man to sell everything and follow Him. This was the point where the rich young man's life could have changed in ways he never would have dreamed of! But instead, he walked away, sad and unable to let go of his possessions, the things he believed to be too valuable to give up. Jesus was sad as well because someone He loved refused Him. But Jesus did not force the young man to follow. Jesus, Himself, showed us the art of "letting go." He loved him but did not force him to stay.

Is there something you need to let go? I invite you to take time this week to reflect upon this story and see what the Holy Spirit is telling you.

———————————

Jesus, looking at him, loved him and said, "You lack one thing; go, sell what you own, and give the money to the poor, and you will have treasure in heaven; then come, follow me."

~ Mark 10:21

Day 118:
If You Only Knew What God Was Offering

If you only knew what God was offering you! You would forget every care, every concern, every worry, and every need. If you only knew what God was offering, you would beg Him to give you only His love and His grace and that would be enough.

The Samaritan woman who met Jesus at the well wanted and needed love. She had already been through five husbands and was living with another man she was not married to by the time she had her encounter with Christ. After five marriages and divorces and now a live-in relationship, do you think she had found the love she was looking for?

The love she needed was finally found in Christ. He sat at the well in the hot sun asking her for a drink. This woman was drawn in by Jesus. Here was a Jewish man that by society's standards should have ignored her. But instead, with His gentle nature, He drew her to Himself and spoke the words of everlasting life that touched her soul in a way no one else could. And Christ wants to do the same for you. Christ wants to show you that He knows the ache you carry with you. He knows the love you are looking for. He wants to give it to you.

Like the woman at the well, we hope for things that may provide some brief happiness or consolation, but in reality they are things that will bring us more pain. So instead, give your complete trust to Christ, especially with the things that are most important to you. Will it be easy? No! It's not easy to loosen your grip and let go of the things that are important to you. But the harder it is to let go, the more you know you need to do it. Learn to trust Christ and His plan for your life. Place your whole life and everything you love in His hands and then sit back and watch! He will make you happier than you could ever imagine!

———————

The water that I will give will become in them a spring of water gushing up to eternal life.

~ John 4:14

Day 119:
The True Victim

---◇---

Jesus—the man who loved, the man who healed, the man who fed, and the man who gave hope to those suffering from despair—was mocked, beaten, tortured and killed, dying the shameful death of a criminal. Imagine you are present at the crucifixion and see all that is taking place. Jesus' mother, Mary, cannot stop her tears, nor can Mary Magdalene or the other women who are watching from afar. The soldiers are laughing and making fun of Jesus as He suffocates and chokes on His own blood. Where are the apostles but John? All those who said they loved Him are hiding in fear. All those who welcomed Him into their town as a king, just one week before, are spitting on Him and shaking their fists at Him. They want him dead. And during it all, Jesus is winning their salvation. And then He says, "Father, forgive them."

Jesus will help you forgive whoever it is in your life that needs your forgiveness. Sometimes the downfall in trying to forgive is trying to do it all on your own. Remember that the very fact that you are willing to forgive is, in fact, a grace from God. So ask Him to stoke that spark of willingness to forgive into a flame and let this flame set your heart on fire with love.

Then Jesus said, "Father, forgive them; for they do not know what they are doing." And they cast lots to divide his clothing.

~ Luke 23:34

Day 120:
The Lesson Of The Leper

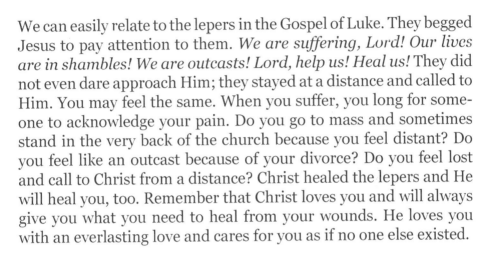

We can easily relate to the lepers in the Gospel of Luke. They begged Jesus to pay attention to them. *We are suffering, Lord! Our lives are in shambles! We are outcasts! Lord, help us! Heal us!* They did not even dare approach Him; they stayed at a distance and called to Him. You may feel the same. When you suffer, you long for someone to acknowledge your pain. Do you go to mass and sometimes stand in the very back of the church because you feel distant? Do you feel like an outcast because of your divorce? Do you feel lost and call to Christ from a distance? Christ healed the lepers and He will heal you, too. Remember that Christ loves you and will always give you what you need to heal from your wounds. He loves you with an everlasting love and cares for you as if no one else existed.

When you recognize God's goodness and the way He takes care of you, be sure to give thanks to Him. Remember the one leper who turned back and thanked Him. This man was a Samaritan. Samaritans understood that according to the Jews they counted for nothing. They were outcasts. But this man, the most unlikely of the bunch, recognized what a great miracle Jesus had performed for him and came back to thank Jesus. We should all follow in his footsteps and remember to thank God for all His blessings, great and small.

Then he said to him,
"Get up and go on your way; your faith has made you well."

~ Luke 17:19

Day 121:
Confidence Is The Key

God wants you to have confidence in Him. When Jesus was on earth, He taught us how to pray both in word and example. When He prayed, Jesus referred to the Father in heaven as "Abba," which means "daddy," a term the Jews were not accustomed to using in prayer. Christ was showing us how to approach God in prayer—with the affection and trust that a child has for his daddy. Even when Christ was beginning His passion, He walked into the Garden of Gethsemane, knelt down by the rock, and cried, "Abba" (see Mark 14:36). In this, your suffering and passion, approach God with confidence and affection and believe He hears you and will help you.

God doesn't sit passively up in heaven and watch life hit you from all angles, nor does He sit idly by while you struggle to deal with your difficulties. God wants you to come to Him with your sufferings, your concerns, your requests, your desires and your plans. He wants you to know that He is waiting for you, every moment of the day and at every turn. And if it is true you should approach God as a trusting child approaches his father, it is even more true that "Abba" will give you what you need. He is waiting for your permission to help you; He is seeking your open heart that welcomes Him and allows Him to work. Are you open to allowing God to help you?

So I say to you, Ask, and it will be given you; search, and you will find; knock, and the door will be opened for you.

~ Luke 11:9

Day 122:
Turn The Other Cheek?!

How do you "turn the other cheek" in your situation? What is it that God is really asking of you as you go through the pain of separating from your ex-spouse? Is He asking you to be a doormat, letting anyone and everyone walk all over you and abuse you? No. Defending and protecting yourself and your children is certainly very important. Turning the other cheek would be loving in a way that is contrary to the way society loves. Society preaches a "feel good" love; as long as it feels good, love, but when it doesn't feel good anymore, stop. This definition is false.

Love is most vividly displayed when things are difficult and painful. A loving person still remains charitable; still seeks the good of the other; and still does not allow angry sentiments to dictate his or her words and actions. It is easy to look at someone who has hurt us and say, "That person doesn't deserve my love." But contemplate Christ on the cross—the torture, the whipping, the insults, the spitting, the pain! That did not feel good, yet Christ endured His torture and pain out of sheer love for us, even though we do not deserve it.

It is easy to love and care for people you like. It is harder to do anything for someone with whom you are at odds. But if you truly want to find healing and peace in your life and move forward to a better place, step outside your comfort zone and stretch your heart a little wider. Ask God for the grace to forgive others and to find love where there is none. Ask God for the grace to love.

But I say to you, Do not resist an evildoer. But if anyone strikes you on the right cheek, turn the other also.

~ Matthew 5:39

Day 123:
Is My Divorce Part Of God's Plan?

Divorce can feel like a sickness so terrible it makes you want to die. The pain seems to be never-ending. But God can take the most horrible situation and bring good out of it. In the same way He allowed Lazarus to die, He allowed your divorce to happen. But is it really part of God's plan? Well, God tells us in Scripture that He "hates divorce." But growing closer to Him through the pain is part of His will. As well as using the opportunity to bring good things about as a result of the bad.

Certainly in times of great distress, you might feel as if God has forgotten you, as if He has left you alone to suffer. Yet, it pains Him to see you suffering. With each cross you carry, no matter how great or small, Christ will carry you and show you a new path; a better way than the one you were on before. He wants you to experience growth, especially growing closer to Him. Trust that He will take care of you.

So if anyone is in Christ, there is a new creation: everything old has passed away; see, everything has become new!

~ 2 Corinthians 5:17

Day 124:
Do You Believe I Can Do This?

It is interesting to see how the blind men asked Jesus to cure them. Jesus didn't just wave His hand and give them their eyesight. He tested their faith. He wasn't testing them to be cruel; He wanted them to recognize that faith in Him was the key. Jesus healed them because of their faith. How much faith do you have in God at this time? As you reflect on all that has happened to you in your divorce and all that is ahead of you, what would your answer be to His question, "Do you believe I can do this?" It is easy to say the words and ask God to help you in whatever you need, but how much do you really believe that He will take care of you? In going through a divorce, it can be particularly hard to trust again, and God knows your reservations. Yet He continually calls you to come closer to Him because He wants you to put your trust in Him alone.

How can you increase your ability to trust in such a difficult time? First, ask God for the grace to grow in your faith and ability to trust in Him. He will give you what you need. Second, proceed in your life as if He has already taken care of the things you need.

So I tell you, whatever you ask for in prayer, believe that you have received it, and it will be yours.

~ Mark 11:24

131

Day 125:
This Is My Blood

When you receive the precious blood during communion, it is under the appearance of wine, yet it is the same blood that covered the whips and chains that were used to scourge Jesus as He was so unjustly punished. It is the same blood which ran down the cross and dripped onto the ground as Jesus hung there, suffering for us. It is the same blood that burst forth from His side when the soldier's arrow pierced His chest. And you are able to receive it! The blood of the new and everlasting covenant, as it is declared during the celebration of the mass. May you receive the grace to understand how precious is His blood. Even though you are not worthy to receive this gift—none of us are—Jesus still gives you the opportunity to come and be one with Him.

Then he took a cup, and after giving thanks he gave it to them, saying, "Drink from it, all of you; for this is my blood of the covenant, which is poured out for many for the forgiveness of sins.

~ Matthew 26:27-28

Day 126:
God's Ways Are Not Ours

Christ suffered more than you will ever know. He was the true, innocent victim convicted and punished unjustly, though suffered out of love for us. If there is anyone who can understand your anger, your outrage at what has happened, it is Christ. Not only did He suffer every injustice, as a completely innocent and loving human being, but he knows all that you have been through better than anyone. He knows the pain, the frustration, the insanity.

But always remember He has a completely different perspective on what is happening because He sees and knows everything. The suffering you bear will bring about good things somewhere else, and this is one reason why God allows you to suffer. What good things will God bring out of your situation? What good things have already happened? Go meet Him in the garden and kneel down with Him at the rock and talk to Him about your situation. Unite your pain to His and embrace your cross with His help. As you kneel with Jesus in the garden and see His sweat turn into drops of blood, know He suffers for your sake, ask Him to help you suffer as He did; out of love for others and the desire for good.

He said, "Abba Father, for you all things are possible; remove this cup from me; yet, not what I want, but what you want."

~ Mark 14:36

Day 127:
It Only Takes A Few Stones

It's easy to focus on the things you don't have or the size of the obstacles you face or how bad things seem to be. And when you're going through a divorce, some obstacles seem insurmountable. But always remember that with God, all things are possible. Recall the story of David and Goliath. David had so very little: a slingshot and a few stones. And Goliath was, well, a giant! David didn't have much to work with. The obstacles he faced were tremendous. Yes, things looked pretty bad for David, but God had given him exactly what he needed. And we all know how the story ends.

Just like David, God has given you exactly what you need for this moment, and He will continue to provide for you. Everything you need to fulfill the purpose God has for you is within your reach. And just as He did for David, God will do extraordinary things in your life.

So David prevailed over the Philistine with a sling and a stone,
striking down the Philistine and killing him;
there was no sword in David's hand.

~ 1 Samuel 17:50

Day 128:
God Will Exceed Your Expectations

In his address given on December 1, 2010, Pope Benedict XVI said:

> If God is supremely good and wise, why does evil and the suffering of the innocent exist? Saints as well, precisely the saints, ask themselves this question. Enlightened by faith, they give us an answer that opens our heart to trust and hope: In the mysterious designs of Providence, even from evil, God draws a greater good, as [Saint] Julian of Norwich writes: 'I learned by the grace of God that I must remain firmly in the faith, and hence I must firmly and perfectly believe that all will end well.'

Yes, dear brothers and sisters, God's promises are always greater than our hopes. If we entrust to God, to his immense love, the most pure and most profound desires of our heart, we will never be disappointed.

Open your heart to God. Bring him your desires. His love for you is more vast, more tender and more enduring than you can ever imagine.

The Lord replied, "If you had faith the size of a mustard seed, you could say to this mulberry tree, 'Be uprooted and planted in the sea,' and it would obey you.

~ Luke 17:6

135

Day 129:
Choosing To Trust God

There are so many uncertainties in life. You have circumstances beyond your control and situations you wish you could manage. Fear and doubt take up residence in your heart. You are frequently filled with worry and a long list of "what-ifs?" Confidence wavers, and your trust in God and His perfect plan falters.

These are the times when you must make a tough decision—the decision to trust God. But feel confident in your decision because with God, all things are possible! God knows your heart. He knows your fears and your worries. He knows the challenges you face. Give it all to Him. Let Him carry your burdens. Trust in Him, and you will find peace in your pain and strength in your struggles.

Trust in the Lord with all your heart, /
and do not rely on your own insight.

~ Proverbs 3:5

Day 130:
Perfect In His Sight

At times you may not like yourself. You may have acted in ways that you're not proud. Maybe you've said things you wish you could take back. When you hear what others have to say about you, it's not always pretty. It may not even be the truth, but you begin to believe it.

Well, let me remind you that God loves you just the way you are. With all your flaws and with all your failings, warts and all. He made you in His perfect image. You are clay in God's hands. He is working on you, every day, to mold you into the person that He made you to be. In God's eyes, you are perfect. You are unique and beautiful in His sight. You are loved, and you are cherished!

So God created humankind in his image, in the image of God he created them; male and female he created them.

~ Genesis 1:27

Day 131:
How Long Must I Pray?

It can sometimes feel like God doesn't answer your prayers. You pray and ask Him for His help and guidance. You confide in Him all the hurts, worries and deepest secrets of your heart. Then you look around and your circumstances have not changed. You wonder, "How long must I continue to pray before God will answer my prayers?"

Consider the story of Zachariah and Elizabeth. They were "advanced in age" and well beyond the age of childbearing. It was unlikely that a woman of Elizabeth's age could possibly bear a child; their situation seemed hopeless. More than that, childlessness was thought of as evidence of God's disfavor. People in their community likely wondered what terrible sin they must have committed. But Zachariah and Elizabeth remained faithful to God and lived good and holy lives. The Lord heard the prayers of Zachariah and Elizabeth, and even though their situation seemed hopeless, He gave them the child they longed for. And not just any child; their child became known as John the Baptist!

God did the impossible for Zachariah and Elizabeth. So continue to pray and know that God is always listening.

Then Jesus told them a parable about their need to pray always and not to lose heart.

~ Luke 18:1

Day 132:
It's Not You, It's Me

So many marriages fail because of spousal infidelity and dishonesty. Many times the failure lies in the fact that what one spouse brings to the relationship is very different than what he or she promised on the day of the wedding. Losing your marriage can leave you feeling totally rejected, unlovable, and unworthy.

But shift your focus and turn your eyes to Christ because He wants to show you the truth—that you are valuable and lovable. Oftentimes you look for self-worth in another person. You gauge your importance by how others treat you and what they think about you. But Jesus is trying to show you that your real value can only be found in Him. Look at Him on the cross and see how He hangs there, completely emptied of Himself—for you! If you were the only human being on earth, He would come down and do it all again— for you! You are the reason He did it all. No one loves you the way Christ does. Let that be the source of your self-worth today, and every day.

Can a woman forget her nursing child, / or show no compassion for the child of her womb? / Even these may forget, / yet I will not forget you.

~ Isaiah 49:15

Day 133:
Dealing With Bad Memories

Like any other traumatic life event, divorce leaves behind the residue of bad memories connected to painful emotions. Some people cling tightly to these memories using them as a shield against future hurts. "I'll never let myself be that foolish/trusting/vulnerable again!" Some people desperately want to free themselves from the chains of the bad memories but don't know how to do this.

The next time you are confronted with bad memories, lay it all down at the foot of the cross. Literally try to imagine yourself laying an armful of heavy stones down at Christ's feet as He hangs on the cross. Give it all to Him. Let Him take them all from you and give you peace in return. This is something you can do each and every time you remember the things that bring you down. Let Jesus bring you the healing and peace in a way that only He can do.

Peace I leave with you; my peace I give to you.
I do not give to you as the world gives. Do not let your hearts be
troubled, and do not let them be afraid.

~ John 14:27

Day 134:
A Gift For God

If you're newly separated or divorced, you may find yourself having to do tasks your spouse once managed or that you did together. For some, paying the bills by yourself is the new undertaking. Dealing with homework for a school-age child is the new challenge for others. It could be yard work, carpool, or all of the above.

It's easy to let resentment build during these new chores, but here is a suggestion for dealing with your burdens. Resolve to do the difficult task and do it to the very best of your ability and offer it up as a gift to God. This offering is just another way, like prayer, to honor the Lord. The benefits of such an undertaking are many. First, you're less likely to resent what is no longer just an irksome chore but an offering for God. However, if you do find yourself feeling resentful, make it part of your offering and have an honest, heartfelt communication with the Lord in the process. Second, a dreaded task will be getting done and done well.

When you look at the mowed lawn or the carpool line, look past your resentment and the unfairness of it all, and see your offering to God and imagine His joy in your offering.

For you, O Lord of hosts, the God of Israel, have made this revelation to your servant, saying, 'I will build you a house'; therefore your servant has found courage to pray this prayer to you.

~ 2 Samuel 7:27

Day 135:
Practice Forgiveness Every Day

In many divorce situations, forgiveness is an ongoing matter. Here's how it usually goes: at some point during or after the divorce, you realize that you're tired of bearing all the hurt and pain. You're tired of being angry at the person who has caused you that pain. You've been learning about forgiveness, and you learn that it's a conscious choice. You're at the point that you're ready to forgive. And you do. You forgive your ex-spouse for every thing—every last thing. And boy, does that feel good! It's a lifting of a burden from your shoulders! You feel lighter already! Regardless of whether or not you've contacted your spouse to forgive him/her, you've done the productive work. You have forgiven! And you feel good! Time to move on.

Then one day, something happens. There's a dispute over the children. Your ex wants to revisit some of the issues that caused your marriage to crumble. Any number of things can happen. And then you are right back in the place of needing to forgive. Again.

This is when you get the chance to practice forgiveness every day. Maybe not every day, exactly, but on an ongoing basis. Forgiveness is not a one-time endeavor, and it's done. Practice forgiveness every day. You'll find plenty of opportunities. You'll also find that in extending your hand in forgiveness, purely as your choice, you will receive more blessings than you can ever imagine. Your life will become more calm and controlled. And you will honor the Lord with your attitude toward your ex-spouse.

Not seven times, but, I tell you, seventy-seven times.

~ Matthew 18:22

142

Day 136:
Don't Be Afraid Of The Dark

As a child, I was afraid of the dark. This was especially true when I was alone in my room at night. Although I knew that nothing changed when I turned off my light, the darkness often filled me with fear. I imagined things that I knew logically did not exist, but my emotions wouldn't listen to my head, and I shivered beneath my covers in fear.

Divorce can feel like you're cloaked in darkness. New challenges and burdens weigh heavily. Confusion, disappointment, hurt and anger descend like a dark fog. Problems are magnified, if not in reality, at least in our own minds.

As an adult, I've come to appreciate the darkness. There's a certain peace and quiet in the dark. Oddly enough, things that aren't clear in the light of day become more clear in the dark of night.

Just like God gives us daylight, He also gives us the dark night. Look at the darkness as a time for quiet, a time for peace. Through this darkness, He will bring you into His light. Know that God is with you, now, as much as ever.

I am the light of the world. Whoever follows me will never walk in darkness but will have the light of life.

~ John 8:12

143

Day 137:
Everybody's Fine

In the 2009 Robert DeNiro film, the children of a recently widowed man try to conceal the truth about their lives to make their father believe that "everybody's fine." Needless to say, everybody's not fine, and they are all struggling with various life situations.

In the time leading up to and during a divorce, you may be tempted to show others that things are just fine. Admittedly there's nothing wrong with putting on a "game face" to the outside world. But your heavenly Father knows your heart. He knows your hurts, your pains, and your troubles. He knows the trials you endure and the heartaches that you suffer. There is no concealing the truth from Him. With Him, you can be just who you are so bring Him your worries and your pain. And allow Him to love you in your brokenness.

Cast your burden on the Lord, / and he will sustain you; /
he will never permit / the righteous to be moved.

~ Psalm 55:22

Day 138:
Only Words

Do you remember the saying we used as children? "Sticks and stones can break my bones, but words can never hurt me." I'm not so sure that I agree.

Our words have awesome power. They have the power to heal, the power to encourage, and the power to comfort. They also have the power to hurt. With just a few cruel or thoughtless words, we can inflict painful and sometimes mortal wounds. No wonder the Book of Proverbs speaks so much about the use of the tongue.

As you navigate through your separation and divorce and during the months and years afterwards, how will you use your words? Will you use them to create an atmosphere of peace and love? Or will you use them to create confusion and doubt? Will you use them to build others up? Or to tear them down? Remember, once you speak, your words are "out there"; there's no taking them back. You cannot undo the damage that they may have done.

Think about how you use your words. Do you use them wisely and for good? Are they timely and well chosen? Do you exercise restraint when things are better left unsaid or a response is better off not given? Do you use your words to please God by being gracious and gentle? When you speak, are you an instrument of God's grace?

Let your speech always be gracious, seasoned with salt, so that you may know how you ought to answer everyone.

~ Colossians 4:6

Day 139:
Mirror, Mirror

Do you like what you see when you look at yourself in the mirror? Are you the person you hoped you would be? The person you've strived to be? Are you the person God wants you to be?

Each of us is placed on this earth for a reason. And God has a unique purpose for you. He loves you and has plans for you. He wants you to live your life with purpose. Think about your dreams. They were given to you by God. Listen to what He is saying to you and follow the direction in which He is gently guiding you. Are there doors opening? Or closing? If you're working according to God's will and if it's in God's timing, things will come together. If you're running into brick walls and finding a roadblock at every turn, perhaps you should consider that you're not acting according to God's will.

Life changes, especially divorce, can be very difficult. But when you leverage the gifts that God has given you and lean into the changes with courage and faith, you may find that the changes are bringing you to the very place that you ought to be.

We have gifts that differ according to the grace given to us: prophecy, in proportion to faith; ministry, in ministering; the teacher, in teaching; the exhorter, in exhortation; the giver, in generosity; the leader, in diligence; the compassionate, in cheerfulness.

~ Romans 12:6-8

Day 140:
The Heart Of Jesus

The New Testament helps us to understand Jesus so that in our difficult times, we can take consolation in the fact that He loves us. He wept with tenderness for Lazarus before He raised him from the dead. He handled sinners with great love and care. When He was alone, He was always in loving conversation with His Father. But sometimes the story we read doesn't translate to our life because of the pain we are experiencing. So Jesus reaches out, even further, to help us see His love for us.

A miracle took place in Buenos Aires in which a consecrated host began to bleed. A prominent doctor was called to take a sample of the host and have it blind tested at a lab, meaning it was submitted without being identified for the scientists. The lab tests revealed that the specimen was tissue from the left ventricle of a human heart and that the specimen was "alive and beating." Further testing with a top cardiologist revealed that this heart tissue was taken from a man who had been tortured and severely beaten.

People say miracles don't happen any more. But each day, through the celebration of the mass and miracles like these, Jesus is trying to show us how much He loves us. He wants us to know how passionate is His love for us and how He thirsts for our love in return. When you are feeling dragged down by the pain of your divorce, contemplate the heart of Jesus, beating with love for you and trying to reach you. His consolation for all that He suffered will be the love you return to Him.

And the life I now live in the flesh I live by faith in the Son of God, who loved me and gave himself for me.

~ Galatians 2:20

Day 141:
What Are You Waiting For?

◇

Do you often find yourself waiting? Waiting for a promotion? Waiting for the latest technology upgrade? Waiting for a circumstance to change? Waiting for someone to change?

What do you do while you're waiting? Do you just wait? Do you place other things on hold? Do you adjust your life around the thing you're waiting for?

God did not intend for you to wait passively. Waiting can be a time that God gives you to focus on Him and all that He has given you. It can be the time when you learn to practice patience and endurance. And it can be a time when you grow most in your faith. Remember that although you're waiting, God is still working. You may not be able to see or feel it, but He is silently at work.

Be assured that He knows your situation and remains in control. Today, make an effort to make your waiting time one in which you praise God as He prepares you for all the good things that lie ahead.

In all your ways acknowledge him, /
and he will make straight your paths.

~ Proverbs 3:6

Day 142:
Name It, Claim It, Tame It

Love is both a virtue and an emotion. In fact, St. Thomas Aquinas taught that all emotions proceed from love. All emotions are directed toward pleasure as their end. So in divorce, when there is no pleasure to be found, only love breached, the result is pain. This is one reason why divorce is such a painful experience.

Since emotions are non-moral until they are acted upon, the anger, frustration, and loneliness you feel are not wrong in and of themselves until you act on them. This can be quite a predicament because retribution is often the sentiment that accompanies these emotions. So how do you manage these powerful emotions in a Christian way when all that you are experiencing seems so unChristian? Use a simple formula—*name it, claim it, tame it.*

Name it: It is unhealthy to ignore or suppress these strong emotions so you must acknowledge them.

Claim it: Say it out loud: I am angry!

Tame it: Emotions must be ruled by your intellect so they don't rule you.

Seek counseling, spiritual guidance, pray, workout, clean out a closet, or any constructive activity so your action will be something positive to help you feel better about yourself and move forward in your healing.

Blessed are those who mourn, for they will be comforted.

~ Matthew 5:4

Day 143:
Carrying Your Cross

A friend of mine recently revealed the agony of his court appearance to finalize his divorce. During the proceedings, he acknowledged that he had allowed his older children to receive the sacrament of confirmation. This angered his ex-wife tremendously. Amidst all the rest of the haggling over custody and property, the judge awarded him with thirty hours of community service to make amends for this "offense." He felt completely humiliated for doing what he knew was right, acting as a good father and a faithful Catholic.

The depths of suffering due to divorce can hardly be described. But I encourage you to look at your suffering through God's eyes. God allows us to endure humiliations so we can understand the humiliation He endured for our salvation. He allows us to be stripped of things that are precious to us so we can focus on Him more clearly and intently. There's abundant grace and virtue in each of your sufferings. The saints suffered many devastating humiliations but were not deterred in their pursuit of holiness. They knew the one thing that could never be taken from them was Christ, and their reward was eternal life in heaven. You may not feel like a saint, but know that these crosses you bear are your path to holiness, and your fidelity pleases God so much!

Blessed are those who trust in the Lord, / whose trust is the Lord.

~ Jeremiah 17:7

Day 144:
Humiliations As A Way To Be Better

---◇---

The humiliations that come along with the divorce experience can bring you to your knees and make you feel worthless. But they can actually be something good if you accept them patiently. They can be stepping stones on the path to acquiring true humility. True and profound humility is a key virtue, one that we can only attain through the practice of it. Just as studying is the way to acquire knowledge, enduring humiliations with patience and charity is the way to acquire true humility.

A great way to do this is by praying the *Litany of Humility* with the goal of cultivating patience and charity. In bearing humiliations out of love for God, you take something that by itself is worthless and transform it into something with great eternal value.

My child, perform your tasks with humility;
then you will be loved by those whom God accepts.

~ Sirach 3:17

Day 145:
Yes, You Can Do It!

I recently enrolled in three months of personal training at my local gym. I admit, exercise and physical discipline are not really my passion in life, but I work out for my health, and I know that this is a good thing. At eight in the morning on Wednesdays and Fridays, I go through an intense and exhausting workout planned by my personal trainer. I hate it, *I hate it, I hate it*—when I'm in the moment—because the workout is very difficult, and my muscles are lazy. But afterwards, despite some soreness, I feel absolutely great. I know that what I am doing is the right thing. I know that what I am doing will pay off. And what makes it even better is that my personal trainer is there the whole time, cheering me on, "You can do it! Come on, just a couple more! Keep going. You're doing great!"

Wouldn't it be fantastic to have a personal trainer for all the various and difficult aspects of life? Someone to cheer you on, *"You can do it! Come on, just a couple more! Keep going. You're doing great!"* As Christians, we do have access to "personal trainers" in our practical and spiritual matters. We have the communion of saints.

All the saints in heaven are watching and waiting for us to pray to them for help. They can intercede with God and help us obtain the graces we need through their earthly example and their heavenly prayers. We also have our Blessed Mother who helps us in ways we are not even aware, and the Holy Spirit who guides us and inspires us at every moment.

If your life is a personal struggle, team with these, the finest personal trainers around, and you will be sure to find great satisfaction and consolation in knowing you are doing the right thing.

Now, discipline always seems painful rather than pleasant at the time, but later it yields the peaceful fruit of righteousness to those who have been trained by it.

~ Hebrews 12:11

Day 146:
My Heart Is Ready

---◇---

In the movie, *The Passion of the Christ*, Jesus' passion and suffering are brought to life before our eyes. We are able to get a glimpse of what those thirty-six hours were really like for Him. We witness how much Christ loved us and how that love led Him to submit to anguish, betrayal, torture and death on the cross. One of the most powerful moments of the film takes place right before He is brutally whipped and scourged by the Roman soldiers. He is bound by His hands at the pillar as the soldiers are mocking Him and selecting their tools of torture, and Jesus looks to heaven and says, "Father, my heart is ready."

My heart is ready. What an incredible approach to accepting suffering! As you carry the cross of divorce, I pray these words will bring you some consolation and peace. Jesus' exceptional attitude of charity and zeal can fortify you in your own trials if you contemplate His beautiful words and follow His example. Is it easy to do? No. But what a great example to emulate, especially knowing that Christ walks closely with you as you carry your cross. He is all the inspiration you need.

And after you have suffered for a little while, the God of all grace, who has called you to his eternal glory in Christ, will himself restore, support, strengthen, and establish you.

~ 1 Peter 5:10

Day 147:
What Do You Need Today?

Some days being a Christian is easy, and some days, not so much. Some days we feel full of gratitude for the gift of our faith, and some days it's easier to hide our Christianity from people. But our faith in Christ is truly a gift and one that can help us rise above the noise of the world. Here is a brief meditation from St. Thomas Aquinas to help you any day you need some special encouragement:

When Jesus is present in us, all goes well and nothing
seems difficult.
When Jesus is absent, everything is hard.
When Jesus does not speak to our hearts, every consolation
is worthless,
but if Jesus speaks only one word, we feel a great joy!
How hard and arid are you without Jesus!
How foolish and vain you are to desire anything outside
of Jesus!
What can the world give you without Jesus?
To be without Jesus is an unbearable hell.
And to be with Jesus is a sweet paradise!
If Jesus is with you, no one can harm you.
Who finds Jesus finds a precious treasure
in fact, he finds a good greater than all goods
and he who loses Jesus loses a very great thing and
loses more than if he had lost the whole world.

If you belonged to the world, the world would love you as its own.
Because you do not belong to the world, but I have chosen you
out of the world—therefore the world hates you.

~ John 15:19

Day 148:
What God Is Offering

Have you ever noticed that the pleasure the world provides is far less valuable than what God has created? You might have three hundred cable channels and can't find anything to watch, but you can go to the ocean and sit for hours watching the sea or go to the mountains and hike for days. It is interesting how you chase after the things of this world when so much of God's goodness is right in front of your eyes, free for the taking and specifically given for your enjoyment.

It is the same with human relationships. Are you chasing after a relationship that is not good for you? Are you holding tightly to someone who mistreats you? If so, consider what kind of a relationship God offers you. God is perfect love, passionate love, and never-ending love. His one desire is for you to be with Him. He is always with you; He never leaves you, betrays you, or mistreats you. God knows you like no other and knows how to make you happy.

If you are hurt, confused, or disenchanted over a human relationship, take time to turn to God in prayer and ask Him to help you understand His plan for your happiness. Let Him give you what you need and show you the way to true peace and happiness.

So we have known and believe the love that God has for us.
God is love, and those who abide in love abide in God,
and God abides in them.

~ 1 John 4:16

Day 149:
Feeling Guilty?

People love to joke about "Catholic guilt" and say things like "You shouldn't feel guilty because as a Catholic, I have enough guilt for everyone!" This exaggerated statement is somewhat humorous but is it true? Well, it depends.

The Church encourages you to form your conscience by understanding the basic moral truths and then continuously dive deeper into them and apply them to your daily life. If you have a well-formed conscience, guilt is a good thing because it keeps you in check and eventually, leads you to joy through the sacrament of reconciliation. However guilt can become a twisted and heavy burden if it is not handled properly. Divorced Catholics, in general, and those who were abandoned or given no choice but to divorce, in particular, bear this burden of guilt, often to an extreme.

Are you struggling with guilt over your divorce now? You need to know that there is a huge difference between someone who willingly destroys his or her marriage to pursue selfish desires, and someone who was faithful to his or her marriage and fought to save it. If you did not want the divorce but found yourself in that position anyway, you need to take some time to look at yourself through the eyes of Christ. Take some time in Eucharistic Adoration and talk with Jesus about this burden you bear. Know that He loves you and is not ashamed of you. He knows your struggles, He's heard your cries and He knows your heart. Let His love for you penetrate your heart and be your guiding inspiration at all times.

For your name's sake, O Lord, pardon my guilt, for it is great.

~ Psalm 25:11

Day 150:
Make Me A Channel Of Your Peace

I have a friend who is very worried and anxious most of the time. She often checks into a day-spa for massages, facials, etc., looking for a way to calm down and feel more relaxed. Isn't this the way the world dictates how to find peace? Through self-indulgent behavior, appeasing ourselves, and staying away from those people and situations that we don't like. But peace can never truly be found through pursuing a self-serving life. Sure, you may find enjoyment in these things (and hey, I love a good massage myself from time to time), but there is no lasting peace in self-indulgence. Why? Because we weren't made for this earth and its imperfection, we were made for God and to live with Him in heaven.

Try this simple exercise: instead of putting yourself in the center of your world and ordering all your relationships, responsibilities and interests, place God in the center of your world and order all that you have around Him. With Christ in the center, you will have His perfect love as your motivation in all you do, and the peace you will receive will be incredible. With God as your focus, and having all your life's components focused on Him, nothing will be able to disturb you. Your foundation will be His perfect love for you!

The priest replied, "Go in peace.
The mission you are on is under the eye of the Lord."

~ Judges 18:6

Day 151:
I Am All The Food You Need

A friend of mine shared this beautiful story with me. She attended a Journey of Hope conference but did not stay at the hotel because she lives locally. On Sunday of the conference, she was running late but was very hungry and debated stopping for breakfast. She felt inspired by a thought that kept coming to her, "I am all the food you need." So in the end, she decided to skip breakfast so she was not late for mass. After mass Fr. Thomas approached her and asked her to help Him consume the many Eucharistic hosts that were left over from communion. She received a great grace consuming the extra hosts because she was in tune with the Holy Spirit's inspiration, "I am all the food you need."

Is there something you are feeling inspired to do by the Holy Spirit? When you hear His whisperings in your heart, trust it. Follow it. He is trying to lead you to something better than what you already have. And when you find yourself encountering those negative and unpleasant situations that divorce forces you to be in, say a quick prayer and ask for His inspirations. He won't let you down.

Our ancestors ate the manna in the wilderness; as it is written,
'He gave them bread from heaven to eat.'

~ John 6:31

Day 152:
Don't Forget

The Eighties was a period in my life that I look back on and say I truly was asleep. I lived for the moment and for my personal gain and lost sight of my true goal. I worked full-time and took college courses and was consumed with the social scene, fashion, music, and school. It was a time in my life where, although I loved God, He was my sidekick instead of my focal point. During that time, I felt as if my life would go on forever, and I had to squeeze the most enjoyment out of it as possible.

Thirty years later, and with full recognition that there's nothing wrong with enjoying life in moderation, I've realized that most of my pursuits back then were a serious distraction from my true purpose in life. Those distractions led me to make the most significant mistake of my life, which resulted in divorce. My pursuits of "happiness" distracted me from my ultimate goal—heaven. I was distracted to the point that I forgot that my home, and my true happiness was not on this earth but in heaven with Jesus, where "He will wipe every tear from their eyes. There will be no more death or mourning or crying or pain, for the old order of things has passed away" (Revelation 21:4).

I offer these thoughts to you, simply because it may be that your divorce situation has distracted you from what's most important. The simple fact is that you belong to God, and heaven is your true home, not this world. The severity of your circumstances may be keeping you disappointed, sad, and worried about today and the future. You may be asking, "Will I survive this pain?" "What does my future hold?" "What do people think of me?" "Am I doing the right thing?" "Am I still loveable?"

Just remember that your enemy, Satan, is using your situation against you. He is also using the world, our modern society, to distract you from your goal. But the communion of saints in heaven await your request for their help in assisting you as you fight the good fight. Take confidence in Christ's grace and power, for He is the Way, the Truth and the Life! He loves you and waits for you. Take some time for Him today and experience His great love!

For the one who is in you is greater than the one who is in the world.

~ 1 John 4:4

Day 153:
When Your Lonely Heart
Demands Attention!

---◇---

One of the greatest crosses to bear during divorce is loneliness. Although intangible, loneliness is just as difficult as bearing the burden of a disease. It affects every aspect of your life and carries with it a pain that is difficult to convey to others.

When a human heart suffers the pain of loneliness, it will, at some point, demand attention. And then, what do you do? First, you need to recognize and acknowledge this normal human reaction to the loss of your marriage relationship. It is not wrong to feel lonely, nor is it silly, nor a sign of weakness. It is just part of the process. But your next step is critical. What will you do with this powerful emotion? Here are some simple ways to deal with loneliness:

Don't fight it. Accept it for what it is. Don't try to put a lid on it but don't wallow in it either.

Don't use a band-aid to make the feelings go away. For example, a band-aid can be excessive eating, drinking, shopping or working; it can be a sexual relationship or pornography; it can be any type of behavior that is not good for us, but that we believe will bring relief. "Band-aids" normally only cause more hurt and pain.

Use your loneliness to your advantage: This is the perfect source of reflection on yourself, the choices you've made, how you would like to improve as a human being, and your relationship with God.

Stay connected with God. Pray and ask for God's grace in your life to carry you through this difficult time and still be able to see the blessings He has bestowed upon you.

Turn to me and be gracious to me, / for I am lonely and afflicted.

~ Psalm 25:16

Day 154:
Second Chances

———◇———

It all changes in an instant! What goes through a person's mind as he faces death? All the woulda, shoulda, couldas? All the things you never said, opportunities you didn't take, loved ones you could have loved better, graces you could have received?

We don't have to wait for death's approach to realize what we woulda, shoulda, coulda done. Every new day is a second chance for us, a clean slate. If we lacked courage yesterday, we can pray for courage today and act upon it. If we were weak yesterday, we can ask for strength today and resolve to be better. If we were angry and resentful yesterday, we can ask for the grace to forgive today and begin learning how to forgive.

Trust that God wants you to be happy and succeed in life. Ask Him for what you need and He will give it to you!

———————

Until now you have not asked for anything in my name.
Ask and you will receive, so that your joy may be complete.

~ John 16:24

Day 155:
Respect For The Mystery

A theater stage is shrouded by a curtain until it's show time. A Christmas gift remains wrapped until December 25th. A blindfold covers the eyes and blocks the view of the surprise until the time is just right. Veils, shrouds, curtains, etc. are not for the purpose of hiding something. They are for the purpose of revealing, when the time is right. Even the Eucharist remains concealed in the tabernacle, not to be hidden from us, but to reveal the glory of Jesus in Adoration and the sacrament of the Eucharist at the appointed times.

Herein lies a lesson for us all in regard to being intimate with another. There is an appointed time, and that appointed time is between two married spouses.

If you are divorced, you should be guarding your gift, the gift of yourself, with utmost care and protection, until the appointed time arrives, and you may reveal yourself again. Safeguard the gift of your heart, mind, body and soul—the total donation of yourself in marriage—with the understanding of its sacredness and importance. Dress yourself in such a way that people can see you honor the gift you possess, and it is precious to you, as it will be to someone else when everything else is right. In doing so, peace and the companionship of Christ will reign in your heart, and your joy will be complete.

I have said these things to you so that my joy may be in you,
and that your joy may be complete.

~ John 15:11

165

Day 156:
Is Someone Watching You?

The popular eighties hit, *Holding Out For A Hero*, says it best—people want someone they can believe in. They want the real thing, an example of authentic virtue in an everyday human being. People are hungry for virtue because virtue is the promise of hope. People want to know that living a good, upstanding life is not only possible these days but a good thing. This is one reason why marriages are celebrated, and divorces are so devastating.

Is someone watching you as you live out the consequences of your divorce? Yes, it is likely, but don't let that scare you. You have made a statement in your life that you are a Christian through your words and actions. So it is only natural to believe that others are watching you as you go through your divorce, hoping to see what real Christians are made of. You already display heroic virtue by remaining close to God as you suffer through your divorce and the aftermath. This speaks loudly to those around you, those who are close, and those who observe from afar. So as you find your way now, be aware of those who are watching your example. Pray for them and always have a kind word, even when you must reference your ex-spouse or your situation. By doing this, you will be winning great graces for yourself and other souls. This will be the treasure in heaven that Jesus asks us to build for ourselves.

But store up for yourselves treasures in heaven, where neither moth nor rust consumes and where thieves do not break in and steal.

~ Matthew 6:20

Day 157:
Calming The Emotional Storm

I'll never forget the advice my mother gave me while I was growing up. She said that whatever I was doing, it should always be something that I would not be ashamed or embarrassed for Jesus or Mary to see. She also told me that I should always invite Jesus and His Mother into my thoughts, no matter if I was angry or sad or happy. Whatever I was doing or thinking, she would say, you should always invite Jesus and Mary to be a part of it. This has stayed with me my entire life and has been a great way to gauge whether I was doing the right thing at any given time.

Going through a divorce presents you with many challenging situations and circumstances. Your head reels from confusion, critical questions, and powerful emotions. Things can get crazy in an instant. Suddenly, seeking retribution for the deep hurt or being happy that things have gone wrong for your ex-spouse seem perfectly just and right. Even the unbridled joy of getting attention from someone who is not your spouse can appear to be something good, when in reality, it is simply a stroking of your ego. When you encounter these situations, don't indulge them, but don't run away from them either. This is the time to invite Our Lord and His mother into your thoughts and discuss how you are feeling with them. Ask for their help and guidance. Ask God to calm the erosive winds of your emotions just as He calmed the wind and the sea.

He woke up and rebuked the wind, and said to the sea, "Peace! Be still!" Then the wind ceased, and there was a dead calm.

~ Mark 4:39

Day 158:
Little Gifts From God

This morning I woke up, and the pain was there as soon as I opened my eyes. I looked out the window to check the weather. The morning sky was filled with red, pink and gold tones as the sun rose from behind the trees and reflected on the clouds. For that moment, life was good again.

I dragged my tired body from the breakfast table to the hallway mirror for one last check before getting in the car. I suddenly remembered the little neighbor child who had waved at me the day before. She didn't know me or my suffering but still had a sweet smile for me. For that moment, the world was a good place again.

I tried to calm my frazzled and worried mind while I drove to my afternoon appointment. I looked up and saw a brilliant blue sky with white clouds. They were so beautiful. They looked as though they'd been painted with a watercolor paint brush. For that moment, it was as if the world stood still, and my heart was peaceful. Just for that moment.

As I was locking up the house for the night, I dreaded the fact that I would be going to bed alone. Suddenly the phone rang. It was my good friend who knew it was late but just wanted to see how I was doing. For that moment, I felt loved.

Your life may be filled with trials, questions, and discontent. Comfort may be difficult to find. But don't you see how God is trying to show you He loves you? That He hasn't forgotten you? It's in these little moments that we hear the simple ways God speaks to us. *I created this sunrise for you to wake up to and enjoy! You're not invisible to me, I see you when everyone else ignores you! Don't worry about things, I will take care of you! You are precious to me, and I will never forget you!* These are God's ways of blessing you in the midst of the Cross you are carrying so you will know you are not alone. He walks beside you on the road to Calvary.

But I trusted in your steadfast love; /
my heart shall rejoice in your salvation.

~ Psalm 13:5

Day 159:
Hidden Manna

If there's anything God wants you to know as you go through your divorce and work to rebuild your life, it is simply that He loves you, and He wants to be your strength. Therefore He will always be trying to reach you and inspire your heart with messages of love. But how can you know which messages you hear are from God?

One great way of hearing God's messages is to begin your day with a Gospel reflection; simply reading and reflecting upon the Gospel of the day's mass. Writings and teachings of the saints are wonderful and speak to you but in God's Word, we find the "hidden manna" that sustains us in every need. After reading and reflecting on the Gospel of the day, write down your inspirations so you can better remember them. That way you can refer to them when prayer feels dry and distant. The "hidden manna" you have found will become your heart's treasure and comfort.

Let anyone who has an ear listen to what the Spirit is saying to the churches. To everyone who conquers I will give some of the hidden manna.

~ Revelations 2:17

Day 160:
If Today You Hear His Voice, Harden Not Your Hearts

So often, Jesus speaks to us through nature, people and circumstances, encouraging us and reminding us of His love for us. Maybe we hear His inspirations, maybe we don't, but they are there.

At times you want to respond to your ex-spouse's words or behavior with anger but catch hold of your emotions and stop. That was God, giving you the grace you needed. At times you may want to explain to your child how rotten your ex-spouse has made everything but instead, you bite your tongue and say nothing. That was God's grace. You may want to say, "I just don't care!!!" and indulge in something that's not good for you but might provide some temporary reprieve. Instead your common sense comes into play, and you decide to do something else. Yep, that was God.

God is always with you, He will never leave you and is always working for your good. Place all that you have and all that you are in His hands. Give Him all your suffering and struggles, all your hopes and desires, all your emotions, your goodness and your sinfulness. Lay it all down at His feet and let Him show you the way.

Today, if you hear his voice, do not harden your hearts.

~ Hebrews 4:7

Day 161:
Hooked On A Feeling

Remember that old 70's song by Blue Swede, *Hooked on a Feeling?* *"I'm hooked on a feeling, I'm high on believing that you're in love with me."*

Getting hooked on a feeling like this is an amazing experience, but how do you know it's the real thing? Attention from the opposite sex can be thrilling, especially after having gone through a divorce and experiencing the rejection that occurs on so many levels. Since you don't want to ever experience that kind of devastation again, make sure your feelings don't lead you down the wrong path. You should be completely prepared and ready to give your heart away, so make sure you are free from anger and resentment toward those who have hurt you by forgiving them. Make sure you have gone through the annulment process and have a decree of nullity. There is nothing that will cause more pain like another failed relationship. You can avoid all that if you have fully prepared yourself and when you do, you will be able to recognize real love from mere attraction.

Blessed is anyone who endures temptation.
Such a one has stood the test and will receive the crown of life that the Lord has promised to those who love him.

~ James 1:12

Day 162:
Why Is Moving Forward So Hard?

The intense pain that comes from divorce can be difficult to manage. You want the pain to go away, but there are no quick fixes or easy solutions. How in the world can you move past this kind of suffering? Will it always be this way?

To a degree, it is true that time is needed for the pain to begin fading away. You have to walk through the fire. But one thing that keeps you stuck is a lack of willingness to forgive those who have hurt you. An element of choice is involved in the healing process. You can choose to hang on to bitterness and a desire for retribution, or you can choose to let go. Letting go is not easy to do, but with prayer, an open heart, and God's grace, it is very possible. It is then you will see that through letting go, you will move forward.

For to this end we toil and struggle, because we have our hope set on the living God, who is the Savior of all people, especially of those who believe.

~ 1 Timothy 4:10

Day 163:
The Joy Of Starting A New Life

---◇---

Divorce brings a multitude of changes to your life, very often, against your will. The pain and suffering that goes along with trying to adjust and begin again can be extremely challenging, especially if there are children involved.

I encourage you today to consider what is happening to you now, and from this day forward, as a new life. But not just some new situation you didn't want but a new opportunity.

Scripture tells us that we are all new creatures in Christ and despite your circumstances, this means you, too. Turn your loneliness and hardships into an offering to the Lord. He will fill you with consolation, joy and inner peace.

Let not your heart be troubled. Approach Him with an open heart and a desire to begin your new life with Him and in Him.

So if anyone is in Christ, there is a new creation: everything old has passed away; see, everything has become new!

~ 2 Corinthians 5:17

Day 164:
The Attraction Factor

People spend a lot of money on salons, clothing and the gym trying to make themselves attractive. But what good is being attractive on the outside, if you're not attractive on the inside?

After going through a divorce, it's important to make a personal assessment to see if you've picked up any behaviors or habits that will make you unattractive on the inside. Taking the time to do this will pay off in a big way. Being someone who is authentic, honest, charitable, and magnanimous has a way of making you someone people want to be around. They are naturally attracted to you. More importantly, you will be truly happy with the person you become, the best version of yourself.

Let your adornment be the inner self with the lasting beauty of a gentle and quiet spirit, which is very precious in God's sight.

~ 1 Peter 3:4

Day 165:
A Gift Only You Can Give

St. Therese of Lisieux offered up her sufferings for sinners. When she was fourteen, she became aware of a man named Pranzini who had murdered three people. He was sentenced to death, yet still showed no signs of remorse. For a month and a half, Therese offered all her prayers and sufferings for this hardened criminal. God gave her a sign: this great sinner took a crucifix and kissed the wounds of the Savior three times in the last moment before his death. Upon learning this, Therese said, "This is my first son." She later wrote, "Suffering alone can give birth to souls for Jesus."

No doubt your divorce has caused you to suffer greatly. Would you consider a spiritual parenthood, such as St. Therese demonstrated for us? What a beautiful way to win souls for Christ and bring eternal value to your suffering. Especially at a time when you most likely feel like your hands are completely tied, and you have control over nothing, this is a wonderful way to offer your suffering to Christ.

Whether you know someone who needs your sacrifices or maybe you read a tragic story in the newspaper, offer your sufferings for sinners and build yourself a treasure in heaven.

I can do all things through him who strengthens me.

~ Philippians 4:13

Day 166:
How Would You Describe Divorce?

People who experience divorce have many descriptions for what it's like when they're trying to explain it to someone else. I've heard people describe it as something like being trapped in a dark room. You can't find the door, and you're walking around with your arms outstretched trying to find the light switch. I've also heard people describe the experience as waking up in a foreign country—nothing and no one is recognizable. Personally it always felt as if I was wandering through a great desert, with little hope of finding an oasis. After my experience, I can tell you, there is an oasis that waits for you.

The sacraments of your faith are that oasis. They are free of charge, and they are waiting for you to come and partake and be refreshed. The graces from the sacraments are like armor that help protect your heart and soul from the corrosive winds of divorce.

Take advantage of every opportunity you can to receive the Holy Eucharist and the sacrament of reconciliation so you have what you need to get you through this difficult time.

In distress you called, and I rescued you; / I answered you in the secret place of thunder; / I tested you at the waters of Meribah.

~ Psalm 81:7

Day 167:
Time With Christ
In The Garden Of Gethsemane

---◇---

Do you feel lonely? Lonely to the point of deep discouragement? Going through a divorce can make it seem like no one is on your side. This is the perfect time to contemplate Jesus in the Garden of Gethsemane as He waited for Judas to lead the soldiers to Him and take Him into custody.

His suffering was so intense His sweat turned to blood. He agonized for the sins of all mankind. He knows that you are suffering a similar pain, a moral suffering, because of the destruction of your family.

Christ became frustrated when He saw the apostles had fallen asleep. All He asked them to do was watch and pray. Jesus knows how you feel in the wake of those who have let you down.

At last, the soldiers arrived, and Judas approached Him, kissing Him on the cheek and calling Him, "Master." Jesus' heart was broken for Judas's hardened one. Christ understands very well your own heart that has been broken by betrayal.

When you are feeling beaten down and discouraged by the suffering caused by your divorce, get away to a quiet place and contemplate Jesus in the garden. Meditate on that scene and place yourself in the story, sitting next to Him. Unite your suffering with His and take consolation in the the joy of the Resurrection.

On the day I called, you answered me,
you increased my strength of soul.

~ Psalm 138:3

Day 168:
Tackling The Fear Of The Unknown

No matter what the circumstances were surrounding the breakup of your marriage, divorce renders a multitude of worries and serious challenges: financial, emotional, social, and spiritual. It is easy to feel like you're drowning in anxiety. Part of that is due to the fear of the unknown, the what nows and the what ifs.

As with every challenge in life, if you can look to the good example of a person who has walked in your shoes before, it's like having a life preserver to keep you going. Consider Mary and Joseph as they returned from the festival in Jerusalem. Three days into their trip, they realized they had lost the boy, Jesus.

Naturally, they panicked. Imagine the anxiety they felt not knowing where He was. There were no cell phones to keep them in touch so all they could do was backtrack. When they finally found Jesus in the temple, He was doing His Father's work. He asked Mary and Joseph why they worried so much. Why didn't they assume everything was okay and that He was simply doing what He was supposed to be doing?

Sometimes Jesus is saying the same thing to you. "Why do you worry? Don't you know I'm doing my Father's work?" When you feel overwhelmed by your worries and concerns, get a Bible and read this passage in the Gospel of Luke. Picture yourself in that scene. Then take heart and trust that God is working circumstances for your good.

He said to them, "Why were you searching for me?
Did you not know that I must be in my Father's house?"

~ Luke 2:49

Day 169:
A Prayer for Guidance

─────────◆─────────

My Lord and My Father, I come before You to seek Your guidance and strength. My life seems to be even more of a mystery than ever, for the life I recognized, and the future I counted on has completely changed, never to return.

It is now that I need You to show me how to use the gifts You have given me. Sadness fills me, but life keeps moving forward, and I need to press on. Give me the grace, Lord, to move forward, too.

I look to Your holy passion and death and observe You as You embrace Your cross, carrying it with love. Grant me the strength to do the same. I observe You in such incredible pain, yet everyone You meet along the way of the cross, You greet with kind words. Lord, show me Your love, that I may imitate Your example.

Help me be stronger, wiser, more charitable, and more trusting of Your plan for me. I know that in the end, You will bring good things out of the bad and for now, the best thing I can do is to follow You.

I believe in You, I trust You, I love You. Amen.

───────────

May I never boast of anything except the cross of our Lord Jesus Christ, by which the world has been crucified to me, and I to the world.

~ Galatians 6:14

Day 170:
A Prayer For Rebirth
Through The Sacraments

Through the sacraments of my faith, I am reborn. God's grace enters my soul like a refreshing breeze that rustles the leaves of the trees in a spring garden.

My soul awakens with new life and rejoices because, once again, I am with my Savior, the One who loves me. Together, we walk through the garden and talk about all that is important to me.

I pray, dear Lord, that You will always be pleased to find Your home in the garden of my soul. May You always take delight in my love for You, a love that blooms like the first rose of springtime. Amen.

Those who eat my flesh and drink my blood abide in me, and I in them.

~ John 6:56

Day 171:
A Prayer for Patience

I am lonely and I yearn for love
I face many choices now
but I will look to God above
for only He can show me how.

How truly beautiful I am
How priceless is my life
How meaningful my suffering
at this point in my life.

The waiting isn't easy
at times, it's very hard.
But patience invites happiness
and comfort from the Lord.

For God has a beautiful plan
designed for me it seems
and He will make me happier
than anything I can dream.

Turn to me and be gracious to me, / for I am lonely and afflicted.

~ Psalm 25:16

Day 172:
Come Rest With Me

Do the powerful emotions that accompany the divorce experience have you feeling depleted of energy and hope? Do angry words and terrible memories plague your mind throughout the day?

Divorce is such an overwhelming experience that it's easy to feel like you've lost yourself. This is precisely the time God is calling you to Himself, trying to draw you nearer to Him so He can refresh you with His love and grace. But how can you hear His voice above the cacophony of emotions overtaking you?

The best way is to go away by yourself to a deserted place and rest with Jesus. This may be a challenging proposition because, despite your need for rest, the day-to-day responsibilities of life dictate your freedom to do so. But even so, you can still carve out some quiet time to be with Him. It can be as simple as getting up a half hour early to read the Gospel passage of the day or as involved as attending a silent retreat and taking an entire weekend to be with God.

Whatever you decide to do, do it with the anticipation of receiving divine consolation and refreshment for your soul. This is His desire for you.

The apostles gathered around Jesus,
and told him all that they had done and taught.

~ Mark 6:30

Day 173:
Should You Stop Pretending
To Get Along With Your Ex?

It's a real struggle to get along with your ex-spouse when you have to put a lid on the resentment you feel. But the anger and bitterness will subside and eventually fade altogether if you let go. Let go of your marriage. Let go of the things you regret. Let go of the need for justice or the need for your ex-spouse to admit to the pain he or she has caused you. Let go of the new husband or wife. Detach yourself from these things, especially the need to have others recognize how much you've suffered. These things are emotional possessions that are obstacles to your healing.

Detachment is a practical decision to let go. It requires action. Many of the saints practiced detachment by embracing only those things that were God's will and letting go of anything contrary to that. What is it that you are tightly holding? These emotional possessions are preventing you from having a healthy perspective on life and relationships. It is important for you to release your grip on them and let them go. Only you can make this decision, but it's worth it. It's time to look forward to your future, one that should focus on you and God as a team. He will lead you from that point.

Anyone whom you forgive, I also forgive. What I have forgiven, if I
have forgiven anything, has been for your sake
in the presence of Christ.

~ 2 Corinthians 2:10

Day 174:
Got Doubts?

Are you having doubts that God can take the horrible circumstances of your divorce and make something good come out of them? Is your first response one of cynicism when someone tells you life will get better? Fair enough. After all the suffering you've been through, that's a reasonable reaction. But it's holding you back.

A holy priest once said that every day the Holy Spirit sends us hundreds of inspirations. They are suggestions that we can act upon or ignore, and sadly, most of us either ignore them, question them, or talk ourselves out of acting on them. Why? Because it might be uncomfortable. The priest stated that if we would only act on every inspiration the Holy Spirit sent us each day, we would be saints in less than a month. Wow!

So if you're feeling discouraged and doubtful, put this idea to the test. Give Him the opportunity to show you the great things He can do for you. Challenge yourself to follow the inspirations you receive. Let the Holy Spirit guide you each day and see where it leads you. My bet is it will lead you to a much happier place.

May the God of hope fill you with all joy and peace in believing, so that you may abound in hope by the power of the Holy Spirit.

~ Romans 15:13

Day 175:
Waiting For That Important Call?

Being single can be very lonely. Even in a big group of friends or surrounded by family, being single and divorced is hard.

Getting back out in the social world and meeting other available men or women can become a bit of a game. How much time do you spend sitting around waiting for that person to call you or to respond to your message?

It can be frustrating, no doubt, but what else is there to do but wait? Much more!

Consider this: How many times has God sent you an inspiration to focus on Him and His love for you, but you missed it because you were busy waiting for someone else's call? You didn't recognize His attempt to reach you because you were too worried about what wasn't happening in your life.

Don't forget that you have a distinct purpose in life, a path to heaven just for you, and God is prompting you to act. Don't let your loneliness or disappointment distract you from what you should be doing. Get going on your mission in life and when the time is appropriate, God will bring you the one He's chosen for you.

The human mind may devise many plans, / but it is the purpose of the Lord that will be established.

~ Proverbs 19:21

Day 176:
God Knows What You Are Going Through

One of the hardest things about going through a divorce and trying to rebuild your life afterward is enduring all the painful details no one notices. It can be as tiny a detail as having to check the "divorced" box on a form. While it might seem minor to someone else, to you, it's a blaring horn that invites judgment and criticism from others. Or it could be the loneliness of coming home to an empty house.

It's at times like these you need to remind yourself that God notices. God knows what you are going through.

Suffering well isn't easy but when you try to suffer with dignity and grace, your heavenly Father sees your efforts, loves you, and blesses you for it. When it seems like no one can relate, God is right there, and He certainly understands your pain. More importantly, your efforts to keep the faith and persevere, despite your circumstances, build up a treasure in heaven that waits for you. Don't lose sight of this. Let it motivate you to keep going and to keep trying. Life will get better.

But store up for yourselves treasures in heaven, where neither moth nor rust consumes and where thieves do not break in and steal.

~ Matthew 6:20

Day 177:
P. F. E. D.

---◆---

There are things you need to remind yourself to do every day. Take your vitamins. Pay the bills. Call your mom. Reduce your salt intake. The list can be endless.

Here is a daily prescription for you to remember that will make a huge difference in your life—P.F.E.D., which stands for Practice Forgiveness Every Day.

Especially if you've gone through a divorce, there is much to forgive; your ex-spouse, the other man/woman, in-laws, etc. Or maybe you are the one who needs the most forgiveness? Are you having trouble forgiving yourself?

Forgiveness after divorce can seem like an insurmountable task, but it's not impossible. God will give you the grace you need to forgive if you ask Him for it in prayers. He wants to help you clean out the anger and resentment from your heart so there is more room for love.

By practicing forgiveness every day, you begin a habit of loving instead of blaming. So each time you feel that anger hitting you, let it go, and say "I forgive you" or whatever it is that helps you release the debt you are holding.

And be kind to one another, tenderhearted, forgiving one another, as God in Christ has forgiven you.

~ Ephesians 4:32

Day 178:
A Prayer For The Grace To Persevere

O good and gentle Jesus, hear my prayer!

I am growing tired of being brave, and my daily struggles leave me feeling empty and discouraged. I know you are with me, but when I pray, my words feel empty; not because I don't love you but because everything seems to be against me. I can't see a light in the darkness.

Lift me up, Lord, and show me your face. Give me hope and grant me the grace to continue my journey, undisturbed by the emotions I feel. Give me an understanding of how You carried your own cross, embracing it and carrying it, out of love for me. In your mercy, grant me the strength to push forward this way, with love and acceptance.

I am the vine, you are the branches. Those who abide in me and I in them bear much fruit, because apart from me you can do nothing.

~ John 15:5

Day 179:
A Grieving Heart

In the third chapter of the Gospel of Mark, you get a special glimpse into the heart of Jesus. Mark writes that Jesus suffered grief at the hardness of the Pharisees' hearts. They were so set on proving Jesus wrong that they would not allow His message of love and conversion to penetrate their hearts, nor their intentions.

If you've experienced a divorce and happen to be the spouse who was abandoned, you can likely relate quite well to Jesus in this passage. Your spouse will not allow your love to penetrate his or her heart, and this causes you much grief and anger.

This is the perfect time to draw near to Christ and contemplate His Sacred Heart; His Heart that has suffered so much for love of us. In contemplating the fact that He loves us, even when we are steeped in sin, His grace will help you to find forgiveness for your spouse and the ability to pray for his or her redemption.

He looked around at them with anger; he was grieved at their hardness of heart and said to the man, "Stretch out your hand." He stretched it out, and his hand was restored.

~ Mark 3:5

Day 180:
Your Suffering Is A Talent

In sacred Scripture, we read about the parable of the talents. It is a story about the gifts God gives us and His expectations for us to use them wisely and not waste them. This parable enables you to look at your own life and take note. Are you using the gifts you've been given wisely?

Did you know that suffering and pain is a talent? Yes, most certainly, and one that is given to you by God to use for your salvation and the salvation of others. How in the world does this make sense? Who in the world can believe that the terrible scourge of divorce is a gift, a talent?

Think of your situation as an opportunity, instead of getting discouraged. Try to understand the deeper meaning of what has happened to you. Focus on how, with hard work, you can refine yourself by virtue of your struggle and excel as a human being through perseverance and ultimately triumph.

Through it all, God gives you all the graces you need to succeed and come out on top.

For they disciplined us for a short time as seemed best to them, but he disciplines us for our good, in order that we may share his holiness.

~ Hebrews 12:10

Day 181:
A Paradox Of Faith

◇

"Suffering is the thread from which the stuff of joy is woven."

– Henri de Lubac, S. J., Paradoxes of Faith.

No one knows fully why our suffering is the path to joy and redemption. It's a mystery that will never be completely understood until you reach heaven. But right now, you are faced with the reality of it on a daily basis. And carrying such heavy crosses can seem, at times, to serve only to underscore your weakness.

But it is your weakness that allows God to work in your life. He needs your weakness to show you His strength. If you are trying to bear your sufferings relying only on your abilities and strengths, step back for a moment and see that by acknowledging your weakness, you are giving Him permission to work in your life. With God, anything and everything is possible.

The more you suffer and the more you allow God to reveal His strength, the greater the joy you will experience at the end of your trial.

Therefore I am content with weaknesses, insults, hardships,
persecutions, and calamities for the sake of Christ;
for whenever I am weak, then I am strong.

~ 2 Corinthians 12:10

Day 182:
Don't Build A Future of Regrets

Do you look for opportunities to tell off your ex-spouse or let them know how you really feel? Do you think of ways to get back at him or her, or make his or her life more difficult because of the pain he or she has caused? This is a natural response to being hurt, but what would actually happen if you followed through?

A great way to handle this temptation is to imagine you are elderly, looking back at your life. Would the older, wiser you regret these angry actions? Sometimes when a moment of anger or rage takes hold, it's difficult to think clearly. So instead of reacting, think of whether or not you will look back and regret taking that action. Take a deep breath and try to let go of your anger.

The effect of righteousness will be peace, / and the result of righteousness, quietness and trust forever.

~ Isaiah 32:17

Day 183:
The Book Of Psalms:
An Oasis In The Desert

Oftentimes finding the words to pray to God is difficult. Your heart may be feeling dry and empty. If you are feeling overwhelmed by your grief and sadness, the Book of Psalms is a great place to go to find understanding, compassion, and consolation.

There, you will find that you are not alone in your frustration over your trials because the Psalms were written for those who suffer. They were also written to inspire hope and provide a reason to trust God and rejoice in His blessings.

Whatever you may be encountering today, you will find a Psalm that can give you the words to pray so you know that God is with you.

*Depart from me, all you workers of evil, /
for the Lord has heard the sound of my weeping.*

~ Psalm 6:8

Day 184:
The Mysterious Benefits Of Prayer

So you've been through a separation and divorce, enduring through a harrowing experience. Many divorced Catholics, in spite of the terrible experience, pray for their ex-spouses frequently, if not all the time. Not only are they answering the call of Scripture to pray for their enemies (Matthew 5:44), but many even still love their ex-spouses despite what has happened.

A friend of mine once told me she offered all her pain and suffering specifically for the soul of her ex-husband. Every tear, every painful question from those who didn't know what happened, and every reminder that her marriage was lost, she offered up to God for the salvation of her husband's soul.

You never know how God will work in a person's life, but you should always have faith in God's ability to work miracles, even out of the worst circumstances. Of course the person you are praying for must cooperate with the graces God provides in order for a change of heart to take place. But the opportunity to affect that change lies in your prayers. God can and does use people and circumstances to reach out to a hardened heart.

If you've wondered whether or not you should pray for your ex-spouse, you definitely should. And in the end, the miracle that takes place might just happen inside your own heart.

We know that all things work together for good for those who love God, who are called according to his purpose.

~ Romans 8:28

Day 185:
Where Have You Gone, Lord?

As someone who is divorced, you may be feeling a spiritual emptiness along with an emotional emptiness asking, "Where have you gone, Lord?"

Does your emptiness lead you to wonder where God's presence is in your life? If this is how you are feeling, I encourage you to reflect on the fifth joyful mystery of the rosary, the finding of Jesus in the temple. Mary and Joseph were long gone from Jerusalem when they discovered Jesus was not with them. In a panic, they searched without success. Three frantic days later, they found Him sitting in the temple doing precisely what He was supposed to be doing.

It's no different in your life. You may not feel God's presence at this moment and that may distress you. But rest assured, He is near, and He is working in your life. He is doing exactly what is needed for you.

He said to them, "Why were you searching for me? Did you not know that I must be in my Father's house?"

~ Luke 2:49

Day 186:
Everything Happens For A Reason?

Have you ever heard someone say that everything happens for a reason? Many people believe this is the case, but that can be a difficult concept to accept when it comes to making sense out of the loss of your marriage.

God created marriage to last so it's safe to say He did not want yours to end in divorce. There was no supernatural reason that you will someday understand. But what is true, is that God can bring good things, yes, even great things, out of the most terrible circumstances. So while you are suffering the effects of your divorce, trust in Him that He will work your circumstances to your good and bring good things out of the bad.

We know that all things work together for good for those who love God, who are called according to his purpose.

~ Romans 8:28

Day 187:
O Holy Contradiction

Scripture tells us that when Joseph and Mary presented Jesus in the temple, there was great joy for all, including Anna and Simeon. Yet in the midst of that joy, Simeon told Mary her heart would be pierced by a sword. What a contradiction!

Although the Holy Family lived a seemingly simple life, they were actually living an incredible life in terms of salvation history. The Son of God, the Mother of God, and a saintly father were embarking on a purpose-driven life that was unknown to the rest of the world. Although Mary didn't have many advanced details, she knew there would be suffering. And Simeon confirmed that fact.

Modern day life is full of suffering. If you've experienced a divorce, you are likely suffering on an extreme level. But like Jesus, Mary and Joseph, you, too, can live an incredible life and play a role in salvation history by suffering with love. You can turn your pain into something extraordinary by offering it up to God for the sake of others. He, in turn, will take your offering and use it for good. Just like He used the terrible suffering of Jesus and Mary to redeem the world, He will take your suffering and use it, too. What a beautiful gift you can give, and in return, receive the blessings and graces you need to carry through.

The inner thoughts of many will be revealed—
and a sword will pierce your own soul too.

~ Luke 2:35

Day 188:
Feeling Lonely?

If you are feeling lonely, it's completely understandable. You've been through so much, and it can be quite difficult to put a smile on your face.

One of the best ways to combat loneliness is to visit others. Visiting the sick in hospitals or spending time at a nursing home are two good places to visit. Oftentimes the sick and elderly are your own family members, but visiting them can be difficult if you know your conversations will dredge up painful memories that you'd prefer to avoid.

In this case, there is one person you can visit who is lonely, too. One who understands everything you are going through—Jesus, in the Blessed Sacrament.

Jesus is present in tabernacles and in adoration chapels everywhere, waiting for you to come visit with Him. He, like you, is vulnerable. He, like you, has suffered. He is the best Counselor, Friend, and Healer you will ever encounter. And the only reason He waits is because He wants to see you.

The voice of the Lord is powerful; /
the voice of the Lord is full of majesty.

~ Psalm 29:4

Day 189:
Praying For Things To Change

A very wise Catholic marriage and family counselor once lamented that she hears her clients say things like, "I've prayed the rosary every day for three years for my ex-spouse, and it hasn't changed him a bit." In response, she would say, "I guess the wrong person got changed."

When we want things to change, we must begin with changing ourselves. This is a tough pill to swallow when so much of what you're going through is out of your control. But if you look at it from a different angle, you will see the wisdom. What other people say, think and do are completely out of your control, but you do have complete control over yourself.

The change must begin with you. Let others witness that change and be influenced by it. St. Francis of Assisi was a great example of this. He believed that if evil was all around, it was himself, and not others, that needed conversion first. He continually converted his own heart so that the world might become a better place.

Do not deceive yourselves. If you think that you are wise in this age, you should become fools so that you may become wise.

~ 1 Corinthians 3:18

Day 190:
Reason And Faith

Having faith in the midst of suffering and trials is a difficult thing to do. Our human nature kicks in and pulls the situation apart, piece-by-piece, in an effort to understand what's happened so we can make sense out of it all. This is a natural reaction and the way people try to get a grip on a disastrous situation.

Questions arise as a result of this exercise. Questions are always good, as they lift our eyes to God to ask, "Why?" Reason, coupled with faith, is how we are made to operate. But to live in faith means that your faith must constantly be evolving and strengthened. Each time your faith is challenged, you must regain the attitude of a child; a child who trusts his Father implicitly.

To live your faith in times of adversity means you must become poor in spirit. It means when nothing makes sense, you accept that God sees you and works these circumstances for your good.

Simon Peter answered him, "Lord, to whom can we go?
You have the words of eternal life."

~ John 6:68

Day 191:
Gratitude For Your Cross

———◇———

We should accept, as we would a favor, every moment of our lives and whatever they may bring, whether it is good or bad, but the crosses with even greater gratitude than the rest. Crosses release us from this world and by doing so, bind us to God.

~ Blessed Charles de Foucauld

How many circumstances do you have in your life today that you find difficult to accept, especially as being a "gift" from God? True, no one likes to suffer. But unless we know suffering, we can never appreciate happiness. Unless we are lost, we can never know the joy of being found.

If you are reading this, you have been given another day of life. This day of your life is a gift from God, whether you wake up with sadness or joy. It is His gift to you. Take this wonderful opportunity to use it wisely and take the time to be truly appreciative for this blessing.

———

Get up and go on your way; your faith has made you well.

~ Luke 17:19

Day 192:
A Prayer For Understanding

Lord, I come before you today with humility, grateful that you are here to listen to me. My heart is not at rest. I am consumed with turmoil over the things that have happened. Things that You have watched take place. I struggle with these events and wonder if they were really part of Your plan for me.

I believe in You, Lord, and I want to stay with You. Please help me today to see something good in all that has happened; to find some positive outcome that would not have happened unless I had experienced these circumstances.

Dear God, You know me better than I know myself. You have loved me since before I was born. In your goodness, have pity on me and if it be Your will, grant me the grace to see my life through Your eyes. Most of all, grant me the grace to have a stronger faith and greater perseverance. Amen.

For it was you who formed my inward parts; /
you knit me together in my mother's womb.

~ Psalm 139:13

Day 193:
God Will Bless You For Being Faithful

It is inspiring to see someone remain faithful to God in the midst of suffering. You may be struggling right now with different temptations; a temptation to stop coming to church, a temptation to overindulge as a means to soothe the pain, or even a temptation to be with someone you know you should not be with. These are all things that might feel good in the moment but would pull you away from your relationship with God.

God knows how hard you struggle to remain faithful to Him, and He blesses you for it. Even if you are not perfect every time, the fact that you are sincerely trying to remain close to Him means everything. Your generous Father will bless you with the graces you need to persevere.

The fear of the Lord is the crown of wisdom,
making peace and perfect health to flourish.

~ Sirach 1:18

Day 194:
Crush The Serpent's Head

———◇———

Are you struggling to fight the good fight, today? Are you trying to change yourself for the better with the little things you do, think, and say but keep coming up against roadblocks and temptations?

You're not alone. And it's important to remember that no one is perfect. Everyone fails. The key is to get back up, dust yourself off, and try again. As you do, keep in mind the supernatural reality of your struggles.

Every time you make the decision to bite your tongue and be charitable to your ex-spouse; every time you put on a smile instead of giving in to tears; every time you say yes to chastity and no to temptation, you are crushing the serpent's head. All these different challenges become great victories when you stand firm in your desire to be better. The devil is always there, whispering lies in your ear because he wants you to believe that you cannot succeed. But each time you choose the right thing, you crush his head.

You are winning small battles in the war over your soul. The glory is in the struggle. Never forget God's grace will carry you through.

———

*No testing has overtaken you that is not common to everyone.
God is faithful, and he will not let you be tested beyond your strength,
but with the testing he will also provide the way out
so that you may be able to endure it.*

~ 1 Corinthians 10:13

Day 195:
A Message From Saint Paul

If you are feeling discouraged in your efforts to live a good life and remain faithful to truth, take heart in these words from St. Paul. He wrote them with the express intent of encouraging the early Christians who, like you, needed a reminder of the great hope that lies in remaining faithful, even when it seems futile:

Therefore, my beloved, just as you have always obeyed me, not only in my presence, but much more now in my absence, work out your own salvation with fear and trembling; for it is God who is at work in you, enabling you both to will and to work for his good pleasure. Do all things without murmuring and arguing, so that you may be blameless and innocent, children of God without blemish in the midst of a crooked and perverse generation, in which you shine like stars in the world. It is by your holding fast to the word of life that I can boast on the day of Christ that I did not run in vain or labor in vain. But even if I am being poured out as a libation over the sacrifice and the offering of your faith, I am glad and rejoice with all of you— and in the same way you also must be glad and rejoice with me.

~ Philippians 2:12-18

Day 196:
You Are Not Far From The Kingdom Of God

If you could only recognize how many times a day the Holy Spirit inspires your thoughts, your life would be very different.

As you go about your day meeting people, driving to appointments, shopping for your family, and fulfilling your responsibilities, God is with you every step of the way inspiring your thoughts. Sometimes He's inspiring you to say something to someone. Sometimes He's inspiring you to not give up hope and be encouraged. The reasons for His inspirations are endless, but the one prominent inspiration He gives you is the reminder that you are not far from His Kingdom.

Many people have no faith. They live for themselves and for today without much thought for the state of their souls or what they will face when they enter into eternity. But you have faith. Despite your sufferings, you believe. You give your suffering meaning by offering it up and taking note of your blessings. Your faith and perseverance in the midst of trials are proof that you are not far from your ultimate goal, Heaven.

And if I go and prepare a place for you, I will come again and will take you to myself, so that where I am, there you may be also.

~ John 14:3

Day 197:
Little Victories Equal Eternal Reward

"In the Saints we see the victory of love over selfishness and death: we see that following Christ leads to life, eternal life, and gives meaning to the present, every moment that passes, because it fills it with love and hope."

~ Pope Benedict XVI, All Saints Day Address 2012

This message bears much significance in the life of one who suffers, for it is through suffering and loss that your soul is transformed. Suffering becomes a gold mine of heavenly treasure for yourself and heavenly gifts for someone else when endured with patience and cheerfulness.

Every setback you face, every unkind word you receive, every deception you become aware of, and everything you love but go without—all these become little victories over selfishness and death when you persevere with love.

If we only knew how many opportunities we have to gain graces and win souls for Christ, we would not regret suffering but embrace it. Your account in heaven will never go bankrupt. It will never disappear because the market plummeted. The reward for following in Christ's footsteps as He carried His cross with love is eternal.

But store up for yourselves treasures in heaven, where neither moth nor rust consumes and where thieves do not break in and steal.

~ Matthew 6:20

Day 198:
The Saints

Is it really worth praying to the saints?

The Church upholds the saints so we can see that it is possible to live a good and holy life, no matter what gets thrown our way. Their example shows us that not only can we live virtuous lives in today's society, but our suffering can have great meaning and become heavenly treasure, instead of just wasted time.

There was a famous athlete who won countless awards and accolades but also suffered from a serious disease. I, like others, considered him a champion and a hero. Until the day he said that he believed all his years of suffering were a complete waste of time. With that revelation, he was no longer a hero. Instead, the saints in heaven are the true heroes we should emulate.

God has allowed you to carry your specific cross, heavy as it may be. He chose it for you because He knows it can make you a saint. Believe in your strength and pray for deeper virtue. Allow your circumstances to change you into a hero and become someone that others will want to imitate.

No testing has overtaken you that is not common to everyone.
God is faithful, and he will not let you be tested beyond your strength,
but with the testing he will also provide the way out so that
you may be able to endure it.

~ 1 Corinthians 10:13

Day 199:
In God We Trust

Many people after experiencing divorce-related betrayal walk away saying, "Never again! I will never let myself be so vulnerable again!" This is a natural reaction but not one that should preside over the way you handle life's difficulties.

You can increase your ability to trust by asking God for the grace to grow in your faith and ability to trust in Him. He will give you what you need. Proceed in your life as if He has already taken care of the things you need.

God can heal you. God can make your life happier than you can ever imagine. Believe in his love for you and trust that He will take care of you.

~ Blessed Mother Teresa

Day 200:
Jesus Is Calling You

Bartimaeus was a blind beggar. Few people paid attention to him. He sat outside the city walls, making noise. He wanted attention. He wanted to be healed.

Most people passed him by, without a thought. Even the apostles, when passing by with Jesus, wanted him to be quiet, to go away. But Bartimaeus could not be silenced. His faith was solid, and he knew Jesus could heal his affliction. But it was more than that; Bartimaeus knew Jesus was the Son of God, the Messiah. When he was finally allowed, Bartimaeus threw away his cloak and came to Jesus.

Don't let your suffering take you away from Jesus. The world will tell you to be quiet and to look in a different direction. But keep your eyes fixed on Jesus. He wants to heal you. He wants to know what He can do for you.

Jesus said to him, "Go; your faith has made you well."
Immediately he regained his sight and followed him on the way.

~ Mark 10:52

Day 201:
Trust, Even When It Seems Impossible

Imagine the scene when Jesus told His disciples they had to eat His flesh and drink His blood to gain eternal life (see John 6). Many of His disciples walked away from Him that day, unable to believe. It was the catalyst for Judas' betrayal. But when Jesus asked those who remained if they would abandon him, too, Peter said, "Lord, to whom can we go? You have the words of eternal life" (John 6:68). Even though Jesus' teaching was difficult, Peter knew Jesus was the Messiah. He knew He was the Son of God.

You may be going through challenging times, yourself, as you go through your divorce or try to rebuild your life after one. It may seem impossible that things will get better. But contemplate St. Peter's statement of simple faith. He didn't demand an explanation from God. He just followed. Even though he didn't fully understand, Peter knew Jesus was God, and there was no other place to go. The only option was to simply follow Christ and gain understanding through following.

Don't give in to your worries and doubts. Trust in God that He will take care of you and give you what you need.

Simon Peter answered him, "Lord, to whom can we go?
You have the words of eternal life.

~ John 6:68

Day 202:
Lost

◆

Many people have described their divorce experience as wandering in the desert or feeling lost in a foreign place. This is not difficult to understand. Divorce creates an upheaval at all levels of living that is shocking. It takes some time to get used to the "new normal."

It's like the terror a small child goes through when he's accidentally separated from his parents and completely without safety. But when his parents find him, they hold him close with tears of joy and tight hugs. The beauty of being lost is being found.

When you are feeling lost, fear not. Christ will find you and hold you close with tears of joy and tight hugs. You are not alone and never will be.

Be strong and bold; have no fear or dread of them, because it is the Lord your God who goes with you; he will not fail you or forsake you.

~ Deuteronomy 31:6

Day 203:
Today Is A New Day

As you begin your day, take a few moments to reflect on the gift that you have been given—a brand new day in which you can start over again. Set aside the problems and stresses from yesterday and breathe in deeply the morning air. You have every moment of this day to spend as you please, compliments of your Creator.

Don't forget, God is waiting to hear from you. He wants to hear what you need for your day, what concerns you have, what struggles you need help with. He wants to communicate His love to you.

Take a few moments to thank Him for this new day and another opportunity to love.

So then you are no longer strangers and aliens, but you are citizens with the saints and also members of the household of God.

~ Ephesians 2:19

Day 204:
God's Merciful Love

Divorce can provoke a tremendous amount of guilt and shame, even if you were the one who was abandoned. These emotions can make you feel as if you are alone in your situation, but it's important to remember we are all broken people. You are not alone in your struggles; you are part of a family who is struggling together. What we need to remember is God's endless mercy.

As long as we are alive and repentant, God will forgive anything, all we need to do is come to Him with an open heart. God is our judge, but He is first our loving Savior and thirsts for our love and salvation. Don't waste precious time beating yourself up for the things you wish you could do over. Instead, pick yourself up and dust yourself off, knowing this is what God wants. Go to confession, go make amends if you can, but never forget God's perfect and merciful love for you.

He saved us, not because of any works of righteousness that we had done, but according to his mercy, through the water of rebirth and renewal by the Holy Spirit.

~ Titus 3:5

Day 205:
Lord, I Believe, Help My Unbelief!

Divorce makes life an unbelievable challenge. Every level of life is affected: material, relational, emotional, and spiritual. One of the most challenging aspects is dealing with the grave disappointment of a lost marriage and broken family.

Never forget that the devil will use this disappointment to convince you there's no hope for you. He actively works to drag you away from your faith. With each disappointment, he is there whispering doubts into your ear.

When you are charged with doubts and overwhelming disappointments, say this simple prayer: "Lord, I believe! Help my unbelief!" This is what the man whose son was possessed said to Jesus in the Gospel of Mark (see Mark 9:24). The humility in the statement is a great way to acknowledge the struggle you're having while still holding firm to your faith in God.

Remember that with each step you take in faith, God strengthens you even more with His grace. He is so pleased that you have not given up.

All things can be done for the one who believes.

~ Mark 9:23

Day 206:
A Heavenly Revenge

One of the most painful things about divorce for the spouse who was abandoned is the overwhelming sense of injustice. You married for life and thought your spouse did, too. You agonize over how your spouse moved on so quickly and now acts as if he or she barely knew you.

This can keep you steeped in anger looking for someone, anyone, to join you in your outrage and acknowledgement of this moral injustice. It's difficult to resolve these feelings in a positive way, but it's not impossible. Remember it takes time to work through these problems. When you are reminded of the need to forgive, remember that forgiveness is a process. It's something to work on every day. You may not see progress today, but if you keep trying and asking God for the grace to forgive, you will achieve this goal.

On the day of judgement everyone will have to account for their earthly lives, which means your spouse will have to account for abandoning you and all the terrible details that went along with it. That is a sort of heavenly revenge.

But don't forget that you, too, will have to stand before God and explain your life. That's why it's so important to work on getting rid of the resentment toward your ex-spouse; to work on forgiving the injustice and stand blameless before God.

Therefore whatever you have said in the dark will be heard in the light,
and what you have whispered behind closed doors
will be proclaimed from the housetops.

~ Luke 12:3

Day 207:
Pain Translated

It's normal to complain to God and to ask Him why He is allowing you to suffer. It's plain to see that the suffering from a divorce spans many facets of life and for a considerable length of time. It tests anyone's patience and endurance.

Suffering creates sinners and saints. When you are carrying a painful cross like divorce, you choose how this suffering will affect you. Will you break down, complain, and go in search of worldly relief? Or will you unite your suffering to Christ and bear it with patience? To suffer is to share in God's glory, if you live it with a supernatural attitude. We must share in Christ's suffering if we are to share in His glory.

But more than that, suffering reveals your inner beauty; your virtues, your hidden talents that come alive in times of necessity, your strength. Just as an oyster knife intrudes and forces the shell open against the will of the oyster revealing a precious pearl inside, so suffering forces your shell open, revealing the precious treasure that lies within you.

For the Lord disciplines those whom he loves,
and chastises every child whom he accepts.

~ Hebrews 12:6

Day 208:
Stand Firm!

Some days it's difficult to have a positive attitude. You are worn down by worries, financial matters, legal matters, trying to heal the hurts from your divorce, and fear of the unknown. It can pile up pretty quickly and hit you like a tidal wave.

At a time like this, it's easy to give in to the temptation to indulge yourself in ways that might make you feel better for a little while but in the long run are not wise choices. Are you tempted to self-medicate with too much alcohol or too much food? Or buy yourself things when you really don't have the money? If you feel this way, it's understandable. But recognize the evil one is using your situation to trip you up and make you fall. Hard.

But know this—you're better than that! You are loved by Christ in a way that none of those things could ever compare. Stand firm in your confidence of God's love, and He will reward you with renewed strength and peace.

For freedom Christ has set us free. Stand firm, therefore, and do not submit again to a yoke of slavery.

~ Galatians 5:1

Day 209:
Don't Settle For A Mediocre Life

St. Teresa of Avila is a great patron for Catholics who are divorced. That might seem odd given the fact that she was never married. She entered the convent at a young age and became a nun at twenty. But the reason why she is a great patron for the divorced lies in her conversion and life afterwards.

The convent Teresa lived in was not much of a house of prayer. It was more like a boarding house for wealthy young women. Teresa came to despise her spiritual mediocrity and resolved never to be content with just doing what everyone else was doing. She committed herself to doing her absolute best in everything, including working to reform the nuns and starting new convents with faithful communities. She was the first woman to be named a Doctor of the Church.

Going through a divorce can make you feel like you've been beaten to a pulp. Every time you fall, you find the strength to get up, and then you get knocked down again. At that point, it's easy to look around at others who are divorced and observe how they are getting through it all. This can be the catalyst to settling for mediocrity. Don't allow yourself to be satisfied with that level of living.

Look to St. Teresa's example and know that with God's grace, you can be a great person, despite all that's happened. You can be a great example for others. You, too, can be a saint. Hold tight to your faith and never give in to living a lukewarm life.

Let nothing disturb you. ...All things are passing. God never changes.

~ St. Teresa of Avila

Day 210:
The Consolation Of Losing

In the parable of the rich young man who approached Jesus seeking the key to eternal life, Jesus knew how good this man was trying to be, but He also knew what was holding him back—possessions.

Possessions, in and of themselves, are not bad, only their ability to get in the way of our relationship with Christ and others. Divorce has a way of stripping you of possessions involuntarily which can make your loss seem quite unjust. But did you ever consider that maybe it is a blessing in disguise?

When you go through a divorce and lose these material things that have kept you feeling safe, it can be very painful. But at the same time, there is a de-cluttering process, a sort of clearing away that happens in your heart and soul. You grieve the loss of possessions, status, and relationships but at the same time, your view of life's landscape, and the things in life that are truly important becomes much clearer and simpler. This is one way God works to bring good things out of the bad. Your great sense of loss is tempered with a new sense of clarity and wisdom.

Take heart and know that God is building you up through all the loss you have endured. Though you may have suffered injustice, no one can take Christ from you. No one can take away your relationship with Him. He will lead you to eternal life.

Then Jesus looked around and said to his disciples, "How hard it will be for those who have wealth to enter the kingdom of God!"

~ Mark 10:23

Day 211:
Living In The Age Of The Broken Heart

What has happened to the family? These days it seems as if there are no happy families anymore. Divorce tears families apart. Abuse destroys the meaning of love and protection. Arguments and hurt feelings estrange parents from children. Adults live full lives that rarely or never include other family members because of disagreements. Couples cohabitate instead of marrying because they fear divorce, yet they eventually go their own ways in the end. The family is under attack like never before. This is the age of the broken heart.

But it's not just your heart and not just mine. Christ's heart is broken. Christ, the One who is Love Himself, grieves over the hurts we inflict upon each other and suffers with those who are left out in the cold. Our Blessed Mother's heart breaks, too. Her only desire is to see the world come to her Son, and her heart is broken as she watches us turn away.

But it's not too late. All is not lost, just yet. Each day is a clean slate, a new chance to change. Society has not yet slipped off the edge of the cliff. You can affect a change, but it must begin with you. Your personal choices, your thoughts, words, and actions; your closeness to God. This is how you can change society. Today, take a step toward real change. Take a step toward doing things differently: with patience, honesty, and kind words. Take a step toward love.

O give thanks to the Lord, for he is good;
for his steadfast love endures forever.

~ 1 Chronicles 16:34

Day 212:
Heartburn Can Be A Good Thing

When the two disciples were on the road to Emmaus after the crucifixion, they were feeling afraid of what the future would bring. They were disillusioned. The hope that Jesus was the Savior was lost. Christ caught up with them on the road. He encouraged these downtrodden men to talk to Him so they could get their disappointment off their chests.

After they had told Him all that had happened, Jesus allowed them to recognize Him. As they conversed with Jesus, their hearts were filled with fiery emotion. Jesus did this out of love for them so they would know they were truly with Jesus.

Jesus does the same for us. When you are disappointed, afraid, sad, or lonely, Jesus may not be speaking to you. He may be waiting for you to talk to Him so you can get all your concerns off your chest. He wants to hear it all from you, and then He wants to show you the way. He wants to give you a heart that burns with love.

Don't let your disappointments weigh you down. Take time to converse with Christ and let Him bless you with His gifts and love.

They said to each other, "Were not our hearts burning within us
while he was talking to us on the road,
while he was opening the scriptures to us?

~ Luke 24:32

Day 213:
You Can't Heal If You're A Victim

During those terrible months and years after my divorce, I played the blame game. Blaming others is a typical, knee-jerk reaction to deep hurt. It is a slippery slope that can quickly become an attitude that causes much worse problems in life. The blame game transformed me into a victim. I was actually avoiding the truth about my situation. It wasn't until I stopped blaming others for my situation that I was able to put my feet on the path toward healing.

The first thing I had to do was accept. I had to accept that my marriage was gone. Unfortunately I was clinging to something that was dead, and I needed to let go of it, even though that would be painful. I had to accept that I could not control my ex-husband. All those things he was doing to hurt me, I could not change. I also had to accept that I, too, carried some of the blame for the divorce. And that was hard.

These were difficult steps to take but once I took them, I began to make progress. This important exercise of accepting the truth in my life made it easier to pray, easier to attend mass, and easier to embrace God. Although I still didn't understand why it all happened, I had stopped blaming God and instead turned to Him for strength.

Are you tangled up in the blame game? If so, take some time to reflect on your circumstances and ask God to enlighten your thoughts and help you accept the truth of your situation.

I will study the way that is blameless. When shall I attain it?
I will walk with integrity of heart within my house.

~ Psalm 101:2

Day 214:
The Problem With Divorce

The Gospels tell us we should have a childlike faith; unless we become like little children, we cannot enter the kingdom of heaven. This is something you've heard and have known for most of your life, but doesn't it seem like divorce changes that? Doesn't the divorce experience make the idea of being "child-like" almost ridiculous?

What does a childlike faith really mean? First, a child has rock-solid trust in his parents. Even though he can barely fend for himself, a child sleeps soundly at night because he knows his parents love him and will protect him; they will take care of him. Next, a child may get hurt or disappointed, but it is short-lived. Children forgive quickly.

Divorce can lead you to determine that you can only trust yourself because you can't trust others. The hurt you bear makes you believe that it is wiser never to forget who hurt you or how they hurt you. But in reality, this kind of "wisdom" is only baggage. It is the unwillingness to let go of resentment; the unwillingness to forgive.

Take time today to reflect upon the hurts you have not forgiven. Pray for the grace to be able to forgive and then, trust your heavenly Father with the outcome.

Forgive your neighbor the wrong he has done, and then your sins will be pardoned when you pray.

~ Sirach 28:2

Day 215:
Dealing With The Loss Of Divorce

Anyone who experiences divorce knows quite well the meaning of the word "loss." Loss takes place on so many levels. Besides the obvious loss of the marriage, divorce can mean the loss of many other relationships, material possessions and self-worth. That's when it's time to look for something else to hold on to. The Bible and all its spiritual nourishment can provide that for you.

During the times in your life when there's not too much stress or too much negativity, it's easy to connect with the Gospel message. But when times become overwhelmingly difficult, it's harder to see the Gospel message through the fog of your trials. You cannot connect with it in a way that makes sense with what you are going through.

A good Scripture passage to embrace during divorce is "the Lord gave, and the Lord has taken away; blessed be the name of the Lord." (Job 1:21). This scripture says it all! When things are good and you're happy, you should be grateful and say, "Blessed be the name of the Lord." And when times are dark and you are suffering, trust and humility should enable you to say, "Blessed be the name of the Lord."

No matter how dark your troubles are, even with the great loss and devastation of divorce, the light of Christ is always with you. He will never place upon you a burden you cannot carry. Know that Christ allows this cross and will make you a better person for it.

The Lord gave, and the Lord has taken away;
blessed be the name of the Lord.

~ Job 1:21

Day 122:
Turn The Other Cheek?!

How do you "turn the other cheek" in your situation? What is it that God is really asking of you as you go through the pain of separating from your ex-spouse? Is He asking you to be a doormat, letting anyone and everyone walk all over you and abuse you? No. Defending and protecting yourself and your children is certainly very important. Turning the other cheek would be loving in a way that is contrary to the way society loves. Society preaches a "feel good" love; as long as it feels good, love, but when it doesn't feel good anymore, stop. This definition is false.

Love is most vividly displayed when things are difficult and painful. A loving person still remains charitable; still seeks the good of the other; and still does not allow angry sentiments to dictate his or her words and actions. It is easy to look at someone who has hurt us and say, "That person doesn't deserve my love." But contemplate Christ on the cross—the torture, the whipping, the insults, the spitting, the pain! That did not feel good, yet Christ endured His torture and pain out of sheer love for us, even though we do not deserve it.

It is easy to love and care for people you like. It is harder to do anything for someone with whom you are at odds. But if you truly want to find healing and peace in your life and move forward to a better place, step outside your comfort zone and stretch your heart a little wider. Ask God for the grace to forgive others and to find love where there is none. Ask God for the grace to love.

But I say to you, Do not resist an evildoer.
But if anyone strikes you on the right cheek, turn the other also.

~ Matthew 5:39

Day 217:
Novena To St. Francis For Peace, Day 1

◆

"Leave all and follow Me."

St. Francis, God called you to a life of poverty and simplicity so that you might know Him intimately and share His peace that surpasses all understanding with others. You left everything behind and followed Him. My divorce causes me to feel connected to you as I have been stripped of relationships, belongings, self-worth, and understanding. I pray to you, now, to petition God on my behalf that He will grant me the grace I need to be a faithful follower during this very difficult time. I believe in His goodness, and I need Him now, more than ever. Help me to stand firmly on my faith and trust in Him. Most of all, I ask for peace in my heart and for this special intention...

I pray these things in Jesus' name. Amen.

———

Our Father, Hail Mary, Glory Be.
St. Francis, patron of peace and families, pray for us.

Day 218:
Novena To Saint Francis For Peace, Day 2

Conversion of Heart

St. Francis, I thank you for the gift of your example to all those who follow Christ. Your early struggles and later sincere conversion of heart is a great witness for me as I wrestle with my own struggles. The circumstances surrounding my divorce make me feel imprisoned by anger, resentment, and worry over things I cannot control. I beg you for the grace to be strong and for the grace to forgive those who have hurt me. Most of all, I ask for peace in my heart and for this special intention...

I pray these things in Jesus' name. Amen.

Our Father, Hail Mary, Glory Be.
St. Francis, patron of peace and families, pray for us.

Day 219:
Novena To Saint Francis For Peace, Day 3

Disapproved Of and Disinherited By His Family

St. Francis, I come to you with a heavy heart, seeking guidance and consolation. Divorce has torn my family apart, and I cannot reverse the incredible pain that has been inflicted on those I love. I look to you, St. Francis, who suffered the rejection and disapproval of your own family as you followed the way of Christ, and I beg you to pray for me to God that He will take this terrible situation and bring good out of it. Most of all, I ask for peace in my heart and for this special intention...

I pray these things in Jesus' name. Amen.

Our Father, Hail Mary, Glory Be.
St. Francis, patron of peace and families, pray for us.

Day 220:
Novena To Saint Francis For Peace, Day 4

Reached Out to Serve Others

St. Francis, I ask for your prayers to God, today, on my behalf. I am so focused on all the worries and negativity of my divorce situation, and I need to refocus myself on goodness and love. You selflessly served others by visiting the sick, cleaning churches, and preaching the Gospel to anyone who would listen. Heartened by your example, please ask God to give me the grace to look beyond my sadness to others who might also be hurting or in need that I may imitate your example of love and service. Most of all, I ask for peace in my heart and for this special intention...

I pray these things in Jesus' name. Amen.

Our Father, Hail Mary, Glory Be.
St. Francis, patron of peace and families, pray for us.

Day 221:
Novena To Saint Francis For Peace, Day 5

Composed Songs and Hymns to God and Nature

St. Francis, lover of all God's creatures, thank you for living a life of charity and service. There was no creature too small for you to tend to, and the love you brought to those who were suffering was constant, until the day you died. You lived with the animals and were inspired by the grandeur of nature. Please pray to God, for me, as I persevere through these difficult times, that I may find peace and consolation through reflecting on nature and all God's beautiful creations. Most of all, I ask for peace in my heart and for this special intention...

I pray these things in Jesus' name. Amen.

Our Father, Hail Mary, Glory Be.
St. Francis, patron of peace and families, pray for us.

Day 222:
Novena To Saint Francis For Peace, Day 6

Cared for Lepers

St. Francis, you cared for lepers, the people no one wanted to be around or have contact with. Being divorced can make me feel like a leper at times because of the loss of relationships and the avoidance of people who do not understand what I am going through. Ask God to grant me the grace to persevere in this struggle and to be more sensitive and kind to others who are going through a divorce. Most of all, I ask for peace in my heart and for this special intention...

I pray these things in Jesus' name. Amen.

Our Father, Hail Mary, Glory Be.
St. Francis, patron of peace and families, pray for us.

Day 223:
Novena To Saint Francis For Peace, Day 7

Sent Food to Thieves

St. Francis, you served everyone without hesitation or discrimination. You even took care of thieves by sending them food with the hopes of bringing them closer to God through your kindness. I am dealing with my own "thieves" and look to your example for encouragement so I can forgive and find a way to be charitable. Please ask God to grant me these graces I need so badly. Most of all, I ask for peace in my heart and for this special intention...

I pray these things in Jesus' name. Amen.

Our Father, Hail Mary, Glory Be.
St. Francis, patron of peace and families, pray for us.

Day 224:
Novena To Saint Francis For Peace, Day 8

Bearer of the Stigmata

St. Francis, you loved God so much that you were blessed with the Stigmata. Although you suffered greatly because of this, you never stopped serving others or preaching the Gospel. Please pray to God for me that I can do the same, despite my great suffering. Most of all, I ask for peace in my heart and for this special intention...

I pray these things in Jesus' name. Amen.

Our Father, Hail Mary, Glory Be.
St. Francis, patron of peace and families, pray for us.

Day 225:
Novena To Saint Francis For Peace, Day 9

Imitator of Jesus

St. Francis, you have walked with me these past days and have been a great source of inspiration for me as I struggle with my difficulties. From today, forward, I will continue to look to your life's example, especially in your imitation of Jesus. Ask God to grant me the graces I need to follow in your footsteps as I continue down this difficult road. Most of all, I ask for peace in my heart and for this special intention...

I pray these things in Jesus' name. Amen.

Our Father, Hail Mary, Glory Be.
St. Francis, patron of peace and families, pray for us.

Day 226:
Real, Faithful, Passionate Love

Having doubts about God's love for you? Here's a little food for thought—Christ loves you with a real, faithful, passionate love.

Christ is a real person, not a character in a book or movie. He is alive today, body and soul. To love someone, you have to know them. He knows you—He's known you from all eternity. If you don't love Christ more than some fictional character, then you don't know Him. He really did die for you, and it really hurt. He really suffered so that you don't have to suffer for all eternity.

Christ's love is a faithful love. There are many reasons to be friends with someone—power, fame, money, etc. But the only real reason that keeps people hanging around is love. Faithful love draws us together across the distance. That is the kind of love that brought Jesus down to earth as a human to die for us. Faithful love is willing to make sacrifices.

Christ's love for you is a passionate love. Passionate love is an attraction so strong that you are willing to suffer for it. You can tell how much someone loves you by the size of the sacrifice they make on your behalf. This is the kind of love we need to return to Christ.

But God proves his love for us in that while we still were sinners Christ died for us.

~ Romans 5:8

Day 227:
Is God Asking You To Walk On Water?

◆

Peter is the apostle to whom many people can easily relate. He was a rough and gregarious type who wore his emotions on his sleeve. He was full of faults, yet humble enough to acknowledge them. And he loved Jesus with everything he had.

St. Peter shows us a real-life illustration of what it is like to be close to Christ and yet still succumb to human frailty. Jesus called Peter and told him to walk on water. He succeeded at first, but then his reason kicked in. His doubts took over, "People can't walk on water!" And he began to sink. But he still cried out to the Lord, who saved him from drowning.

What a great example for you as you struggle to rebuild your life after divorce. Are there areas in your life where God is asking for your trust? Is He asking you to take a step out of the boat to walk on the water?

If you are consumed with doubt, just trust in Jesus. Trust that what He's asking you to do is a good thing. Take that step out of the boat and walk. If you begin to sink, simply cry out to Jesus. He will keep you from sinking.

―――――――――

Peter answered him,
"Lord, if it is you, command me to come to you on the water."

~ Matthew 14:28

Day 228:
From The Death Of Divorce
To The Resurrection Of New Life

Divorce is a terrible thing to go through. The loss that is experienced happens on many different levels. The whole, intact family unit is lost. The love and trust between spouses is lost. Relationships with friends, family, and neighbors are lost. Property, reputation and self-esteem are lost.

All these losses, piled one on top of the other, are devastating and can make even the most faithful person look to God and ask, why?

In his first letter to the Corinthians, St. Paul gives you the answer you need at this time: "What you sow does not come to life unless it dies" (1 Corinthians 15:36).

We all must die to ourselves. What you are experiencing is precisely that, dying to yourself. You are experiencing a little of what Christ did for all of us. He gave everything—every drop of blood, every ounce of strength. He spared nothing to show us how much He loves us.

He sees what you are going through and loves you all the more. Your losses are bringing you closer to Him in the purest way. Let His love carry you through and wait with hope for your resurrection.

So if anyone is in Christ, there is a new creation: everything old has passed away; see, everything has become new!

~ 2 Corinthians 5:17

Day 229:
Advice For Carrying A Heavy Cross

Feeling weak under the heavy weight of your cross today?

Cardinal Timothy Dolan wrote: "The Cross is the classroom of sanctity, the professor of perfection, the arena of heroic virtue!"

Never forget that God gave you this particular cross because He knows it will transform you—if you allow it to happen. Complaining about your circumstances is normal and easy but greeting the day with a smile, despite the pain, is noble and a great example for those who encounter you.

_____

No testing has overtaken you that is not common to everyone.
God is faithful, and he will not let you be tested beyond your strength,
but with the testing he will also provide the way out
so that you may be able to endure it.

~ 1 Corinthians 10:13

Day 230:
Tempted, But Not Conquered

Are you facing a constant temptation right now? Are you tempted to give someone a piece of your mind? Are you tempted to give in to someone pressuring you to be physically intimate? Are you tempted to do something you know is wrong?

Well, you are normal. Thank goodness for that. We all face temptations on a daily basis. But you don't have to be a victim of temptation. You can stand strong and defeat those temptations if you use the tools you have at your fingertips.

First, say this prayer when you are feeling tempted: "Lord Jesus, let your blood wash over me and protect me from the temptations of the devil."

Then, turn your eyes away from whatever you are being tempted by. St. Augustine said: "From the look comes the thought and from the thought comes the desire." If your eyes are the window to your soul, let them reflect God who dwells within you.

Last, remember the devil is not as strong as a soul in the state of grace, and you, coupled with God's saving grace, will win this battle.

For the one who is in you is greater than the one who is in the world.

~ 1 John 4:4

Day 231:
You're Still Catholic?

One evening I went out to dinner with a friend from work. We enjoyed working together, and we wanted to get to know each other better without taking away from company time. She told me all about herself, and I did the same, including the divorce I had gone through a few years prior. Her response to me was, "Wow, you're still Catholic?" I did not hesitate to confirm that answer.

"Let me see," she said. "Your Catholic husband left you high and dry, and now the Catholic Church says you can't date or be in a relationship with anyone until you go through another legal proceeding? I don't know, it seems like a lot of hassle. If it were me, I'd just go do my own thing and be happy."

I was sad to hear her words. I knew she had no understanding of what it meant to be truly Catholic; truly faithful to Christ in the good times and the bad.

You may feel tempted to just walk away, too. Divorce is hard, no question. But the mere fact that you stay faithful to God is a delight to Him. How dear to His heart are all your acts of confidence and perseverance, even though others challenge you. And whether or not you "feel" it, Christ is closer to you now, more than ever before. Don't give in to mediocrity but place your trust in God, who, as St. Teresa of Avila says, loves us more than we love ourselves.

Therefore, since we are surrounded by so great a cloud of witnesses, let us also lay aside every weight and the sin that clings so closely, and let us run with perseverance the race that is set before us.

~ Hebrews 12:1

Day 232:
How To Find God

When going through troubled times, many people complain that they cannot find God. It's a unique experience that can be confusing, "If God loves me so much, where is He when I need Him the most?" Praying becomes a desolate and difficult experience.

God is, of course, present with you at every moment. Part of the reason you are having trouble finding Him is because there are too many obstructions in your way. You need to let go of doubt, worries, and attachments to things of this world because they will get in the way.

St. Alphonsus Ligouri said, "If a crystal vase is filled with dirt, the sun cannot penetrate it. The light of God cannot illuminate a heart that is attached to the things of this world." Identify those things that are filling your heart and preventing God's love and grace from filling your heart. Then, place it all at the foot of the cross and experience your Savior.

But whenever you pray, go into your room and shut the door
and pray to your Father who is in secret;
and your Father who sees in secret will reward you.

~ Matthew 6:6

Day 233:
Share Your Suffering

One of the truly heartbreaking aspects of going through a divorce is the terrible scourge of anger that embeds itself in the human heart. Hearts were created to be a source of love. So to find your own heart so complicated and compromised by the emotions that accompany the loss of a marriage can be devastating.

But you are not alone in your struggle. There are many, now, that share your experiences and many that have gone before you—in particular, Jesus, your Savior.

I guess what helps all the suffering make sense is the understanding that everyone suffers injustice, and these lessons are there to make you think harder, reflect more, and improve yourself.

Most of all, suffering helps you learn the virtue of humility, recognizing that other people will do as they please. All you can do is control yourself.

Take some time this week to reflect upon your situation and ask God for the help you need. And then, be comforted by the fact that many people, including me, are praying for you!

For I am longing to see you so that I may share with you some spiritual gift to strengthen you.

~ Romans 1:11

Day 234:
Let Not Your Heart Be Troubled

We live in troubled times. Everything that is moral, just, and right seems to be turned upside down, mocked, and disdained. All that is immoral is held up as good, just, and what everyone should do.

These contradictions make it very difficult to cope with the disaster of divorce, especially when children are involved. But let not your heart be troubled, as Scripture says, because Christ will bring you the peace and understanding you need if you remain connected to Him in prayer.

From simple conversations to all twenty decades of the rosary, it doesn't really matter what type of prayer you choose. What matters is joining your heart with His, sharing your worries and concerns with Him, and opening your heart to whatever He wants to give you. This is how you can have peace in the midst of chaos.

Peace I leave with you; my peace I give to you.
I do not give to you as the world gives. Do not let your hearts be
troubled, and do not let them be afraid.

~ John 14:27

Day 235:
We All Need Somebody To Lean On

Many people who get divorced fall away from their faith because no one is there encouraging them to stay. Have you experienced this?

When you wondered if you would be allowed to attend mass and receive the sacraments, was someone there to help you answer those questions? When you were overwhelmed by grief and needed someone to talk to, someone who would listen and not judge, was someone there for you?

Hopefully, your answer to these questions is "yes." But many people cannot answer that way, which is tragic.

As you rebuild your life and move past the pain of your divorce, resolve to be the kind of person that will be there for others. You can understand the pain and agony that divorce inflicts. You've asked the tough questions and had to wrestle with many critical issues that surround a Catholic experiencing divorce. Resolve to be there for someone else who needs someone to listen, answer, and support them. Taking the time for even one soul builds you an everlasting treasure in heaven.

This is my commandment,
that you love one another as I have loved you.

~ John 15:12

Day 236:
Searching For The Light
At The End Of The Tunnel

Sometimes divorce can seem like a never-ending tunnel of darkness. You know the end is ahead of you somewhere, but you can't find it. You feel like you may be stuck forever trying to find your way out. If you are feeling this way, it is understandable but know that Jesus is walking through that darkness with you. At this time, He wants to be your strength and your guide through that darkness. He wants you to rely on Him.

It is through our reliance on Him that we will gain strength and find the way out of the darkness. Jesus tried to tell Peter that despite all his talents and goodness, he would fail if he relied on his own strength. Peter ignored Jesus and failed three times: when he fell asleep in the garden, when he cut off the soldier's ear, and when he denied Christ. Often when we hit a brick wall, we can look back and see we relied on our own strength instead of calling upon Christ.

Today, take some time to dialogue with God and offer Him your struggles so that He can take them and bring good out of them.

God, the Lord, is my strength; /
he makes my feet like the feet of a deer, /
and makes me tread upon the heights.

~ Habakkuk 3:19

Day 237:
Don't Make Negative Resolutions

Rebuilding your life after divorce is a daunting task and the struggles are enormous. It takes a courageous person to really make the most of it. Through personal refinement, reflecting on what happened in the marriage to cause the divorce, and then, working to change those faults, you identify what contributed to the divorce.

In doing so, you may adopt some resolutions to practice each day. When you do, make them positive resolutions, not negative ones. For example, instead of saying "I won't speak angrily to my ex next time," try, "I will pray for more peaceful encounters with my ex-spouse."

Practicing a virtue is always more effective and life-changing than avoiding a sin.

"I know that there is nothing better for them than to be happy and enjoy themselves as long as they live."

~ Ecclesiastes 3:12

Day 238:
The Blank Check

When you are born, it's like God gives you a signed, blank check. Your life is full of possibilities. He's endowed you with gifts that are unique. God says, "Here is my gift of life to you! Run with it! Make the most of it!"

The pain and ugliness of divorce can completely overshadow this understanding of what life is supposed to be. The rejection, anger, and lack of forgiveness can make you feel as if life is completely void of joy and possibility. This is precisely the point where you can make a radical change. You can give God a signed, blank check back.

That blank check says, "I trust you, Lord." At a time when everything seems dismal, and you don't know what the future holds, placing your trust in God is an act of faith and love that will be rewarded. He will take your blank check, invest all the trust you give Him, and the return will be greater than you can hope for. Trust Him.

My refuge and my fortress; / my God, in whom I trust!

~ Psalm 91:2

Day 239:
A Prayer For Healing

---◈---

Dear Jesus, Healer of all infirmities and suffering, I approach you with faith and a deep desire to know you more intimately. I want to know your heart as much as possible because my suffering leads to questions that I will only understand if I am close to you. I know the healing of my wounds is part of your plan, and I listen attentively to your words that they may soothe my heart and bring me peace.

In your great love, grant me the grace to be patient as you work in my life and bring good fruit out of the bad things that have happened. I praise you and thank you for all your blessings and protection. Amen.

Our Lady of Sorrows, pray for us!

Day 240:
Come To The Quiet

Divorce can seem like a loud, abrasive, irritating, and noisy racket that won't go away. But the quiet times you reserve for prayer are the perfect remedy for this. Times when you approach God and rest in Him as a child falls asleep in his daddy's lap. Are you able to have this childlike relationship with our heavenly Father?

Jesus was the first to call God, "Father." People did not have that type of relationship with God. The idea of God as "Father" was a revolutionary one, and Jesus taught us we should call Him "Abba" or "Daddy" as a child would.

It can be difficult to approach God as a child, especially when your heart is engulfed in anger. But if you take some time to pray and seek God as "daddy," He will be there and provide the peace and quiet you need, as well as the blessings of a loving Father.

For you did not receive a spirit of slavery to fall back into fear, but you have received a spirit of adoption. When we cry, "Abba! Father!"

~ Romans 8:15

Day 241:
Confession: A Spiritual Toolbox

One of the greatest struggles of divorce is learning how to deal with all the powerful emotions you feel. Anger, resentment, loneliness, sadness, and the pain of incredible loss—all these feelings can overwhelm you like a tidal wave. The trick is managing your emotions so they don't manage you. This takes personal strength. But what do you do when you are lacking this strength?

Avail yourself of the sacrament of confession. This sacrament is like having a spiritual toolbox. It is so much more than just going inside a small room and listing your sins. Confession gives you the opportunity to discuss your circumstances and feelings with someone who will give you good advice, who cares about your soul, and wants to see you happy. And because it is a sacrament, you receive the graces and the strength you need to manage these emotions and have a better life.

The best thing is the sacrament of confession is always at your disposal. You can go any time if you call and make an appointment. It's not just limited to Saturdays. If you are lacking the strength you need, consider going to confession.

Lord, hear my voice! / Let your ears be attentive /
to the voice of my supplications!

~ Psalm 130:2

Day 242:
Still Not Convinced?

The culture of divorce is a deceptive one. It promises an instant fix to the pain and loneliness people feel after divorce through the encouragement of sexual intimacy with others, filling that terrible hole with self-indulgent behavior. But this prescription for healing is nothing but smoke and mirrors, designed to lead you down a path to further pain and destruction. There is nothing good that can come from this, and the Church teaches that true healing can only come through Jesus and His sacraments.

However, many people who go through a divorce don't believe this is true. Are you one of them? Maybe you are not convinced that doing God's will can make you happy? Do you doubt that you can be holy and happy?

God inspires your thoughts many times each day, hoping you will act upon them. For one week, put aside your doubt and act on the inspirations He gives you. Make a concerted effort to really put the "holy and happy" idea to the test and see what you think at the end of the week. Make a note of what happened when you followed His lead. God will not disappoint you!

May the God of peace himself sanctify you entirely;
and may your spirit and soul and body be kept sound and blameless
at the coming of our Lord Jesus Christ.

~ 1 Thessalonians 5:23

Day 243:
When You Doubt God's Presence

◇

Divorce is devastating. Very few are over quickly, most are drawn out battles with painful words, shocking betrayals, and bitter fights. For anyone going through such torture, it can seem as if God is silent, absent, and leaving you to fight alone.

This is not the case, but it does feel like you are left to your own devices. How exhausting it is to feel as if you have no confidant, no protector, and no safety net to fall back on!

Keep your faith in God, for He is surely with you and will use your circumstances for your good, even if it seems all is lost. It's much easier to see God's work in your life when you reflect on the past than recognize it in the thick of your struggle.

Take some time to make note of God's blessings in your life in the past. Let those blessings help reinforce your faith that God will take care of you.

Wake up! Bestir yourself for my defense, /
for my cause, my God and my Lord!

~ Psalm 35:23

Day 244:
Don't Let Your Feelings Fool You

Love is an emotion, but in its truer sense, it is a decisive act to will the good of another person.

This is important to remember when you are trying to improve yourself, especially when working on forgiving someone who has hurt you. You might say you forgive them, but in your heart, you still feel resentment. You believe that you haven't truly forgiven until you don't feel the negativity anymore, but don't let your feelings fool you.

Just because you don't "feel" a positive emotion connected with what you are trying to accomplish, does not mean you are failing in your struggle to be better. You have made the decision to forgive, and you need to accept that this is enough. It is God's grace that sweetens your heart and removes the resentment. What matters the most is that you put forth the effort and leave the rest to Christ.

Let the favor of the Lord our God be upon us, / and prosper for us the work of our hands— / O prosper the work of our hands!

~ Psalm 90:17

Day 245:
If It Helps You Pray, Do It

Do you feel uninspired to pray? Is your heart conflicted with powerful emotions like resentment, worry, anger, self-pity, or jealousy? After experiencing divorce, these are all typical reactions. But these emotions can certainly make prayer a mundane and difficult task.

It might help you if you know the basic rule of prayer: if "X" helps me pray, do it. If "X" doesn't help me pray, don't do it.

For some people, the rosary is a staple in their prayer life. No matter where they are or what situation they are in, the rosary is their lifeline. But the rosary might seem too complex or too rote for some people. Other people prefer to be outdoors, in nature, to help elevate their thoughts to God. Others prefer the quiet solace of a morning mass or an adoration chapel.

If you're having trouble praying, try something different. Read the book of Psalms, or maybe, a book of daily reflections to help your dialogue with God. The important thing is to "feed" your conversation with Jesus. It's like having a diving board to dive into the pool of prayer.

No matter what works for you, remember that your best bet for recovering from divorce is staying connected to God. He loves you and will not forsake you.

I am the vine, you are the branches. Those who abide in me and I in them bear much fruit, because apart from me you can do nothing.

~ John 15:5

Day 246:
Serenity Through Service

When bad things happen, you can easily become consumed by doubts, worries and negativity. You focus intently on yourself and block out the things that don't concern you until the crisis is over. But doing this never helps to relieve stress or bring clarity. In fact, allowing this to happen will likely make things worse for you.

A great way to overcome this obstacle to peace is to focus on others instead of yourself. Do you know someone who needs your help in some way? Can you bring someone dinner and visit with them or offer to help with a fix-it job?

There are many things you can do to help someone else which will give you a break from worrying about your situation. Paying attention to others' needs will bring you happiness. Through helping others, you can allow God to work in your life and take care of these details that are stressing you out.

For truly I tell you, whoever gives you a cup of water to drink because you bear the name of Christ will by no means lose the reward.

~ Mark 9:41

Day 247:
A Prayer For The Grace To Forgive

Dear Lord, I come to you with a heart that is heavy with resentment. The hurt I carry with me is taking its toll, slowly closing the door of my heart to love. I have been unjustly hurt, and I don't want to forgive, yet I beg You to grant me the grace to forgive the one who has hurt me, even though the very thought of doing so is painful to me.

Turn my eyes now to You and show me Your wounds. Show me Your bloody face. Show me Your torn flesh. Help me to always remember that You are the True Victim who suffered the most unjust hurt ever known to humankind. Give me the grace to be sorrowful for my sins that nailed You to the cross and whisper in my ear Your loving words, "Father forgive them for they know not what they do." With Your tenderness, O Lord, I know my heart will melt and be filled with Your love, that I may forgive my offender. Amen.

But I say to you,
Love your enemies and pray for those who persecute you.

~ Matthew 5:44

Day 248:
Mary, Your Guide Through The Darkness

St. Bernard said about Mary, "If you follow her guidance, you will not go astray. If you pray to her, you will not give up hope. If you think of her, you will not go wrong. If she upholds you, you will not stumble. If she protects you, you will not be afraid. If she leads you, you will reach the goal."

Today, take a few moments to say a special prayer to your heavenly Mother. Ask her to obtain for you the graces you need to persevere through your trials. Ask her especially to lead you through the darkness to her Son, Jesus Christ, and let her gentle guidance console you.

When Jesus saw his mother and the disciple whom he loved standing beside her, he said to his mother, "Woman, here is your son."

~ John 19:26

Day 249:
The Way

It seems that anything in life that is worth having involves suffering of some sort—childbirth, growing up, relationships, financial security, good health, etc. It all involves some level of work, self-denial, and pain. But in the end, the fruit of the labor makes the suffering worthwhile.

When going through a divorce, it can be a bit puzzling to wonder what can be good about losing a marriage and intact family. What in the world can be good about all the emotional scars left on parents and children alike?

God uses every bad situation for the good of those who love Him. These "goods" often come in the form of virtues. Divorce teaches you how to suffer with patience, and how to persevere when the odds are stacked against you. It reveals your real inner strength. It teaches you the importance of forgiveness. And in the end, you walk away with the gift of becoming a new person; one that can lead someone else through the darkness of divorce when needed.

Jesus said to him, "I am the way, and the truth, and the life.
No one comes to the Father except through me.

~ John 14:6

Day 250:
When Life Lacks A Personal Touch

One of the toughest things to deal with in the wake of divorce is the lack of human touch. Especially for those who live alone, it can be days, weeks and sometimes longer between any type of personal, physical contact with someone such as a hug or simply a handshake.

A friend of mine once told me his favorite part of Sunday mass was when the congregation prayed the "Our Father" together and held hands. He said that made him still feel connected to a family. That was his only physical contact with another human being until the following Sunday.

If you are suffering from this lack of physical contact, it can be very hard to deal with. But try to remember that life won't always be this way. A change will come, and when it does, Christ will bless you with exactly what you need.

In the meantime, contemplate Him on the cross, bleeding and dying, with no one to heal His wounds. Unite your suffering with His and let Him draw you into His incredible work of salvation.

For it is a credit to you if, being aware of God,
you endure pain while suffering unjustly.

~ 1 Peter 2:19

Day 251:
The Gifts God Waits To Give You

We know, of course, that when we get to heaven, we will live with God in complete happiness, unending joy, and perfect bliss. But have you realized that God doesn't want you to wait until you get to heaven to experience the wonderful things He wants to give you?

God wants to live with us here on earth, now, today! How, you might think, can this be possible, especially when you are enduring such pain and suffering? The key is to stop worrying and trust God with your situation. Give Him all your burdens and the gift of your complete trust and then let Him work. Your first gift will be the gift of peace and there will be much more to follow—yes, even in the midst of your pain. There is so much that God has waiting to give you.

But don't stop there. Realize that God also wants to live in the world through you! He needs you to pass on to others the lessons you are learning, the peace you experience when you trust Him, and the hope that all is not lost. It is in this way that you, and those around you, can experience the joy of being close to Christ. The example you give as you go through your suffering will be a beacon of light to all those who witness you.

In the same way, let your light shine before others, so that they may see your good works and give glory to your Father in heaven.

~ Matthew 5:16

Day 252:
The Best Way To Recharge Your Battery

When Jesus was in His public ministry, He had little time to Himself. The people He served were very needy, much like children. Crowds followed Him from one end of the sea to the other, and it was difficult for Him to have any time alone, even with His apostles. But Jesus found His rest, consolation and strength in communicating with His Father in prayer. He would find a hiding place and pray, returning refreshed and ready to face whatever the day brought.

If you are feeling overwhelmed, try some creative ways to fit prayer into your busy schedule. Try getting up earlier each morning to spend some quiet prayer time with God, or take some time in the evening when the kids are asleep. Even pausing at noon for a few brief moments of prayer is a good thing and will help you find your rest and refreshment in God.

I am the vine, you are the branches. Those who abide in me and I in them bear much fruit, because apart from me you can do nothing.

~ John 15:5

Day 253:
Don't Look Back

◇

As someone who has been through a divorce, the experience will always be a part of you. Time and God's grace will heal the wounds, make forgiveness possible, and allow the painful memories to fade away. You will always be affected by what happened to you, but it doesn't define who you are.

Sometimes the most difficult part of rebuilding your life after the loss of your marriage is realizing this terribly important fact. You were created to be an important person in this world with a mission to fulfill given to you by God that no one else can fulfill. Despite your divorce, and all the other hurts in your life, you still have things you've got to do and a purpose to fulfill. So don't spend too much time dwelling on what's happened.

You always need to learn from the past and incorporate those lessons into everyday life. But as you stand up, dust yourself off, and look to the future, know that God has many good things waiting for you. You are doing exactly what He wants you to do.

No one who puts a hand to the plow and looks back
is fit for the kingdom of God.

~ Luke 9:62

Day 254:
Victim or Victor?

Gratitude is crucial to the healing process. Without it, you will remain stuck in the mire of resentment and self-pity, and these are major stumbling blocks to finding gratitude. Don't allow the victim mentality to steal your chances for finding peace.

When you are tempted to blame your trials and sufferings on someone else, look to the true Victim, Jesus Christ. He hung on the cross out of love for us and said "Father, forgive them..." If you make the effort to practice Jesus' example, you will be victorious in overcoming your suffering and experience new life in Christ.

But if you do not forgive others,
neither will your Father forgive your trespasses.

~ Matthew 6:15

Day 255:
Love The Sinner, Hate The Sin

What was the cause of your divorce?

Abuse? Infidelity? Indifference?

Now you find yourself here in the aftermath trying to rebuild. You desire peace, you desire happiness, and you desire healing. You are not alone—all of us want this. A huge step in obtaining these things is forgiving those who have hurt you.

We all know forgiveness is a struggle. No one talks that much about the practical applications of forgiveness. The concept easily becomes vague and something out of reach.

One good way to begin the process of forgiveness is to look at the person who has hurt you and remember that God loves that person, too, just as much as He loves you. God wants you both to be in heaven with Him for eternity and if that person is good enough for God, he or she should be good enough for you.

Viewing your offender in this light is something positive you can do to begin separating the sinner from the sin. Once you are able to do this, forgiveness becomes less challenging and more natural.

Come now, let us argue it out, / says the Lord: / though your sins are like scarlet, / they shall be like snow; / though they are red like crimson, / they shall become like wool.

~ Isaiah 1:18

266

Day 256:
The Lost And Searching Sheep

Do you feel unwelcome at church since your divorce or separation? Do you believe you don't have a place anymore at your parish or in the Church at all?

Do not be afraid! No matter what has happened, no matter what anyone has told you about being divorced and Catholic, you are still an important part of the Church, the mystical Body of Christ.

In the Gospel of Matthew, we read about the Shepherd who leaves His flock to find the lost sheep. You may be the spouse who was abandoned, or you may be the spouse who left. No matter what the circumstance, YOU are the one that Christ is seeking. You are the sheep He loves so much that He will do anything to keep you close to Him. We are all wounded by sin, whether it is our own sin or the sin of another. Jesus is looking for you. He wants to bring you home and heal you.

In this Gospel story, we see that none of the sheep received as much attention as the one who had strayed. God's mercy is overwhelming. Take some time today to contemplate how His mercy envelops your life.

And if he finds it, truly I tell you, he rejoices over it more than over the ninety-nine that never went astray. So it is not the will of your Father in heaven that one of these little ones should be lost.

~ Matthew 18:13-14

Day 257:
Through Him, With Him, In Him

What makes life worth living? Many people would say happiness and love. But what happens when those two things are missing from your life? Does that mean that life has no meaning? No! But when you go through a divorce, it can often feel that way. Happiness and love suddenly seem out of reach, and it's natural to feel an emptiness.

But to say that a life with suffering and challenges is a life without meaning is false. We all know that with change comes suffering, and with suffering comes a new strength and a new hope. In fact, if you think about it, pretty much all the good things in your life have been a result of some sort of suffering or self-denial.

As Christians, suffering takes on a whole new meaning that non-believers don't have, namely, hope in Christ and eternity with Him. Therefore, we can look at our suffering in this way, "Through Him, with Him, and in Him."

Through Him: Offer your trials to the Father through His perfect Son, Jesus.

With Him: View your difficulties as a chance to walk the road to Calvary with Christ.

In Him: Endure your struggles in imitation of Jesus, with great love.

For from him and through him and to him are all things.
To him be the glory forever. Amen.

~ Romans 11:36

Day 258:
In Imitation Of Mary

During certain months and feast days, the Catholic Church focuses her attention on Our Blessed Mother. You can receive special blessings and graces by paying special attention to your heavenly Mother through rosaries, novenas, masses, etc.

As someone who is going through a divorce or perhaps in the rebuilding phase, you can obtain these special blessings and graces by imitating Mary in your own suffering. We know that Mary's life was filled with hardship and many sorrows, and she certainly can relate to what you are enduring.

The two most admirable virtues Mary possessed were her humility and her obedience. Her humble "yes" to God's will meant that all people would be saved, despite everything she would suffer. In your pain, is it possible that you can also say "yes" to God and endure your suffering as Mary did—with patience and love?

Although you may not understand why God allowed your divorce to happen, your patient endurance of this trial can bring great graces and conversions, especially if you offer it all up for someone else's salvation. Your "yes" in response to God's plan, even in the midst of suffering, becomes a treasure you store up in heaven.

Then Mary said, "Here am I, the servant of the Lord; let it be with me according to your word." Then the angel departed from her.

~ Luke 1:38

Day 259:
From Suffering, Good Things Come

We know that God brings good things out of suffering if we allow Him to enter our lives. The fact that God has allowed this to happen to you is because He respects the gift of free will that He gave you. But it doesn't mean that He doesn't love you, or that He wants you to suffer needlessly. It is precisely when bad things happen that Christ is ready to create new, good things for you. He is simply waiting for your permission to take the situation and bring good out of it.

Take your broken heart to the foot of the cross and say to Christ, "Why, Lord? Help me!" He will come down from the cross, put His arms around you and say, "I know you are suffering. I love you. And now I want to show you the way through your suffering into happiness."

And even the hairs of your head are all counted.

~ Matthew 10:30

Day 260:
A Paradigm Shift

There's a popular cliché that goes, "Let your attitude determine your altitude." Sometimes these sayings can seem trite and rather insulting, especially when we are going through hardship. If it's so difficult to begin with, how can someone else make it sound so easy to overcome? When you encounter others who have never been divorced, and they dispense advice they think is helpful, you can often feel exasperated.

One of the great truths of life is that there will be suffering and, at some point or another, everyone encounters difficulty. Hearing things like "just get over it!" or "just accept that this is your life now, and it will be easier to start moving forward" are easy to comprehend in thought, yet they are difficult to accept in your heart.

Acceptance is the first and necessary step in rebuilding your life and one that should not be taken lightly. It truly is a process. But there are things that can make the work of acceptance a little easier. First, offer your suffering for others who need your prayers. Second, understand that God has chosen you to participate in His work of salvation through your offering of pain. And third, God is lovingly tending to your soul as you work through all these things. Understanding all these things can indeed make your burden easier to bear; knowing you are a vine that will bear much good fruit.

The man went away and told the Jews
that it was Jesus who had made him well.

~ John 5:15

Day 261:
How To Be A Better Person
Because Of Your Divorce

Experiencing the pain that comes from going through a separation and divorce can make it difficult, even impossible, to be grateful for anything. Still, it's important to recognize that finding reasons to be grateful is important because it enables you to move forward to a new phase in life. Gratitude enables you to look back at what happened and say, I have survived that pain, and I am better for it.

I have said this to you, so that in me you may have peace. In the world you face persecution. But take courage; I have conquered the world!

~ John 16:33

Day 262:
God Is Waiting To Give You Good Things

It is hard work going through the process of rebuilding your life after divorce, constantly wondering what the future holds. Few people take the time to sift through the debris of their failed marriage to discover the truths, learn the hard lessons, and resolve to make the future better than the past. But make no mistake, taking time to do this results in becoming a better version of yourself. Through your efforts, you will be better equipped to receive the good things God has in store for you.

So take some time to reflect on your failed marriage, trying to learn the truths and discover the hard lessons. Ask the Holy Spirit to enlighten and guide you so you can become the best version of yourself.

So if anyone is in Christ, there is a new creation: everything old has passed away; see, everything has become new!

~ 2 Corinthians 5:17

Day 263:
Bearing The Judgments of Others

Ignoring the judgments of others who do not know your circumstances can be one of the most difficult aspects of the divorce experience. That shameful, pernicious label of divorce can make you feel as if you are wearing a conspicuous scarlet "D" on your chest. You feel like people you meet in passing can tell just by looking at you that you are divorced. It is true, people tend to judge what they do not know. The key to overcoming these judgments is to focus yourself on how God sees you. Never forget how precious you are to Him.

As I live, says the Lord, every knee shall bow to me, /
and every tongue shall give praise to God.

~ Romans 14:11

Day 264:
Let Go Of the Label "Divorced"

It is crucial to stay close to your faith and receive the sacraments frequently as you move forward in your healing process. However, you may find this difficult because of others in your parish or family who may be critical of your situation because they do not understand. I encourage you to be patient and draw closer to the sacraments as a means of comfort and support. You will find doing this will strengthen you and help prepare you even more for a new relationship. Don't hide yourself behind the label of "divorce." Give yourself permission to let go of the stigma.

So we do not lose heart. Even though our outer nature is wasting away, our inner nature is being renewed day by day.

~ 2 Corinthians 4:16

Day 265:
Help Your Children Heal

Children feel the same powerful emotions adults do, but they are incapable of expressing their feelings the same way. This means they carry raw, unaddressed pain with them every day of their young lives into adulthood, where it can finally be expressed but by then, it has done incredible damage.

Help your children have happier futures by giving them opportunities to talk about the hurt and offer age-appropriate answers when questions arise. Children who know they can count on parents who love them can overcome many obstacles in life.

Keep alert, stand firm in your faith, be courageous, be strong.

~ 1 Corinthians 16:13

Day 266:
The Church Is Not A Hotel For Saints

We all fail. We all make mistakes. That is part of the human condition. What should you do if you know that you have made choices that are spiritually harmful to yourself and others and want to make things right with God? Go to confession.

Fortunately God does not leave us to our own devices when we sin. The sacrament of reconciliation is there for anyone who wants to make a fresh start. Why not have that burden of guilt lifted so you can live a happy life? Remember the Church is not a hotel for saints, as some have said, it is a hospital for sinners.

Let us approach with a true heart in full assurance of faith, with our hearts sprinkled clean from an evil conscience and our bodies washed with pure water.

~ Hebrews 10:22

Day 267:
Divorce Does Not Define Who You Are

<hr />

"Divorce" does not and will never encapsulate who you are as a person. You are a living, breathing human being with a mind and a body; a heart and a soul. You are loved by a God who created you and gave you a distinct purpose in life. Divorce does not invalidate your role as an important family member, friend or member of society. It does not erase all the good qualities you possess or all the good things you've done. It certainly does not negate all the incredible potential you have for living the rest of your life.

You are not the sum of one word, nor are you validated by a social status. Divorce is something that happened to you. It is not who you are.

<hr />

Let endurance have its full effect,
so that you may be mature and complete, lacking in nothing.

~ James 1:4

Day 268:
Being Happy Boils Down To This One Thing

Are you feeling emotionally stuck as you work to rebuild your life after divorce? If so, I extend an invitation to you to remember that being happy is a conscious decision. You can move forward by choosing to say goodbye to the past and hello to the future. Let today be your clean slate; your new beginning.

Take this opportunity to reflect upon the changes you would like to see happen in your life, and make your own list of things you can do to make those changes happen. What will your list be like? Start the annulment process? Forgive your ex-spouse? Choose to be happy instead of depressed? Only you know. But one thing is certain—if you make the decision to change the things you can control and choose to be happy, you will discover a new life.

May the God of hope fill you with all joy and peace in believing, so that you may abound in hope by the power of the Holy Spirit.

~ Romans 15:13

Day 269:
When You Feel Invisible To Others

If you're divorced, you may also feel like you're invisible, like you don't count or no one would notice if you weren't around. But always remember, God sees you.

Every ounce of extra effort you give, every prayer you utter, every time you push yourself to do better, and every time you feel like giving up—He sees and He knows it all.

It's during the painful times that God wants to help you most. That's one great lesson of enduring loneliness—that through the absence of those you love in your life, Christ comes more into focus. What a great opportunity to come closer to Him and to realize your self worth rests in His eyes, not in the opinions of others.

Be strong and bold; have no fear or dread of them, because it is the Lord your God who goes with you; he will not fail you or forsake you.

~ Deuteronomy 31:6

Day 270:
Don't Let Your Ex-Spouse Get To You

Most men and women who go through a divorce harbor a great deal of resentment toward their ex-spouse for some amount of time, often because of infidelity and abandonment. This is normal. If you are struggling with this, try to remember—you cannot control your ex-spouse's words, thoughts or actions. If you can accept that reality, you begin the critical process of letting go. Just keep in mind that the only person you can control is yourself.

Therefore, my beloved, be steadfast, immovable,
always excelling in the work of the Lord,
because you know that in the Lord your labor is not in vain.

~ 1 Corinthians 15:58

Day 271:
Jesus' Example Is All You Need

In every situation we encounter in life, it is good to remember that while Jesus was on earth, He encountered the same struggles and challenges we do. Jesus did not divorce, but He certainly experienced the betrayal and abandonment of the ones He loved. He experienced the sorrow of a broken heart.

It is always appropriate to look at His earthly life and see what we can glean from His example so we can use it as guidance and inspiration as we forge ahead. "Father, forgive them" is the supreme example Christ set for dealing with those who have hurt us. If you find it difficult to forgive, ask God for the grace to do it and ask Him to be beside you every step of the way.

For if you forgive others their trespasses, your heavenly Father will also forgive you; but if you do not forgive others, neither will your Father forgive your trespasses.

~ Matthew 6:14-15

Day 272:
Are You Ready To Love, Again?

Many people who go through a divorce want to find a new relationship they can be happy in again. They believe they still have many good things to bring to a relationship and are hopeful of finding the right person. If you are one of those people, it's important to make sure you're really ready before you jump back into a new relationship. Are you prepared?

When speaking in terms of getting ready to love again, note that Christ went through a very similar process. He lived thirty-three years, and only three of those years were spent in public ministry. The rest of the time He spent preparing for the time in which He would show everyone how to love. Christ is always our best example. Make sure you are not only prepared but completely free to enter into a new relationship, and then you will succeed.

God is love, and those who abide in love abide in God,
and God abides in them.

~ 1 John 4:16

Day 273:
Don't Use Dating As A Band-Aid For Your Broken Heart

Trying to form a romantic attachment to someone new before your heart is strong and ready for that kind of commitment will only compound your woundedness. That is why so many people go from relationship to relationship without ever finding the peace and fulfillment they seek.

Don't make the mistake of entering into a relationship before your heart is prepared to give and receive love again and run the risk of making some very painful mistakes. Consider going through the annulment process. There is so much to gain from going through with it if you approach it with a heart that is open to seeking God's will. You will find healing, and it's a great way to prepare yourself for a new love.

Beloved, let us love one another, because love is from God;
everyone who loves is born of God and knows God.

~ 1 John 4:7

Day 274:
Should You Go Through
The Annulment Process?

If you are wrestling with the decision to go through the annulment process, I encourage you to talk to your pastor or spiritual director about it. Give yourself the gift of time to ensure you have done the hard work you need to do to fully heal from your divorce.

The annulment process will help you take a bold and honest look at yourself, will help you to learn from your mistakes, will provide an opportunity for spiritual growth, and will enable you to regain complete confidence in the direction you take in life.

Whether or not you decide to get married again, an incredible experience awaits you as you discover the most reliable source of healing found in God and the Church; the only place we can experience the perfect, healing love of Jesus.

You desire truth in the inward being;
therefore teach me wisdom in my secret heart.

~ Psalm 51:6

Day 275:
Feeling Kicked Down Because Of Divorce?

Keep your eyes on the goal and trust that God will take care of you. The best way to handle the pain of divorce is by facing it, not running from it or putting a lid on it. Facing this kind of suffering takes a great deal of courage. It requires accepting the loss with humility, forgiving those who have hurt you, and admitting the truth about mistakes that were made on the part of both spouses. Take the steps you need to detach from what is holding you back. When the temptation to do the things that will divert you from your goal comes up, say a quick prayer for strength, (God, help me!), and remind yourself why you set this goal.

I can do all things through him who strengthens me.

~ Philippians 4:13

Day 276:
Heart On Fire

If you have ever seen a picture of the Sacred Heart of Jesus, you will see Him pointing to His heart from which flames are burning, representing His love for us. But there are also thorns surrounding His heart. Those thorns represent all the souls who are indifferent to His love. Souls who know Jesus but forget about Him, ignore Him, or don't have time for Him. This is what causes Him the most pain and why He reaches out to us at every moment of our lives.

As you struggle with carrying your cross, don't allow it to distance you from God; don't do it alone. Unite your cross to Christ and let Him carry it for you. Let Him show you His love and the many blessings He has waiting for you.

But God proves his love for us in that while we still were sinners Christ died for us.

~ Romans 5:8

Day 277:
Find Your Refreshment In God

When Jesus was in His public ministry, the crowds followed Him from place to place; people begged him to cure their sick and to work miracles. The Pharisees harassed Him everywhere He went, and even the apostles were rather needy individuals. But Jesus found rest, consolation and strength in spending time with His Father in prayer. This is when He found refreshment.

As you go through this process of rebuilding your life after divorce, it may feel a little overwhelming to have so much to work on. You may have many pressing responsibilities, concerns about your future, or worries about your children's welfare. It's important, then, to stop and take time to pray as Jesus did. Find your rest and refreshment in God.

My soul melts away for sorrow; /
strengthen me according to your word.

~ Psalm 119:28

Day 278:
Time and Eternity

Let's always keep two words at the forefront of our day-to-day existence: time and eternity. Time, because each moment of the day you spend looking backward, you waste. You will never get those moments back. You need to look forward because God still has many good things He wants to show you; things He wants you to experience that will make you happy. And eternity, because everything we do here on earth, counts in eternity. Let's make everything count.

Strength and dignity are her clothing, /
and she laughs at the time to come.

~ Proverbs 31:25

Day 279:
The Greatest Prayer Chain

When we are going through the trials and tribulations of life, we ask others to pray for us. We rely on their petitions to God on our behalf. But did you also know that as you work and struggle to move past your divorce, all of heaven is waiting for you to ask them for help as well?

The communion of saints, namely the blessed souls who have gone before us to heaven, can pray for you and petition God on your behalf. All that is necessary is to ask them for their help. St. Teresa of Avila, St. Pope John Paul II, St. Padre Pio—there are countless saints waiting to offer you their assistance. When you become overwhelmed, pray and seek help from the saints; they are one of the greatest spiritual resources you have.

First of all, then, I urge that supplications, prayers, intercessions, and thanksgivings be made for everyone.

~ 1 Timothy 2:1

Day 280:
When Trusting God Is Difficult

The Scriptures describe Mary as kind, patient, humble, thoughtful and generous. But probably her most astute display of virtue was her unwavering trust in God and obedience to His will, despite her suffering. Everything she did was in accordance with His Divine plan, even when she had good reason to fear the future or be skeptical.

Divorce makes it easy to believe you cannot trust anymore, as if God has somehow left you to fend for yourself. If you are feeling this way, I encourage you to contemplate Mary's example. Since the world is imperfect, place your trust and hope in the only thing that is perfect, her Son. Ask your mother in heaven to obtain for you the graces she knows you need. Ask her to help you live today, instead of waiting to live when everything becomes just right.

In all your ways acknowledge him, /
and he will make straight your paths.

~ Proverbs 3:6

Day 281:
Use God's Gifts To Keep You Motivated

The emotional duress that comes with experiencing divorce is often like a tidal wave that hits and destroys you. It becomes hard to get out of the bed in the morning, hard to take care of responsibilities, and hard to relate to the people we encounter each day. But it's so important to keep trying and keep picking yourself up off the floor. If you lived your life simply at the whim of your feelings, basing all your actions on how you felt at the time, you would be living like an animal. An animal has no ability to reason and has no free will.

But God gave human beings these gifts. When you use your free will to motivate yourself to do something good, especially during times of adversity, there is an ennobling effect that results in your personal growth and maturity. So many times we see people who have suffered greatly during their lives, and as a result, have great character, integrity and strength. It is in taking steps like these, praying even when you don't feel like it, that those great virtues come into place.

For God did not give us a spirit of cowardice, but rather a spirit of power and of love and of self-discipline.

~ 2 Timothy 1:7

Day 282:
A Prayer To The Holy Spirit
In Times Of Distress

Come, Holy Spirit!
Replace the tension within us with a holy relaxation.
Replace the turbulence within us with a sacred calm.
Replace the anxiety within us with a quiet confidence.
Replace the fear within us with a strong faith.
Replace the bitterness within us with the sweetness of grace.
Replace the darkness within us with a gentle light.
Replace the coldness within us with a loving warmth.
Replace the night within us with your light.
Straighten our crookedness, fill our emptiness.
Dull the edge of our pride, sharpen the edge of our humility,
Light the fires of our love, quench the flames of our lust.
Let us see ourselves as you see us
that we may see you as you have promised
and be fortunate according to your word:

"Blessed are the pure in heart, for they will see God."

~ Matthew 5:8

Day 283:
Begin With Love, Continue With Love, End With Love

St. Teresa of Calcutta is one of the greatest examples of how to live life while carrying a heavy cross. In the 2007 book, *Mother Teresa: Come Be My Light*, which published her private letters, it was revealed that she suffered the "dark night of the soul" where God seemed non-existent. Yet, no one ever would have suspected this while she was alive. St. Teresa of Calcutta seemed full of love, life, and faith. Her actions revealed a sacrificial love that mirrored Christ's love for us. She may have had doubts, yet she never wavered because her faith was great. She trusted that He was there, even if she couldn't feel His presence.

The heartache and destruction that come with divorce can easily lead to cynicism, deep resentment, and doubt. The world will exacerbate that in any way it can. If you are struggling with these things, I encourage you to get to know Saint Teresa of Calcutta and pray for her intercession. Ask her to show you how to go through your own dark night without losing your trust in God.

Beloved, let us love one another, because love is from God; everyone who loves is born of God and knows God.

~ 1 John 4:7

Day 284:
A Childlike Faith

*We have been trained in the habit of looking at our dark side, our
ugliness, and not at the purifying Sun, Light of Light,
which He is, who changes the dust that we are into pure gold.
We think about examining ourselves, yet we do not think before the
examination, during the examination, and after the examination,
to plunge ourselves, with all our miseries, into the consuming and
transforming furnace of His Heart, which is open to us
through a single humble act of confidence.*

~ I Believe In Love, Fr. Jean C. J. d'Elbée

I encourage you to take time and reflect upon God's immense, merciful and passionate love for you and approach His heart with the humble confidence of a child.

*God is love, and those who abide in love abide in God,
and God abides in them.*

~ 1 John 4:16

Day 285:
When You Want To Scream,
Try This Instead

Maybe you had a diary as a kid and figured that journaling was something you grew out of in the eighth grade, but rebuilding your life after divorce presents a great time to rethink that. Journaling is a great way to get the thoughts and anxieties out of your head and onto paper. It is the perfect place to say exactly what you are thinking and make yourself feel better without hurting anyone. You can be perfectly honest.

Whenever you feel your emotions building and getting out of control, or when you just want to say what you can't say to your ex-spouse, start writing. Say everything you want to say, exactly as you want to say it. No holds barred. You can always throw it away or burn it later on. The main thing is that you've gotten it out. Your journal can be the one safe channel where you can let it all hang out. Try it, it works.

Do not fear, for I am with you, / do not be afraid, for I am your God; /
I will strengthen you, I will help you, /
I will uphold you with my victorious right hand.

~ Isaiah 41:10

Day 286:
Healing From Divorce Requires One Thing

God does not want your life to be hell on earth because of your divorce. He wants to show you how to find peace and joy amid all the trials of life. He wants to show you how His love transforms any and all situations, if you grant Him access to your heart. If you don't open your heart to the possibility of forgiveness, you are blocking His ability to bring good things out of your terrible circumstances.

Do you feel like if you forgive, you are losing? Do you feel as if your offender is "off the hook" or somehow bears no responsibility for their offense? I assure you, nothing could be further from the truth. A lack of forgiveness has a direct, negative impact on your physical, emotional and spiritual well-being.

Taking that unbelievably difficult first step in forgiveness can be very hard. If you are battling the idea of forgiving your ex-spouse, I invite you to lay down your arms and remember that if you want to heal from your divorce, forgiveness will be the path to your peace.

Peace I leave with you; my peace I give to you.
I do not give to you as the world gives.
Do not let your hearts be troubled, and do not let them be afraid.

~ John 14:27

Day 287:
Thinking About Dating? Take It Slow

Not all people rush into new relationships after their divorces, but many do and it's easy to see why. Divorce is a very lonely experience that has a devastating effect on your attitude and self-worth. Dating someone who thinks you're attractive, smart, and interesting has an intoxicating effect. You can become addicted to that feeling instantaneously. Unfortunately, this leads to mistaking the feeling for real love and can result in a rush to get married, and eventually a second divorce.

The best way to approach dating again after you've received a decree of nullity is to take it slow. Spend time as friends first so your relationship can grow naturally without the hot-and-heavy pressure to be sexually intimate. Give your new relationship the opportunity to put what you've learned from your mistakes into practice.

I have said this to you, so that in me you may have peace. In the world you face persecution. But take courage; I have conquered the world!

~ John 16:33

Day 288:
Don't Make This Mistake

Not everyone who gets divorced finds Sundays lonely, but a great many divorced Catholics do. It can be hard to go to Mass by yourself and muster up an attitude of worship when all those happy families are a reminder of what you've lost. If you struggle with attending mass, I encourage you, do not make the one mistake that so many others make—not going to mass.

It's tempting to stop going to Mass because you find it hard to face the rest of the parish, but going to mass is important. You need the spiritual inoculation, you need the Eucharist, and you need the connection to your parish family. Take the opportunity to sort out your feelings while you are in God's presence. You don't have to be a super-Catholic, just give as much effort as you can and let God's grace do the rest.

God is our refuge and strength, / a very present help in trouble.

~ Psalm 46:1

Day 289:
Riding The Emotional Roller Coaster

Did you know that a 2002 Chevy Corvette can go from 0 to 60 mph in 1.97 seconds? What a ride! What also happens at an amazing speed is how quickly emotions can take hold and control you. Happiness, anger, jealousy, and frustration—all of them can grip you in a split second.

Controlling your emotions is a tough battle after divorce because of their illogical frequency. They show up, unannounced, like a group of rowdy kids wreaking havoc on an otherwise calm situation. The challenge is to gain control of those emotions. How do you find the balance between knowing when to act on your righteous anger and when to just let it pass?

The balance lies in being merciful with others in the same way Jesus is merciful with us. Your offender may deserve your wrath, but showing mercy will slow your anger and help you react calmly.

In my distress I cry to the Lord, / that he may answer me.

~ Psalm 120:1

Day 290:
The Transforming Effects Of Suffering

Not everyone who suffers through adversity learns from it. Some people allow themselves to become bitter and resentful. Are you able to see that God wants to transform you through your circumstances? He doesn't want you to just get along or make lemonade out of lemons, He wants to transform you into a new person. He's allowed your circumstances so He can use them to change you.

I've often heard the heavier the cross, the greater the joy you will experience when it is lifted. If you trust in God, follow Him to the best of your ability and bear your crosses with patience, you will experience that joyful transformation. Life will still throw you some fast hardballs. The process of trust and patience will become a constant theme, but in the end, that's where the transformation lies. Let your circumstances change you into a stronger, more virtuous person.

It is good for me that I was humbled, / so that I might learn your statutes.

~ Psalm 119:71

Day 291:
Learning The Importance Of Letting Go

It can be difficult to accept the finality of divorce, to let go of your ex-spouse, and to work on forgiveness. In my personal experience, much of the pain I suffered through in the first month after my ex-spouse left was because I was in win-back mode. I refused to accept the premise of divorce, and I did everything I could to win him back. I even asked him to consider reconciliation. It took me a long time to accept the fact that I couldn't make him love me. I had to let him go and accept that he was free to make his own choices.

Trying to save your marriage is a good thing, but if there comes a time when the door to reconciliation is closed, locked, and bolted, it's time to begin the process of detachment. Through detachment, you will be able to say that is his choice, or that is her choice.

This can be a painful proposition, but sometimes what you don't see is the pain you cause yourself by clinging to something that's gone. You have to let go. In letting go, you will find peace. That peace will make the idea of forgiveness become palatable.

---

*In all your ways acknowledge him, /
and he will make straight your paths.*

~ Proverbs 3:6

Day 292:
God Heals Your Heart
Even When You Can't Feel It

Healing is a gradual process, but it's not just time that has an effect on this process. Sometimes God is healing your heart, but you just don't realize it. It's a lot like getting a suntan. You go to the beach, swim in the water, play a little frisbee, and lay out for a while without noticing a thing, but when you go back inside, you've got a tan.

It's the same with healing. Oftentimes, it's in the looking back that you see how far you've really come and all that God has been doing for you. Sometimes you just have to get out there and move forward so you can look back and recognize exactly how much you've progressed.

I encourage you to approach this conversation of healing with God by asking, "What do you want me to learn, Lord? What are you trying to show me?" If you are being faithful to Him, and you keep this spirit of child-like trust, He will bless you abundantly.

Then your light shall break forth like the dawn, / and your healing shall spring up quickly; / your vindicator shall go before you, / the glory of the Lord shall be your rear guard.

~ Isaiah 58:8

Day 293:
The Surprising Thing
About Sustaining A Loss

There was a couple who was having their dream home built. They invested a lot of money into buying the land, having the floor plans drafted, and selecting all the details. There were coffered ceilings, granite in the kitchen, and so on. But halfway through the process, they fell upon difficult financial times and lost the house, including all the money they had put into it. It was a devastating blow.

Sometime later, the wife recognized the whole thing was for the best. She was now able to see how micro-focused she had become on money, materialism and the approval of others. She did not see wealth as something bad, but she saw how easily she had become consumed with this house. She saw how easily her focus had drifted away from her relationship with God.

Sometimes when you suffer the loss of someone or something you love, it is possible that person or thing was an obstacle to your relationship with God. Take some time to reflect on the positive things that have happened because of your divorce. Is it possible that you have come closer to God since your divorce?

But those who wait for the Lord shall renew their strength, /
they shall mount up with wings like eagles, /
they shall run and not be weary, / they shall walk and not faint.

~ Isaiah 40:31

Day 294:
What Does It Really Mean To Be Healed?

A common question among people trying to rebuild their lives after divorce is what does it really mean to be healed? Does it mean you will never feel the terrible pain anymore?

Pain is not a one-dimensional phenomenon. There are multiple layers that contribute to your overall suffering. For example, you may have had traumatic events during your marriage that are associated with this pain, such as the loss of a child or an irreparable breach between family members. If you felt unloved by your own parents or even if you just have unresolved guilt over things you've done in the past, the feeling of failure that comes with divorce drags these other emotions out into the open.

It is important to take the time you need to properly heal. You need to be able to turn over every stone, analyze every detail, and make peace with it all to feel comfortable enough to detach from it and move forward. Living a self-indulgent lifestyle, which is the worldly answer to grief, is never satisfactory. It will never be enough. It takes grace to heal and grace to overcome. Only God can dispense the graces we need to truly heal.

Those who wait for the Lord shall renew their strength, / they shall mount up with wings like eagles, / they shall run and not be weary, / they shall walk and not faint.

~ Isaiah 40:31

Day 295:
Don't Fall Into This Trap

Maybe you're having a difficult time because you can't imagine being happy again. Maybe your divorce has convinced you that this pain and loneliness is your new normal, and you just can't imagine what it would be like to be truly happy again. If that's how you feel, don't fall for it.

God didn't put you on this earth to be unhappy. He wants you to be happy. He wants you to trust Him with your future because He can bring good things out of the most deplorable situations and the most reprehensible circumstances. It might seem impossible to bring good things out of your mess. But one thing is for sure, God is going to blow you away with what He can do. Your best imagining of what is to come is nothing compared to what God can do with your life.

We know that all things work together for good for those who love God, who are called according to his purpose.

~ Romans 8:28

Day 296:
Stay Healthy By Practicing Forgiveness

Some years ago, a friend of mine started attending a support group to find healing from her divorce. She was struck by a particular woman who was extremely angry that her husband had left her. Every week, she would go and listen to this woman be angry. She looked at the woman's face, wrinkled with anger, and thought, I don't want to look like that. My friend knew she needed to figure out how to let go and forgive because she recognized she would never grow or improve in any way unless she did.

There are many reasons why a person gets angry; many of them are justifiable. But the kind of anger that causes wrinkles and health problems is prolonged anger, which is a result of harboring resentment toward particular people or people in general. This lack of forgiveness can wreak havoc in your life and the lives of others.

Divorce is a terrible scourge to bear, but there are far too many people in this world who refuse to forgive those who have hurt them. They end up suffering the consequences, one of which is poor health and premature aging. Why be one of them? Make the choice to forgive today and start living your life in freedom and happiness.

Truly I tell you, unless you change and become like children, you will never enter the kingdom of heaven.

~ Matthew 18:3

Day 297:
Don't Forget To Forgive Yourself

In this process of recovering from a divorce, much is said about finding a way to forgive those who have hurt you, and this is important and necessary. But sometimes you might be so challenged by the idea of offering forgiveness, you may not recognize the need to forgive yourself. If you haven't forgiven yourself, you won't be able to move forward. You will remain stuck.

It takes two people to create a marriage, and it takes two people to create a divorce. No matter what role you played in it, have you considered you might be holding yourself accountable for something and that is holding you back? If so, go to confession and ask for God's forgiveness so you can keep moving forward. That's something God wants everyone to do, in every situation—accept the failure, ask for forgiveness, and move forward.

Our Father in heaven, hallowed be your name. Your kingdom come. Your will be done, on earth as it is in heaven. Give us this day our daily bread. And forgive us our debts, as we also have forgiven our debtors. And do not bring us to the time of trial, but rescue us from the evil one.

~ Matthew 6:9-13

Day 298:
The Problem With Becoming Cynical

Pain caused by the betrayal of people you trust is devastating. Becoming cynical is nothing more than a knee-jerk reaction to being hurt. Cynicism is not really protection, it is just a false sense of security.

Cynicism actually circumvents the possibility of happiness, not the possibility of hurt. Does this mean you should be a doormat, letting anyone and everyone walk all over you and abuse you? No. Then can you protect yourself from future betrayal and still be able to love? Yes. The answer is found through being merciful and forgiving. Beholding those who have hurt you through merciful eyes is the key to maintaining love in its purest form; a childlike love.

"My grace is sufficient for you, for power is made perfect in weakness."
So, I will boast all the more gladly of my weaknesses, so that the power of Christ may dwell in me.

~ 2 Corinthians 12:9

Day 299:
More Thoughts On Time And Eternity

Everyone is busy with obligations, responsibilities and pressures. It's easy to lose sight of the forest because we're so focused on the trees. Make sure to remember that one of the greatest gifts you've been given is the gift of time. Make the best use of it you can, not just in fulfilling the small details but living each day well.

Every moment of our day is a gift from God, a gift of life that is not only for the here and now, but a gift we should use wisely. Always begin your day with prayer. As you take care of your day-to-day details, stop every now and then, and thank God for all His blessings. Take the time to listen to someone who needs your attention and really be present to them. Make sure the people in your life know you love them. These things will bring meaning to your moments and help you live your life well.

This is my comfort in my distress, / that your promise gives me life.

~ Psalm 119:50

Day 300:
Strength Through Suffering

Divorce happens because someone made a terrible choice and did so of his/her own free will. Free will is a gift from God that He will never take away, despite the fact our choices cause untold suffering for many. But every time a bad decision is made, it creates an opportunity for God to bring about great things, even miracles, in the lives of those who are suffering.

Suffering also strengthens us; it has a sort of tempering effect. For example, did you know that homebuilders often use wood that has been cut into short strips and glued back together to make one long plank because they are stronger that way? The same thing takes place with emotional and spiritual suffering. If you allow it to happen, suffering can change you and make you stronger and wiser because of the experience.

Don't be afraid to look for the silver lining to the storm cloud. Have faith that God will bring good things out of what has happened. It's His specialty.

---

*Cast your burden on the Lord, / and he will sustain you; /
he will never permit / the righteous to be moved.*

~ Psalm 55:22

Day 301:
Live The Everyday Details
With Great Love

God offers each of us opportunities to become saints according to our state in life. Each one of us must carry different crosses. Going through a divorce can be one of the heaviest burdens to bear. The path to sainthood is in living the small details of your life with great love.

These are the steps that all the saints have taken. Famous or not, they have endured their crosses with humility, forgiveness and patience. There are many ways each of us can live everyday details with great love. I offer you this encouragement in the hopes you will find peace and healing for yourself and firm footing on the path to heaven.

For surely I know the plans I have for you, says the Lord, plans for your welfare and not for harm, to give you a future with hope.

~ Jeremiah 29:11

Day 302:
Practicing Virtue

As you rebuild your life after divorce, it's important to look back and see if there are any personal behaviors or habits that may have contributed to your divorce that you should change or work on improving. When you try to change a habit, it is important to replace the specific action with a different one.

Once you have identified the problem areas you would like to improve, choose one of the virtues to practice as a way to counteract the negative habit. For example, if you find yourself complaining or being pessimistic, work on cultivating a sense of gratitude. If you tend to be self-centered or focused on your own needs, practice generosity. These small things can make a huge difference in your ability to be happy.

For God did not give us a spirit of cowardice, but rather a spirit of power and of love and of self-discipline.

~ 2 Timothy 1:7

Day 303:
Words Matter

When a marriage fails, communication is usually the first aspect of the relationship to break down. It gets worse as the separation and divorce ensues. Many painful words have been spoken and agonizing conversations have taken place. In the process, bad communication habits are formed: yelling, swearing, accusing, and walking away.

The great thing about rebuilding your life after divorce is that you have the opportunity to change these things. If choosing the right words when you are angry is difficult, or if you have become used to blurting out profanity as a knee-jerk reaction, try repeating a simple mantra when you are calm, like 'Lord, give me the grace to love', or 'Lord, help me to be more patient.'

Moreover, remember that your body is supposed to be a temple of the Holy Spirit. You consume the Body of Christ when you receive communion. Let your mouth, heart, and mind be a source of the goodness you receive and a testament to the God of love you follow.

Or do you not know that your body is a temple of the Holy Spirit within you, which you have from God, and that you are not your own?

~ 1 Corinthians 6:19

Day 304:
Sowing The Seeds Of Love

———◇———

Everyone needs a support system as they pursue their endeavors, and in healing from divorce and doing the hard work of building a new life, this is a very important aspect to consider. When you pursue a college degree, you are surrounded by other students pursuing an education. When building your career, you network with like-minded people to help yourself move ahead in your industry. Your goals for personal and spiritual growth are the same. It is important to have friends who support your efforts to grow and are willing to assist you, if necessary.

Make sure you surround yourself with people who support you and understand you. You will make much better progress and find less distractions to hold you back.

Other seeds fell on good soil and brought forth grain, some a hundredfold, some sixty, some thirty.

~ Matthew 13:8

Day 305:
There Is Life After Divorce

Going through a divorce forces you to accept a terrible change—your "new normal." At times, especially during the first six months or so, it's easy to succumb to the feeling that you will always feel angry, sad, depressed, or lonely.

But don't fall into that trap. There is life after divorce. You won't always feel as bad as you do in the beginning. Your divorce does not define who you are, and you must remember this as you move forward. This too shall pass, even though it seems impossible. Let this experience change you for the better. Let it make you stronger, wiser, and a better person because of the experience.

The God who girded me with strength, / and made my way safe.

~ Psalm 18:32

Day 306:
Where Is God When I Need Him Most?

Where is God when I need Him most? Have you ever felt this way? This was my overwhelming sentiment when I was going through my divorce. I felt completely abandoned by God, as if He could see me but refused to speak to me.

In time, I came to realize that the opposite was really true. It wasn't that God was absent. In fact, He was closer to me during this time than before. But the pain that resulted from the terrible choice my ex-spouse had made seemed to drown out any sense of love from God. It became an obstacle to being with God.

Remember that God's presence in your life does not depend upon whether or not you feel it. He is always there. Sometimes the distance you feel is His doing, which simply means He wants you to search for Him and draw closer to Him. Other times, there may be something in your life that has become an obstacle between you and Him. No matter what the situation is, trust that He is there, listening to you, and waiting to help you.

But you, O Lord, do not be far away! /
O my help, come quickly to my aid!

~ Psalm 22:19

Day 307:
Pope Francis' Encouragement For Rebuilding After Divorce

Pope Francis's papal exhortation, *Evangelii gaudium (The Joy of the Gospel)*, was written to assist us in our resolutions to rebuild our lives and become better people. His opening words are a refreshing approach to personal renewal:

> *I invite all Christians, everywhere, at this very moment, to a renewed personal encounter with Jesus Christ, or at least an openness to letting him encounter them; I ask all of you to do this unfailingly each day... The Lord does not disappoint those who take this risk; whenever we take a step toward Jesus, we come to realize that he is already there, waiting for us with open arms.*

Let today be your day to encounter Christ and give Him permission to begin the process of personal renewal in you.

O Lord, be gracious to us; we wait for you. / Be our arm every morning, / our salvation in the time of trouble.

~ Isaiah 33:2

Day 308:
If You're Looking For Revenge, Look To St. Joseph

Scripture and tradition both reveal to us that Joseph, the foster father of Jesus, was a fine, upstanding man. He was well-known in his community and well-respected as a carpenter and man of faith. In the Gospel of Matthew, he comes to find that his fiancee is pregnant—and not by him. He must have felt incredibly hurt and betrayed, but the Gospel tells us that despite this assumed betrayal, Joseph was "unwilling to expose her to shame." This speaks volumes about the great kindness and generosity Joseph showed in a situation that would have anyone up in arms with rage, ready to retaliate with revenge.

But revenge is never the right way to go and certainly not something that will bring you peace. You may have just reasons to want to get back at your ex-spouse for his/her betrayal, but let not your heart be troubled as the Gospel of John tells us. God's grace can overcome any hurt or any evil. All you need to do is call on our Lord and ask for the grace to imitate St. Joseph. Ask Him for the grace to learn how to temper your feelings of revenge toward your ex-spouse with prudence, patience and love. In practicing this kind of selfless love, you will see a new you emerge from the old you.

You shall not take vengeance or bear a grudge against any of your people, but you shall love your neighbor as yourself: I am the Lord.

~ Leviticus 19:18

Day 309:
Advice For Those Struggling
With Sexual Impurity

These days, it's difficult for the average person to remain chaste with all the sexual images, messages and innuendos thrown in our faces at every turn. When you try to be good but end up struggling with sexual sins, it can be discouraging because, although your intentions are good, you keep failing.

The devil likes to step in and convince you that you can't change, telling you, "You're a hypocrite. Don't even try because you're just going to fail." But truth be told, we're all hypocrites and we all struggle. The key to overcoming the devil's lie is understanding that struggling is pleasing to God because He sees you are trying. Pride is what makes you feel discouraged. Forget your pride. Do your best and when you fall, don't beat yourself up. Just get up, go to confession, ask God for the grace to be better, and try again. That's what God wants.

I appeal to you, brothers and sisters, by our Lord Jesus Christ and by the love of the Spirit, to join me in earnest prayer to God on my behalf.

~ Romans 15:30

Day 310:
How To Avoid The Pity-Party Trap

When you're feeling discouraged about your circumstances, it's easy to fall into the pity-party trap and become completely depressed. When you find this happening to you, there is a great way to avoid self-pity and start feeling good about yourself—focus on others and find little ways to love them.

St. Teresa of Calcutta talks about loving others in doing the little things, the ones that often go unnoticed. Picking up someone else's dirty dishes as you leave the table. Taking the trash out without being asked. Spending time listening to your co-worker ramble and not muttering under your breath while you do. Taking time to get to know your neighbor next door who could really use your wisdom and guidance. Little things. And they don't really go unnoticed because your Father in heaven sees them, and He's really the one that matters.

In her book, *No Greater Love*, St. Teresa of Calcutta spoke these beautiful words of wisdom, "What we need is to love without getting tired. How does a lamp burn? Through the continuous input of small drops of oil. What are these drops of oil in our lamps? They are the small things of daily life: faithfulness, small words of kindness, a thought for others."

Next time you are tempted to feel sorry for yourself, try showing someone a small gesture of love, and you will feel better.

The second is this, 'You shall love your neighbor as yourself.'
There is no other commandment greater than these.

~ Mark 12:31

Day 311:
Therese of Lisieux's "Little Way"
Can Help You

One of the most difficult emotions to deal with during divorce is the feeling of being alone. It's not uncommon to feel as if your divorce has completely alienated you from others. If you feel this way, this is a perfect time to rely on your heavenly family, the Communion of Saints, for help and encouragement.

For example, St. Therese of Lisieux said she would spend her time in heaven doing good on earth, and she meant it. She has performed countless miracles since her death and has answered prayers of the faithful with showers of roses. She is a great saint for those who are divorced because she suffered the disdain and disparagement of many of the nuns who worked and prayed right beside her in her own convent. It was this poor treatment by her fellow sisters that makes her a saint who understands how your divorce might make you feel like an outcast.

St. Therese's way was one of love, humility, and simplicity. It is a great example for anyone who is trying to deal with the intense emotions of anger and feeling betrayed.

I give you a new commandment, that you love one another.
Just as I have loved you, you also should love one another.

~ John 13:34

Day 312:
Need Encouragement?
Consider St. Francis

If you're looking for some encouragement in your circumstances, a wonderful saint for anyone who is going through a divorce is the beloved St. Francis of Assisi. St. Francis was a saint who called himself a "poor little man of God." No doubt, you've heard much about his gentleness and compassion. But he's an especially good saint to turn to for wisdom and encouragement if you feel the divorce process has stripped you of possessions that were important to you.

Saint Francis was born into a wealthy family and was not a saint at an early age. As a wealthy adult, he lived the high life for a long time. When he felt called to follow Christ, he gave everything away. If you are having difficulty dealing with the loss of your home or other possessions, you might consider praying to St. Francis for help in detaching from these things and letting go of what happened.

No slave can serve two masters; for a slave will either hate the one and love the other, or be devoted to the one and despise the other. You cannot serve God and wealth.

~ Luke 16:13

Day 313:
Step Out In Faith

---◇---

I often hear people who are suffering through tragedies such as divorce ask, "Why would God allow this to happen?" But my question is, why do people always blame God for what happens to them? Don't they recognize God gave everyone a free will?

God may not force you to choose what is right, and He may not step in and block your way when you're about to do something terrible, but He will take the aftermath of your divorce and use it for your good. So don't let your divorce turn you into a victim. Don't play the blame game. Embrace your cross and let it change you.

Remember, things are not always what they seem. You are in the thick of the situation, and your emotions might be overwhelming you, but God knows your pain. He is very aware of what is happening in your life, and He is trying to help you learn and grow through these circumstances. Take a step out in faith and trust that God has a plan for your life.

We know that all things work together for good for those who love God, who are called according to his purpose.

~ Romans 8:28

Day 314:
Handling Your Emotions

Emotions aren't always fair to us. They treat us with little regard to where we are or who is with us. Oftentimes they cause us to blurt out angry statements in front of people we love. Or we begin crying in the middle of a busy intersection as we're trying to make a left-hand turn. Emotions tend to have their way with us when we're hurting.

As you progress in your healing process, there are a few things to remember that will help you when you're feeling overwhelmed.

First, give yourself permission to feel the way you're feeling. Putting a lid on your emotions will backfire, sooner or later, because they will take over. If you allow yourself to feel whatever emotion is plaguing you, it will pass sooner, and you will survive it.

Second, remember to pray. You don't have to pray a Rosary or a novena to communicate with God; just talk to Him. When it hurts, talk to Him about what you're going through in silent prayer. Ask Him the questions you want answers to as they pop into your mind. Little conversations with God, like this, will keep you tethered to Him. He will pour graces down upon you that will strengthen you.

God is our refuge and strength, / a very present help in trouble.

~ Psalm 46:1

Day 315:
Can Loving Your Enemies
Prepare You For Marriage?

If we call ourselves Christians, we must take the command to love very seriously, but this can be difficult to do after divorce. Your ex-spouse, ex-in-laws, the "other" man or woman could all be targets of the righteous indignation and wrath you feel. It may seem literally impossible to imagine treating any of them with love or charity. This reaction is very normal and justified but despite that, God still calls us to love.

In the Gospel of John, Christ told His apostles that to be His disciples, they must love one another. And in the Gospel of Matthew, He says don't even Gentiles love their brothers? These are great teachings to keep in mind when you're feeling repulsed by the thought of treating those who have hurt you with charity.

But here's another thought to ponder, especially if you would like to marry again in the future, if you find it impossible to love someone who's hurt you, even for a moment, how in the world will you be able to love someone who's hurt you for a lifetime? There are no perfect spouses, and marriage is hard work. Working on loving the ones who have hurt you now is good training for making a future marriage work.

But I say to you that listen, Love your enemies,
do good to those who hate you.

~ Luke 6:27

Day 316:
No One Is Too Lost For God

When Jesus was entrenched in His public ministry, He was constantly criticized for dining with notorious sinners, especially the scamming tax collectors, the ones who brought fear and loathing to the people of their towns. They were the people who no one wanted to deal with because they did terrible things. If you bring that example into today's world, it would compare to Jesus sitting down and having dinner with the terrorists who brought down the Twin Towers on 9/11. A shocking insight, isn't it?

He didn't just eat with them, He talked to them, and He had in-depth conversations with them. He tried to change their hearts through friendship and truth. He followed through with His teaching to love your enemy. Jesus never minced words, and His directive here applies to us today, no matter how much hurt we feel. You may not be in a position to sit down and have a heart-to-heart with your ex-spouse, but you can pray for him or her.

This is what Jesus is trying to impress upon us. He loves all of us so much that no one is lost to Him—not even your ex-spouse. No matter how insidious his or her crimes against you are, Jesus wants your ex-spouse to go to heaven. You have the opportunity to help make that happen by praying on his or her behalf.

But love your enemies, do good, and lend, expecting nothing in return. Your reward will be great, and you will be children of the Most High; for he is kind to the ungrateful and the wicked.

~ Luke 6:35

Day 317:
Advice For Finding A New Relationship

We are all familiar with the parable of the rich young man in the New Testament who walked away from Jesus because he could not let go of his possessions. He followed the commandments with zeal but in the end, he was too attached to his stuff. He just couldn't let go of it.

This same mentality can be present when you are looking for a new relationship after divorce. It can become the coveted possession when you're feeling lonely or want to prove to others that you are still loveable and attractive. Finding that new, exciting relationship becomes the thing you must have. The danger, then, is once you have it, you run the risk of not being able to let go of it, even if that person is wrong for you, because if you do, you have yet another failed relationship.

If you would like to be in a good relationship again, I encourage you to make sure you've gone through the annulment process and have a decree of nullity. Then ask God what He wants for you as you search for the right relationship. Seek His guidance and don't settle for less than what you know is right for you.

For wisdom will come into your heart, /
and knowledge will be pleasant to your soul.

~ Proverbs 2:10

Day 318:
The Blessed Mother Can Help

Often when we pray, we are asking God to change something about our circumstances to make them the way we want. It's only natural to want to alleviate our pain and suffering but maybe instead, our prayer should be, "Your will be done, Lord."

This can be the hardest prayer of all at times. It's hard to let go of what we want and just let God work in our lives. If you struggle with accepting the way things are for you now, I invite you to consider the example of our Blessed Mother, Mary, because she can be of help to you.

Her entire life was a beautiful prayer of acceptance. She accepted the role of mother of God which was just the beginning. When Simeon told Mary her heart would be pierced by a sword, she could have said, "Wait a minute, I didn't sign up for this." But she did not. Her entire life was about doing God's will.

Let Mary's example help guide you in seeking what God has in store for you today and in your future.

Then Mary said, "Here am I, the servant of the Lord;
let it be with me according to your word."

~ Luke 1:38

Day 319:
Struggling To Be Chaste?

---◇---

Why is the decision to remain chaste so difficult? There are many factors that contribute to this, but society's message that 'if you're not having sex, there's something wrong with you' compounds the struggle. Magazines, billboards, television shows, movies and music all attack every sensibility we might have toward living a chaste life. If you are struggling with the idea of committing to celibacy until you marry again, don't believe the lie that something is wrong with you.

The truth is, you elevate your status as a human being when you practice chastity by not giving in to your base instincts. When you resist temptation, you are in control of your desires, instead of your desires controlling you, which brings freedom. Each time you resist the temptation, your level of spirituality and maturity is upgraded with virtues and graces that fortify you for the next temptations that will come.

This kind of freedom brings joy. You could indulge in what feels good and what the rest of society says is "normal," but that's a form of slavery. In choosing to please God, not only is that freeing, but it brings an unprecedented clarity to your heart and mind.

But as servants of God we have commended ourselves in every way: through great endurance, in afflictions, hardships, calamities, beatings, imprisonments, riots, labors, sleepless nights, hunger; by purity, knowledge, patience, kindness, holiness of spirit, genuine love.

~ 2 Corinthians 6:4-6

Day 320:
Getting Through Divorce
With Sanity And Peace

After experiencing a divorce, it can seem like you will never heal from such a devastating wound. People around you might think you should just get up, shake it off, and keep going, when in your mind, everything has come to a screeching halt. So how do you get through the post-divorce years with your sanity and peace?

There are many things you can do, but one great way to affect your situation, immediately, is to pray the Stations of the Cross as often as possible. Praying may be difficult for you at this time which is a natural reaction to losing something precious to you. Praying prayers that guide you, instead of trying to find the words to say, are often a big help in getting yourself back on track.

In your mind and heart, you can witness the immense suffering Jesus chose to bear out of love for you. Knowing that His burden was heavier than anyone has ever carried, that His suffering was more severe than anyone has ever endured, and that He did it all because He loves you brings a kind of consolation nothing else can. It provides hope that when the time comes for you to put this cross of divorce aside, there will be a kind of resurrection for you in a new life. Good Fridays always yield Easter Sundays.

And not only that, but we also boast in our sufferings, knowing that suffering produces endurance.

~ Romans 5:3

Day 321:
Feeling Disconnected From the Church?

As a separated or divorced Catholic, you are an important part of the Catholic Church, and you are welcome in your parish. You are encouraged to participate at mass and in the sacraments but also to attend parish functions, such as men's groups, bible studies, women's reflections, volunteer opportunities, etc. A civil divorce does not prevent you from fulfilling your duties. So if you are an Extraordinary Minister of the Eucharist, Lector, Usher, or involved with some other service to your parish, stay with it. It is important for you as a divorced Catholic to be a part of a community and receive that sense of belonging you're looking for.

St. John Paul II was well aware of the alienation divorced Catholics can feel. He stressed in his address to the Pontifical Council for the Family: "Let these men and women know that the Church loves them, that she is not far from them and suffers because of their situation. The divorced and remarried are and remain her members, because they have received Baptism and retain their Christian faith" (Address to the Pontifical Council for the Family, 24 January 1997).

Remember that, despite your divorce, you are an important member of the Body of Christ, the Church.

Rejoice with those who rejoice, weep with those who weep.

~ Romans 12:15

Day 322:
Suffering Is A Bridge
Between Crosses And Blessings

Suffering plays an essential role in a Christian's ability to understand redemption. There is no change without pain. There is no growth without discomfort. If you've been through a divorce, you know the truth of this well.

Beyond this basic understanding of suffering is the recognition that suffering acts as a bridge between the crosses you bear and the blessings you receive. Suffering is not God frowning upon us, it is not a curse. It is a spiritual refinement that can be brought about by no other means.

There is glory in suffering when it is united to Christ's suffering. Offering up your struggles and sufferings, no matter how big or small, changes you, strengthens you, and builds a higher level of virtue. Let your trials change you into a better, stronger, and more perfect person.

Beloved, do not be surprised at the fiery ordeal that is taking place among you to test you, as though something strange were happening to you. But rejoice insofar as you are sharing Christ's sufferings, so that you may also be glad and shout for joy when his glory is revealed.

~ 1 Peter 4:12-13

Day 323:
The Cure For Suffering Injustice
Is Forgiveness

Many years ago, two snipers killed random citizens in the Washington D.C. area as they made their way up the East Coast. Eventually they were captured and charged. A national news anchorman interviewed the husband of one of the victims, asking him if he felt the death penalty was the right kind of justice to avenge his wife's murder. His answer was, "No. I'd like to see them go to jail and be given the chance to be rehabilitated. I don't need retribution. They should have the chance to make themselves right with God and go to heaven."

His statement is so contrary to the way people normally think. Everybody wants retribution, a public apology, or the offender to lose their job. Divorced spouses fight bitterly for years. But how does any of this make us happy?

We all have to forgive, and we have to do it from our hearts. Deep hurts and wounded hearts need TLC, no doubt, but in the end, the best medicine for suffering due to injustice is forgiveness. I hope that if you are harboring resentment or anger toward those who have hurt you, you will consider asking God for the grace to forgive them. It will truly make a difference in your life and free you from the things that are holding you back.

This is my blood of the covenant,
which is poured out for many for the forgiveness of sins.

~ Matthew 26:28

Day 324:
Your Suffering Is
Another Man's Consolation

One way to help reduce the pain and suffering of divorce is to spend time with someone who is in the beginning stages of that experience. It's amazing how the experience of having walked in someone else's shoes, so to speak, can bring the other person a great deal of consolation when you share it with him.

As a Catholic who has experienced the pain and anguish of divorce and is now moving on to a new, happier phase of your life, I encourage you to use your experiences to help others. Not only can you help someone through one of the toughest times in life, but you would be performing a spiritual work of mercy, namely, comforting the afflicted.

Always be ready to make your defense to anyone who demands from you an accounting for the hope that is in you.

~ 1 Peter 3:15

Day 325:
You Want God To Be Available To You, But How Available Are You To God?

Losing a marriage and intact family can easily take a toll on your relationship with God. Prayer is often the first thing that goes out the window. Yet, God is waiting for you, to help and console you.

As you work on rebuilding your life, why not make an honest assessment of how available you are to Jesus? Why not take this opportunity to boost your level of devotion to Him? All it takes from us is a simple act of love. I love you, Jesus. Thank you, Jesus. He will give you all the graces you need. Every trial you encounter, He will be with you, helping you.

As the Father has loved me, so I have loved you; abide in my love.

~ John 15:9

Day 326:
Single Parents Are Saints In Training

I've known many men and women who despite their bitter circumstances became examples of unthinkable charity toward their ex-spouses. One gentleman, Sam, worked in the same office everyday with his ex-wife. He had to find a way to work alongside her, despite the fact she had left him and their teenage children for another man. For Sam, finding another job was not an option so, instead, he attended daily mass at the nearby cathedral and offered it all up for his ex-spouse.

The daily struggles of single parents go largely unnoticed by most of us. The health and well-being of their children compel them to push through their worries of the present and the fear of the unknown to offer their suffering to Christ for others. They cling to their faith and allow their circumstances to bring them closer to God. It is amazing to witness.

My hat goes off to all you single parents who are walking the road to sanctity. Never forget the trials you are enduring are purifying you, and you are a bright light for the world to see.

I give you a new commandment, that you love one another.
Just as I have loved you, you also should love one another.

~ John 13:34

Day 327:
Find Him In The Interior Castle
Of Your Heart

All of us who have been married and divorced know the awkward discomfort that comes with being in the same room with happily married couples and intact families. We don't wish for anyone else to go through a divorce. In fact, we wouldn't wish it on our worst enemies. But it can be really hard to be in the presence of happy couples who are a reminder of what you don't have anymore. It's a silent suffering we don't talk about.

One powerful way to ease that sort of suffering is by imitating St. Teresa of Avila's popular form of prayer called "The Interior Castle." She describes a person's soul as a great castle with seven mansions, each level preparing the soul to meet Christ in the seventh mansion. It is a beautiful and effective way to find peace with Christ amid the chaos of the world.

A friend of mine used this form of prayer. When she had to face a room full of married couples at a parent meeting for school, she prayed that God would be with her and spent a few moments meditating on meeting Christ in the interior castle of her own heart. She said this of her experience: "I may have arrived alone, but I was never alone that evening. My Beloved was an attentive and loving presence who brought joy to me as we watched His children and mine."

As the Father has loved me, so have I loved you.
Now remain in my love.

~ John 15:9

Day 328:
Release Your Burden!

At a recent conference for divorced Catholics, Archbishop Gregory related his own experience as a child of divorce and how his parents managed their lives after they went their separate ways. He shared that one of the most important things a divorced person needs to do to move past their divorce and into a new phase of life is to let go of the emotional baggage.

"We drag these burdens around with us as if they are important possessions," he said in a dramatic tone, mimicking a person dragging a heavy load. "But all they do is prevent us from having a deeper relationship with Christ, and a deeper relationship with each other." When we insist on clinging to our baggage, we forget that Christ has cleared all that away and makes each of us new.

So how do you sort out and deal with your relationship baggage?

The best way to begin to deal with the contents of your baggage is through prayer and honest reflection. Ask God to give you the graces you need to discern the truth about what's happened.

Rejoice in hope, be patient in suffering, persevere in prayer.

~ Romans 12:12

Day 329:
Don't Fear The Fear of The Unknown

While working to heal from divorce, it is important to recognize that the only thing you have control over is yourself. You can't control your ex-spouse. You can't control your in-laws. You can't control the judges presiding over your case, the lawyers representing you and your ex-spouse, your neighbors, your witnesses, etc. You can only control your own thoughts, words, and actions. Self-control is freedom. It brings great peace. It paves the way for you to do great things with your life.

This is why it is incredibly important to pray and stay close to God during your divorce. Is it easy? No, not at first. But it's essential. Try to make prayer a habit in your life, even if it's just for a few moments in the morning, and see the difference it makes for you.

Do not worry about anything, but in everything by prayer and supplication with thanksgiving let your requests be made known to God.

~ Philippians 4:6

Day 330:
Are You Missing The Signs?

Your life may be filled with trials, questions, and discontent. Comfort may be difficult to find. But don't you see how God is trying to show He loves you? He shows you in the brilliant sunrise, when you wake and start your day. He shows you in the neighbor that stops to check in and see if you're okay. He shows you in the accident you almost were involved in but were saved from at the last minute.

He hasn't forgotten you!

It's in these little moments that we hear the simple ways God speaks to us. *I created this sunrise for you to wake up to and enjoy! You're not invisible to me, I see you when everyone else ignores you! Don't worry about things, I will take care of you! You are precious to me, and I will never forget you!*

These are God's ways of blessing you in the midst of the cross you are carrying so you will know you are not alone. He walks beside you on the road to Calvary, and He will never leave you. I encourage you to take some time and reflect on the past few days to see if there were gifts God gave you that you missed.

Are not five sparrows sold for two pennies?
Yet not one of them is forgotten in God's sight.

~ Luke 12:6

Day 331:
When You're Battling Depression

---◇---

Depression after divorce is a normal experience because the losses sustained occur on many different levels. Loss of the marriage relationship and intimacy; loss of children, friends, possessions, reputation, etc. This is "circumstantial" depression, different than chemical depression but a very real depression, all the same.

Depression due to loneliness is just as big an issue. Many people, married or not, suffer from this type of depression. What can you do if you find yourself suffering from this problem?

Remember God's love for you is like an immense ocean, and you are a tiny drop of water. He wants you to get lost in His love. No matter how bad you may feel or think you are, never forget that you are precious in His sight. Jesus came into the world, suffered and died for you. If you were the only person alive, He would still do it, specifically for you, because He loves you and wants you to be with Him in heaven. Going to Mass and Adoration is a perfect way to let this great hope penetrate your depressed feelings.

The name of the Lord is a strong tower; /
the righteous run into it and are safe.

~ Proverbs 18:10

Day 332:
Meeting Sorrow
With A Sense Of Gratitude

When you can accept the bad times that have been a part of your life but find ways to still be grateful and count your blessings, you become a better person as a result of the suffering. You make huge strides in your emotional growth and healing.

Acknowledging that your suffering has made you a stronger person, or appreciating others more because they were a support to you, or seeing how you've learned to do new things you never thought you'd do is an attitude that spills over into everything. This is what will attract other people to you. Compassion, patience, perseverance, gratitude—all these virtues bring a new dimension to your personality and bring something more to offer in your next relationship.

For surely I know the plans I have for you, says the Lord, plans for your welfare and not for harm, to give you a future with hope.

~ Jeremiah 29:11

Day 333:
Prayer, Psalms, and Peace

One of the greatest crosses to bear during divorce is loneliness. Although intangible, loneliness is just as difficult as bearing the burden of an illness. It affects every aspect of your life and carries with it a pain that is difficult to convey to others.

A good remedy for this pain is prayer. But when you're going through a divorce, prayer might be the first thing you stop doing because it gets hard. Your emotions get in the way, and the pain you feel takes over your thoughts. But remember, prayer is simply communicating with God. God doesn't demand that we are perfect people in order to communicate with Him. He comes to meet you where you are. So if you find you don't have any words to say to God, try using the Psalms as your directive for prayer.

The Psalms are always a wonderful source of prayer and reflection, particularly because they're all about the human condition and reaching out to God. Psalm 25:16 reads: "Turn to me and be gracious to me, For I am lonely and afflicted." Let your loneliness become a bridge between you and God and rely on Him for the strength and the grace to get through this part of your life. Realize the peace that will come when the loneliness ends.

Answer me when I call, O God of my right! / You gave me room when I was in distress. / Be gracious to me, and hear my prayer.

~ Psalm 4:1

Day 334:
You Are The Salt Of The Earth

I often wonder why God allows me, a wretched sinner, to have another glorious day? Why does He continue to shower me with blessings? I believe He allows me to continue on because He loves me; because He wants to use me as His hands and feet. He wants me to serve Him. He wants me to serve others.

God allows our experiences—painful, scary, happy, surprising, shocking—to season us. Coupled with His graces and blessings, we can take these experiences and help others who are distressed in some way. We become the light of the world through our examples of perseverance and hope.

If you're feeling scared, hopeless, or discouraged because of your divorce or your fear of the unknown, don't allow these experiences to make you, the salt of the earth, become tasteless. Take heart and trust that God is using your circumstances to prepare you for great things. You can use your experiences to help others and give them hope.

You are the salt of the earth; but if salt has lost its taste, how can its saltiness be restored? It is no longer good for anything, but is thrown out and trampled under foot.

~ Matthew 5:13

Day 335:
It Doesn't Matter
What Other People Think

When I went through my divorce so many years ago, I went on to rebuild my life feeling like I was wearing a "Scarlet D" that everyone could see. I was horrified that I had to identify myself on an employment or loan application as divorced. I felt I needed to explain to everyone that the divorce wasn't my choice, but that was not always possible. I was frustrated by the fact that the person who got my personal information was just going to think what they were going to think.

But I had to remember, and oftentimes it was a friend or a family member who reminded me of this, that there was so much more to me than being divorced. I had gifts; I had talents; I had a lot to offer someone in a new relationship when the time was right. The suffering I had endured through my divorce and afterward had deepened my faith in God, and I became a better Catholic. I had accepted my faults that contributed to the breakdown of my first marriage and worked hard to change that. In a way, I felt like I was better prepared for a relationship than I ever had been before. I had to believe in myself and ignore the ones that judged me.

Always remember that in God's eyes, you are precious to Him.

O taste and see that the Lord is good; /
happy are those who take refuge in him.

~ Psalm 34:8

Day 336:
The Good, The Bad, And The Ugly

Managing your memories and emotions after divorce can be a quite a challenge. It can be a constant battle, especially if you have direct contact with your ex-spouse on a frequent basis. But this is a critical step in the healing process. It is not only an indispensable tool for your future, but it will also help bring back your self-confidence.

The key to making this happen is praying for God's grace to help you let go and praying for the ones who have hurt you. This is not easy to do at times, but the old adage is true, it's difficult to remain angry at someone when you are praying for them. God's grace can soften any heart and heal all wounds. This takes the sting out of the bad memories.

Learn from the good and the bad. Oftentimes you must dig through a lot of garbage to find what's hidden. But when you unearth that treasure, you can experience a new level of faith.

We know that all things work together for good for those who love God, who are called according to his purpose.

~ Romans 8:28

Day 337:
Turn Your Pain Into Passion

Are you still feeling the pain of your divorce, even though you thought by now it would be different? Don't worry, this is a normal experience. Divorce is a traumatic event so you will always feel some sort of pain associated with memories of your divorce although the sting will dull as time goes by.

A great way to deal with the suffering is by turning your pain into passion.

Passion is a Latin word which means "to suffer." Although this word has taken on quite a different meaning these days, the original definition was the willing suffering of Christ. The word "passion" is intended to describe the transcendence of human desires to a love that is willing to suffer. How does that apply to you?

You can resolve to live each moment in a way that gives meaning to your suffering, such as offering it up for someone you know who is also suffering. Or you can offer it up for the souls in Purgatory. This practice will do more than make you feel like you're doing something worthwhile, it will build your treasure in heaven.

Do not fear, for I am with you, / do not be afraid, for I am your God; /
I will strengthen you, I will help you, /
I will uphold you with my victorious right hand.

~ Isaiah 41:10

Day 338:
Weapon Of Choice

The experience of divorce can leave you feeling helpless and completely out of control, but through reciting the Rosary, you have the most powerful protection against evil.

"The holy Rosary is a powerful weapon. Use it with confidence and you'll be amazed at the results." ~ St. Josemaria Escriva

"The Rosary is my favorite prayer." ~ St. John Paul II

Whether it's been a while since you've prayed the Rosary, or you recite it daily, I highly encourage you to pick up rosary beads and start praying. Here are just a few of the benefits of praying the Rosary:

- It gives us victory over all our enemies.
- It makes it easy for us to practice virtue.
- We grow closer to Jesus through contemplating His life.
- It expiates our sins and enriches us with graces and merits.
- It obtains many graces for us from God.

I hope you will take a little time to pray and know that I offer my daily Rosary for you.

I am not asking you to take them out of the world,
but I ask you to protect them from the evil one.

~ John 17:15

Day 339:
My Ex Was Making My Life Miserable Until I Did This

My phone rang and the caller ID revealed my ex-spouse's number. I instantly felt my stomach do a somersault, and I tried to imagine what the problem prompting his call would be this time. My hands shook a little. My palms were clammy. Not because I was afraid, but because I was angry and fatigued by the thought of yet another battle.

I didn't like being angry and was rather disappointed because I felt I had made some good progress in overcoming the anger. Frankly, this was kind of a surprise. It happened so fast and in such an acute manner. If I really had made such progress, how was it that the mere sight of his name on my phone's screen could set me off and ruin my day? I didn't like that at all.

The answer to my problem was simple. I had a lot of forgiving to do. Forgiveness seemed impossible when I had such righteous anger. Yet, these powerful emotions were like a thermometer registering a 105 degree temperature, a symptom of a much bigger problem.

Do you still struggle with forgiving your ex-spouse and anyone else who has hurt you? If so, I invite you to take fifteen minutes when you can, and pray the Sorrowful Mysteries of the Rosary or the Stations of the Cross. Contemplating the passion of Jesus is a great way to learn to forgive.

And for this reason I suffer as I do. But I am not ashamed, for I know the one in whom I have put my trust, and I am sure that he is able to guard until that day what I have entrusted to him.

~ 2 Timothy 1:12

Day 340:
In The End What Matters
Is How Much You Loved

You stand in the kitchen waiting for the coffee maker to finish making coffee so you can get on with your day. When you get your coffee, you go to work, waiting for 5:00 pm to roll around so you can go home. You do this each day, waiting for the end of the week. As the weeks pass, you wait for the next month and then the next year. As the years go by, what are you waiting for? You wait for the seasons of life to change. Being young, middle-aged, old. The only thing left, then, is to pass from this life to the next and stand before the Lord.

Scripture tells us that in the end, God will judge us on how much we loved others. It's important, then, to keep this in focus and not allow the finer details of everyday life to distract us from the goal of reaching heaven. Live every detail of each day with as much love as possible. Pray for those who have hurt you and work on being more patient, understanding, and kind. These seemingly tiny things all add up to fighting the good fight, and when you've passed from this life to the next, you will hear God say, "Well done, good and faithful servant."

For I was hungry and you gave me food, I was thirsty and you gave me something to drink, I was a stranger and you welcomed me, I was naked and you gave me clothing, I was sick and you took care of me, I was in prison and you visited me.

~ Matthew 25:35-36

Day 341:
When Life's Stress Is Too Much To Bear, Remember These Words

Trying to rebuild your life after divorce can be cruel and unusual punishment. It's devastating emotionally, financially, and interpersonally. It can be tempting to stand in the moment and feel as if there is no hope for your situation to get better. But don't allow this discouragement to drag you down.

Think of Jesus in the boat with the apostles during the storm. Remember they were frightened to death, and when Jesus awoke, He got up, rebuked the wind and the raging waters and all was calm. Then He said to the disciples, "Where is your faith?"

Life can be overwhelming, no question. But in those moments when all seems lost, remember Jesus' words, 'Where is your faith?' Making a simple act of faith, 'Jesus, I believe in you! Help my unbelief,' can bring the calm you need in any situation. Be assured that God will help you.

But strive first for the kingdom of God and his righteousness, and all these things will be given to you as well.

~ Matthew 6:33

Day 342:
Faith Requires Darkness

Faith does not remove the darkness, it does just the opposite;
it requires it.

~ Fr. Tadeusz Dajczer, The Gift of Faith

People have many descriptions about what it's like to go through a divorce. They liken it to falling down a well and not being able to get out. Or wandering in the desert and never coming across an oasis. One of the most powerful descriptions of the suffering is that it feels like you are wandering in a dark room with your hands patting the walls, trying to find the light switch so you can turn it on. But you can't find it. You can't turn on the light.

This is why so many people beg God to tell them why He's allowing this divorce to happen to them. You can't see a good reason for it, and you can't understand God's way of doing things. But inevitably when we come out the other end of the suffering, we begin to understand, even if it's not a complete understanding.

It's much easier to see God's work in your life when you look back. You can't always understand in the present. For this reason, you should never give up your hope in God. Although you may not understand what He is doing or why He is doing it, trust Him that in His love for you, He knows what He is doing. He will bring you into the fullness of light if you hang in there and trust Him.

Trust in the Lord with all your heart, /
and do not rely on your own insight.

~ Proverbs 3:5

Day 343:
Tiny Mercies

———◇———

I didn't know it at the time of my divorce, but I found out later that a neighbor was praying fervently for me through my suffering. This thought helps me every time I'm down, and I know it helped then, too. I have tried to live up to her example ever since.

I call these "tiny mercies," and I believe there are many people who perform these tiny mercies each day whether we know it or not. You probably have people praying for you and aren't aware of it. We know that God works all things for the good of those who love Him, and it's through these tiny mercies that God brings blessings into your life and begins the work of renewal in your soul.

———

Let us therefore approach the throne of grace with boldness, so that we may receive mercy and find grace to help in time of need.

~ Hebrews 4:16

Day 344:
A Shower of Graces

Suffering is a mystery that we won't fully understand until we get to heaven. However, we do know that God will provide us with what we need to survive the suffering so we can come out the other side a better person because of it.

God has a mountain of graces set aside for you so when you pray, share your suffering with Him and ask for the graces you need. God is actively present every moment of your life; calling you to Him and drawing you closer to Him. He will shower you with the graces you need each day through your prayers and reception of the sacraments. Trust God, for He is always there to carry you!

And now I commend you to God and to the message of his grace, a message that is able to build you up and to give you the inheritance among all who are sanctified.

~ Acts 20:32

Day 345:
Man On Fire

In the midst of suffering, it is easy to see only the bad things that are happening. The crosses, the sacrifices, and the indignities you bear can have you so focused on the negative that you become unaware of the positive; the good things that may be happening. Though your heart may be steeped in darkness, there is a purpose to this fire you are walking through.

Through this fiery furnace of suffering, you are being transformed into a new person; a stronger, wiser, purer human being. In learning these hard lessons, you will be a better person because of the experience. Give this fire of purification the chance to ignite your heart and transform you into a new person.

With weeping they shall come, / and with consolations I will lead them back, / I will let them walk by brooks of water, / in a straight path in which they shall not stumble.

~ Jeremiah 31:9

Day 346:
Your Heart Is Like A Vineyard

God never gives up on us, no matter how wretched our lives seem to be. He is always with us, especially in times of trial. Throughout your life, God has tended to your heart as if it were a vineyard, carefully plucking weeds through the graces of the sacraments, forming your conscience and fortifying it with many graces and blessings with the hope it will bear fruit.

You can return this tender love God has given you by offering Him the fruit of His labor. Do not squander His graces by ignoring them or demanding justice for your situation in place of these gifts, but offer God the fruit of your heart: forgiveness toward those who have hurt you, the merciful treatment of your enemies, and your humble trust in Him.

Joy and gladness are taken away from the fruitful field.

~ Isaiah 16:10

Day 347:
Dealing With The Pain Of Rejection

The rejection that comes with divorce occurs on many levels. The rejection of friendship, love and romance, physical intimacy, and trust are all difficult crosses to bear. How in the world can one recover from such betrayal? Well, you can begin by putting it into perspective.

The world is a spiritual battlefield and to win the battle takes much love. Yes, love, even in the face of rejection. You may have loved much up to this point, but you have not loved with perfect love, the way Jesus did. The rejection He experienced is so much greater than our own. Now you have the opportunity to console Christ through your efforts to love those around you, especially those who have hurt you. If you ask Him, He will show you how.

Then he began to teach them that the Son of Man must undergo great suffering, and be rejected by the elders, the chief priests, and the scribes, and be killed, and after three days rise again.

~ Mark 8:31

Day 348:
Persevering When All Seems Lost

Are you feeling overwhelmed by your losses? Does it appear that there is no light at the end of the tunnel? God knows your pain. He wants you to hope in Him and the future He has in store for you because He will not leave you desolate and abandoned. He will bring the Easter Sunday that inevitably comes with your Good Friday. Until then, you must persevere.

But do not be discouraged by this premise. Perseverance in challenging and difficult times builds spiritual muscle and strengthens you for future trials. Pray constantly, pray deliberately, pray with faith, and God will lead you out of your suffering in His perfect time. Saint Monica prayed for her son Augustine's conversion for more than thirty years. If she ever had stopped praying or given up hope, we would not have St. Augustine, Doctor of the Church, today. So, take heart, pray, and hope in Christ's mercy.

Are any among you suffering? They should pray. Are any cheerful?
They should sing songs of praise.

~ James 5:13

Day 349:
Why Won't You Give Me
This Part Of Your Life?

After my divorce, I was so broken and felt fairly hopeless that I would ever be happy again. One day as I sat in my car at a red light, I saw a happy family crossing the street, and my heart was yet again struck by the loss of my marriage. I was reduced to tears. It was at this moment I heard a gentle voice in my heart say, *Why won't you give me this part of your life?* That was the unmistakable voice of God, and He was so gentle and so loving, I could not refuse Him. Through my tears, I resolved from that moment forward to trust in God's plan for my life.

If you are struggling with this kind of sadness, or feeling hopeless about the future, I encourage you to take this same step. Remember that God's love will never fail you; He wants you to be happy, and He will take your brokenness and turn it into something amazing. Let that begin today through resolving to trust Him and His plan for your life.

Let us hold fast to the confession of our hope without wavering,
for he who has promised is faithful.

~ Hebrews 10:23

Day 350:
The Healing Love of Christ

Your divorce causes you to suffer greatly and search for relief and peace. But the world cannot give any of that to you. The world does not know peace, and it cannot offer you what it doesn't possess. Cast your gaze, instead, upon the cross where Jesus hangs out of love for you. It is here you will find peace. It is here you will find the consolation of Christ's sacrifice on the cross.

Jesus suffered His passion and crucifixion out of love for you. He hangs on the cross with a posture of love. His head is bent to kiss you. His arms are outstretched to embrace you. His heart is opened to receive you. Lay your suffering at the foot of His cross and receive the love He is offering you. Then let Him be your model as you carry your own cross.

He heals the brokenhearted, / and binds up their wounds.

~ Psalm 147:3

Day 351:
The 1% Rule

Rebuilding your life after divorce can seem like an insurmountable task at times. There is so much to reconstruct, from finances and stable living arrangements to emotional healing and new friendships. How does one accomplish all this when burdened with the pain of a lost marriage?

There is a way to rebuild without guilting yourself into a hole or stressing yourself out. It's called the 1% Rule. The 1% Rule simply says do one thing better than you did the day before and after a week, a month, six months, you will see marked improvement. That one thing could be biting your tongue when you want to say something spiteful. It could be placing your children in God's hands when they leave with your ex-spouse instead of worrying about them every moment they are away. Whatever that one thing is each day, it will add up over time to real, affirmative progress.

---

*Do your work in good time, and in his own time
God will give you your reward.*

~ Sirach 51:30

Day 352:
The Light At The End Of The Tunnel

How long does it take to heal a broken heart after divorce? Some say just two years, others say three years for every year you were married. People have varying opinions on this. I believe the healing process is different for everyone and is rarely a "one size fits all" process.

The most important task in the healing process is taking time for yourself. This does not mean you are always alone, it just means you take the time to reflect on what has happened and how you will move forward. It means you commit to the hard work of forgiveness and letting go. Your willingness to be honest with yourself about the past and to face the future with a sense of hope plays a big role in getting to the light at the end of the tunnel. When you get there, you will be a completely new person.

For God alone my soul waits in silence, / for my hope is from him. /
He alone is my rock and my salvation, /
my fortress; I shall not be shaken.

~ Psalm 62:5-6

Day 353:
Healing Through Forgiveness

———————◇———————

Forgiveness is a critical key to healing because of the spiritual, moral, and emotional effect it has on us. This can be a bitter pill to swallow, sometimes, because of the seriousness of divorce, but forgiveness is the vehicle that can significantly move you forward in your healing process.

Forgiveness is a huge monster to tackle on your own so remember, you are not alone. Pray to God and ask Him for the grace to forgive, then trust that He will give it to you. Make that a daily prayer.

Don't beat yourself up. Forgiveness takes time and is an everyday process. Just remain open to God's grace. That's all you have to do to allow Him to work on your heart.

Remember that Christ is very close to you as you suffer. He loves you with a passionate and never-ending love. In your journey toward forgiveness, lean on Him. Ask Him for what you need. He is waiting to give it to you and will not leave you alone in your suffering.

———————————

Whenever you stand praying, forgive,
if you have anything against anyone; so that your Father in heaven
may also forgive you your trespasses.

~ Mark 11:25

Day 354:
An Exercise In Gratitude

Change is a guaranteed result of divorce. Divorce changes life on almost every level possible: physically, financially, emotionally, and intellectually. This change typically has a damaging effect on one's self-esteem. But change also has a positive side to it. One positive aspect to what you're going through is the opportunity to rediscover yourself.

This is not meant to be a fluffy "love yourself" kind of thing but an exercise in gratitude. The rejection experienced with divorce can take a severe toll on your self worth so it's important to remember your value, particularly to God. Take time to reflect on the things that make you who you are—your talents, your gifts, and your personality. God has gifted you with strengths and unique abilities that bring happiness to others. No matter what has happened, you are still an important member of your family, your parish and society.

So God created humankind in his image, / in the image of God he created them: / male and female he created them.

~ Genesis 1:27

Day 355:
Feeling Lost and Defeated?
Open Yourself to Christ

Christ's example of weakness is par excellence: He was born into the world as a tiny, helpless infant who had to rely on other people for everything! He hung on the cross at Calvary in what the world saw as complete powerlessness, yet it was the greatest triumph in salvation history. Even today, He appears powerless in the tabernacle, for anyone can take Him out and do what they want: honor Him or desecrate Him.

When you are weak, feeling lost and defeated, stripped of your belongings and precious things, open yourself to Christ, for this is when He has the room to start working in your life. He will be the strength found within your weakness.

He has pity on the weak and the needy,
and saves the lives of the needy.

~ Psalm 72:13

Day 356:
The Hidden Masterpiece

There used to be a show back in the sixties that showcased brilliant artistry. Two or three children would be selected from the audience, brought up on the stage, and asked to scribble on a blank piece of paper attached to an easel. Then selected artists would create a beautiful picture out of the scribble. It was incredible the way they could make a beautiful masterpiece out of a child's simple drawing.

Think of this show if you feel that divorce has destroyed your possibilities for happiness in your future. If you believe that God is almighty and all-powerful, don't you think that He can take your scribbles and turn them into great masterpieces? This is exactly what He wants to do! Place your worries and anxieties about the future in God's hands, then let Him take your scribbles and turn your life into a masterpiece!

I am about to do a new thing; / now it springs forth, do you not perceive it? / I will make a way in the wilderness / and rivers in the desert.

~ Isaiah 43:19

Day 357:
Getting Back to Basics

It can be confusing at times to know which are the rights steps to take after a divorce. Should I move away so I don't have contact with my ex-spouse? Will finding a new relationship make me feel better? Should I stop going to church because it's just too painful? Sometimes going back to the basics is the best way to find your answers.

Just consider these simple questions:

- Will doing _____ bring me closer to God? If our goal in life is to spend eternity with God in heaven, then this should always be the first question we ask ourselves.
- Will doing _____ make me a more loving person? In other words, will this enable you to grow in love for God and others?
- Will doing _____ enable me to use my gifts and talents? God endowed you with gifts and talents for a reason—so you can use them for His glory and the good of others.

This is a great way to discern your answers and be confident in your decisions.

I will instruct you and teach you the way you should go; /
I will counsel you with my eye upon you.

~ Psalm 32:8

Day 358:
Create In Me A Clean Heart, O Lord

Create in me a clean heart, O Lord! This is the perfect prayer to say when the temptations of life tug at you. Struggling with your desire for physical intimacy? Working on taming your temper? Wrestling with thoughts of retribution toward your ex-spouse? Call upon God for strength and grace with this powerful little prayer. It can work wonders.

Don't struggle alone! Ask God to create in you a clean heart, a forgiving heart, a humble heart; for these are the stepping stones to healing and happiness in life.

Create in me a clean heart, O God, / and put a new and right spirit within me. / Do not cast me away from your presence, / and do not take your holy spirit from me. / Restore to me the joy of your salvation, / and sustain in me a willing spirit.

~ Psalm 51:10-12

Day 359:
Offer Christ Your Humiliations

If we contemplate Jesus' passion, we see the cruelty with which the soldiers treated Him. Here was Christ, King of King and Lord of Lords, Creator of the universe, yet He was laughed at, beaten, mocked, and stripped of everything.

In your own way, through your divorce, you have lost so much. You, too, have been stripped of the things that you needed to live. Seeing Jesus so cruelly humiliated acts as a reminder to offer Him the many humiliations you have suffered as a result of your divorce. Ask Him to help you to let go of the hurts, the humiliations, and the embarrassments so you can focus totally on Him, your salvation.

The Lord God has opened my ear, / and I was not rebellious, / I did not turn backward. / I gave my back to those who struck me, / and my cheeks to those who pulled out the beard; / I did not hide my face / from insult and spitting. / The Lord God helps me; / therefore I have not been disgraced; / therefore I have set my face like flint, / and I know that I shall not be put to shame.

~ Isaiah 50:5-7

Day 360:
Old Baggage, New Beginnings

Emotional baggage is the inevitable by-product of divorce. It's there whether we like it or not. Some people actually cling to it as if it were a prized possession or a shield to protect their hearts from further hurt. In reality, it's nothing more than a stumbling block. Many people don't take into consideration that emotional baggage is only there if we allow it to be there.

You don't have to be chained to your baggage forever. Detaching yourself from it takes courage, humility, and determination. Courage, to honestly face the truth of what happened. Humility, to learn the lessons that will follow. And determination, to make the future better by letting go of the past. If you can do these things, you will experience the freedom and peace that come with your new beginning.

For freedom Christ has set us free. Stand firm, therefore, and do not submit again to a yoke of slavery.

~ Galatians 5:1

Day 361:
The Mystery of Faith and Suffering

There was a time when I believed that since I was faithful to God, I should always be happy. Little crosses were to be expected, but I believed I was protected from deep suffering. When the devastation of divorce came my way, I was brought to my knees in disillusionment. *How could You allow this to happen to me, your faithful servant?*

We won't fully understand why God chose suffering as a means to perfection until we face Him at the end of our earthly lives, but one thing is true, He uses our suffering to purify and strengthen us.

You are being perfected in your suffering. Don't fight this process, embrace it. Allow it to purge your anger and pride and make you into a better person. He will support you and bring real meaning to your suffering.

Therefore, let those suffering in accordance with God's will entrust themselves to a faithful Creator, while continuing to do good.

~ 1 Peter 4:19

Day 362:
Receive Help Graciously

Many people have difficulty accepting help from others, even when they are in dire straits. They don't want to be pitied or looked down upon. But that is not how people who sincerely want to help see it.

Your suffering offers those who genuinely want to help the opportunity to be the hands and feet of Christ. What a great blessing to everyone involved! Don't deny them the chance to love Christ through service to you. God will bless you, and through them, He will show you the depths of His love.

For it is a credit to you if, being aware of God, you endure pain while suffering unjustly.

~ 1 Peter 2:19

Day 363:
You Just Never Know
What God Has Planned

There is a priest who went through tremendous suffering when he was a young adult. He was leading a happy life that was going in a good direction, when he suddenly was afflicted with a terrible brain hemorrhage that kept him bedridden for months. He endured terrible suffering during this time of great uncertainty.

If you speak to him today, he will tell you he believes he would never have become a priest if it weren't for that period of suffering. It was God's way of refocusing his attention on things that were more important than what he had been focused on. It was what helped him detach from his own will and embrace God's will, and today, he is happier than he could have ever imagined.

What great things could God be trying to show you through your suffering?

The Rock, his work is perfect, / and all his ways are just. /
A faithful God, without deceit, / just and upright is he.

~ Deuteronomy 32:4

Day 364:
Christ's Transfiguration
Is A Message To You

When children are growing up and becoming young adults, we try to impress upon them that life is not all about finding comfort or being entertained all the time. It's about growing, changing, and being transformed. It can be a hard principle to instill.

When Jesus was transfigured on the mountain with Peter, James, and John, this is exactly what He was trying to impress upon them. But they did not understand. Peter wanted to stay, so much so that he offered to erect tents for Moses and Elijah. Peter was sincere, but he was missing the point.

You were sincere in trying to save your marriage, and God did not want it to fail, but through this terrible event in your life, He will transform you. Let go of the past and let God work in your life. Don't stay where you are, let God transform your heart and bring you new life.

While he was still speaking, suddenly a bright cloud overshadowed them, and from the cloud a voice said, "This is my Son, the Beloved; with him I am well pleased; listen to him!" When the disciples heard this, they fell to the ground and were overcome by fear. But Jesus came and touched them, saying, "Get up and do not be afraid."

~ Matthew 17: 5-7

Day 365:
Litany For The Divorced Heart

O Jesus, Good Shepherd, hear my prayer!

From the temptation to spite those who have hurt me,
deliver me, Jesus!
From the temptation to speak ill of my ex-spouse,
deliver me, Jesus!
From the temptation to ease my pain through indulgent behavior,
deliver me, Jesus!
From the desire to pity myself,
deliver me, Jesus!
From the temptation to blame,
deliver me, Jesus!
From the temptation to give up hope,
deliver me, Jesus!
From the temptation to turn away from you in rebellion,
deliver me, Jesus!
From the temptation to doubt your plan for my life,
deliver me, Jesus!

That I may be willing to forgive those who have hurt me,
Jesus, grant me the grace to desire it!
That I may suffer out of love for you,
Jesus, grant me the grace to desire it!
That I may see my ex-spouse as you see him,
Jesus, grant me the grace to desire it!
That I may accept responsibility for my failings,
Jesus, grant me the grace to desire it!
That I may trust you more each day,
Jesus, grant me the grace to desire it!
That in my darkness, I will seek your light,
Jesus, grant me the grace to desire it!
That in my loneliness, I will draw nearer to you,
Jesus, grant me the grace to desire it!
That my cross may strengthen me,
Jesus, grant me the grace to desire it!
That I may be confident in your love for me
and trust you in all things,
Jesus grant me the grace to desire it!

HOLIDAY REFLECTIONS

The Secret To
Valentine's Day

———◇———

Valentine's Day is upon us, and for those who are divorced, celebrating love is very hard to do. That is, of course, unless you know the secret.

I've heard people say they avoid the "pink" aisle in stores at all costs. I've heard some say they take the money they would have spent on their spouses and spend it on themselves instead. One woman even sent herself a bouquet of roses to her office with an "anonymous admirer" note to defray the embarrassment of her divorce in front of others. It's entirely reasonable to avoid feeling bad, but what is everyone trying to accomplish in doing these things? It's simple. They want to believe they are desirable, valuable, and worthy of being loved. Do you know what the secret is to finding that kind of peace of mind?

The secret is simple—find your self-worth in Christ; understand how much He loves you and how much He sacrificed for you. Try to imagine being passionately loved, the most wildly passionate love you have ever dreamed of. Now realize that this is how God loves you. You are worth everything to Him, and He demonstrated that when He hung on the cross and gave you everything He had to give. You are the one He wants, and He pursues you every moment of the day. He wants to give you the love, peace and happiness you've been waiting for.

God created you with one purpose—to be with Him in heaven. Until that day, your life is spent seeking that happiness. The secret to being happy on earth is looking to God for that fulfillment, not looking to find it in others. Part of the reason why people date, marry, divorce, and start all over again is because they are searching for the fulfillment, peace and happiness that only Christ can bring. This is not to say that dating and marriage are bad—on the contrary. But when your spouse fails you, you should remember that he or she is imperfect, just as you are, and cannot fulfill you in the way God's love can. St. Valentine, or Valentinus the martyr, was happy to die because he knew the love of Christ. He knew that being with Jesus in heaven was worth far more than anything the world could offer him. And it still holds true today. Nothing we can get here on earth, not valentines, nor roses, nor chocolates, nor relationships can match the love and generosity of God.

So on Valentine's Day, focus on God's love for you. Take some time, preferably in the morning when it's quiet, and sit with God. Ask Him to help you find your strength and self-worth in His love. Ask Him to increase your faith! Share with Him all your worries, hurts, concerns and hopes. He loves you and He will bless you for it!

———————

Do not fear, for I have redeemed you; /
I have called you by name, you are mine.

~ Isaiah 43:1

LENT AND EASTER

Ash Wednesday, A Lenten Fast

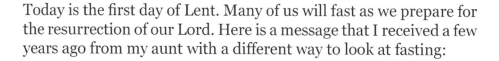

Today is the first day of Lent. Many of us will fast as we prepare for the resurrection of our Lord. Here is a message that I received a few years ago from my aunt with a different way to look at fasting:

Give up harsh words. *Use generous ones instead.*
Give up unhappiness. *Take up gratitude.*
Give up anger. *Take up gentleness and patience.*
Give up pessimism. *Take up hope and optimism.*
Give up worrying. *Take up trust in God.*
Give up complaining. *Value what you have.*
Give up stress. *Take up prayer.*
Give up judging others. *Discover Jesus within them.*
Give up sorrow and bitterness. *Fill your heart with joy.*
Give up selfishness. *Take up compassion for others.*
Give up being unforgiving. *Learn reconciliation.*
Give up words. *Fill yourself with silence and listen to others.*

Then I turned to the Lord God, to seek an answer by prayer and supplication with fasting and sackcloth and ashes.

~ Daniel 9:3

Come Suffer With Me

Anyone suffering because of divorce can easily believe that Lenten sacrifices are an unfair burden; a sort of double-whammy. "Lord," you might say, "Aren't I suffering enough, already? Can't my every-day life just be my sacrifice during Lent?" This seems to be a reasonable request. Jesus, Himself, had much the same prayer when He was in the Garden of Gethsemane the night before He died, "Father, if it is possible, let this cup pass from Me" (Matthew 26:39). Christ understands your humanity better than anyone and offers you, personally, a beautiful gift in return during this season of Lent.

Jesus finished that passage saying, "yet, not my will Father, but your will be done." Christ knew that although He would suffer immensely, His Father's plan was the better way to go. And so Jesus' gift to you is an invitation to say "yes" to the Father's will and then accompany Jesus on the road to Calvary. "Come suffer with Me," He says to you, "Accompany me as I carry my cross to the top of the hill and share with me your anger, your hardships, your betrayals, your pain. And in doing so, if you offer your suffering for the good of souls, I allow you to partake in My work of salvation for the world. You will experience My love in a way that you have never experienced before. Your presence is a consolation to Me, and as you keep Me company, I will make your burden light."

For my yoke is easy, and my burden is light.

~ Matthew 11:30

383

Palm Sunday Reflection

We welcome Him as King, and in less than a week, we will crucify Him like a criminal.

Dear Lord, as I contemplate this scene from your passion today, I think of all the times I personally welcomed You into my heart and then closed it off to You. My heart has been broken, and I mistakenly believed that building a wall would protect me from further hurt. When will I finally learn that my heart was made for You, to love You and to share that love with others?

Today, grant me the grace to recognize You as my King and to worship You always. To know that my healing lies with You. To know that in Your divine providence, You will take care of those whom I cannot. And to always remember, You will work the bad things that have happened to me for my good.

Grant me the grace to embrace my cross with love, as You do, and walk with You to Calvary where my sincere prayer will always be heard:

Jesus, remember me when you come into your kingdom.

~ Luke 23:42

Holy Week Remembrance
Of Christ's Passion And Death

As we begin our Holy Week observance, I invite you to join me on the path to Calvary with Jesus through meditation. In order to experience a deeper meaning of Christ's suffering, we will focus on the issues that you face as a divorced man or woman, with an effort to unite these experiences with the Passion and Death of Jesus Christ. In finding healing from divorce, it is important to reflect on Christ and all that He suffered for our sake. Through this reflection, we can more profoundly understand the Paschal Mystery and witness the undying and passionate love that Jesus has for us.

Monday of Holy Week:
Precious Tears

There are many types of tears—tears of sadness, tears of joy, tears of laughter, and so on. Tears are the natural result of reacting to strong emotions, and if you've been through a divorce, you understand that, at times, tears are "precious." They are almost like drops of blood that are being shed, born out of the pain you feel. Others have also cried these precious tears.

When Jesus visited Lazarus, Martha and Mary shortly before He was to be crucified, Mary was so moved by recognizing her own sinfulness before Jesus, her Lord and Savior, that she sat at His feet, washing them with her tears. Those precious tears cleansed her heart with true contrition and a desire to give her heart entirely to the Lord. She dried His feet with her hair and anointed Him. In doing so, she demonstrated her true love for Jesus and the understanding that He was her Savior.

Our Blessed Mother, Mary, also shed those precious tears at the foot of the cross as she watched her innocent Son suffer. Who can soothe a mother's anguish over the death of her child? Who can console our Lord as He hangs on the Cross dying a cruel death? You can. **We all can!**

You can do this through your faithfulness to Him as you suffer the loss of your marriage. Let Jesus know that His death was not in vain through your meditation of His Passion and development of a genuine sorrow for your sins. Console Him by not giving in to the frustration, loneliness and disappointment of your divorce. Sit at His feet and let your precious tears wash away whatever does not belong and whatever is keeping you from being close to Him.

Mary took a pound of costly perfume made of pure nard, anointed Jesus' feet, and wiped them with her hair.
The house was filled with the fragrance of the perfume.

~ John 12:3

Tuesday of Holy Week:
One Of You Will Betray Me

---◇---

"After he received the piece of bread, Satan entered into him" *(John 13:27).* These are heavy words like boulders. They carry so much meaning.

Judas accepted the temptation laid before him, and Satan entered his heart. Judas had spent time with Jesus. He had experienced the powerful significance of being called by Christ to follow. He experienced the joy of personally knowing Jesus and saw how much He loved. He witnessed the incredible healing that took place from the miracles Jesus performed. None of it was enough! None of it was enough to melt Judas' hardened heart. Judas no longer belonged to Jesus. He had allowed his love and his sensibility to be deceived by human respect. His heart was hardened and dishonest. He had not accepted Jesus' teaching on the Bread of Life. Was that the beginning of the end for Judas?

As someone who has experienced divorce, it is easy to see your own betrayals in this scene. Did someone you love suddenly harden their heart against you? Did someone you love allow their love and sensibility to be deceived by human respect? Sometimes it's like the flip of a switch, the person you loved from the beginning is suddenly gone, and someone you don't recognize is left in their place. Sometimes this happens abruptly, and sometimes it happens gradually over the years. Either way, the pain of betrayal can be an unforgettable experience in life. But take consolation in the example Jesus gave. Jesus, being completely human and completely divine, understands your pain like no other. He suffered the ultimate, unjust betrayal. Christ is closer to you in your moments of suffering than at any other time. He hurts because you hurt. Unite your suffering to Christ and help each other carry the cross. And then, look forward to sharing the Resurrection with Him because all things are made new in Christ.

After he received the piece of bread, Satan entered into him.

~ John 13:27

Wednesday of Holy Week:
Midnight in the Garden of Gethsemane

When you have some time to yourself, relax, close your eyes, and imagine yourself in the Garden of Gethsemane with Jesus on the night before His crucifixion. Peter, James, and John are snoring about fifty feet away. You see Jesus on His knees, tense, upset, and overwhelmed by the understanding of the suffering He is about to endure. And in His divine humanity as He sweats drops of blood, He prays, "My Father, if it is possible, let this cup pass from me; yet not what I want but what you want" (Matthew 26:39). God's will was for His Son to suffer and die.

What is going through your mind as you watch this scene? Does it make you wonder if God actually hears your prayers? Does it make you wonder why God allowed so much suffering in your own life? Why is suffering the path that God chose? Why does He allow it? Why did He allow His only Son to die a horrific death? The reason is because God knows what He is about. His ways are not ours, and His plan is always greater than what we can imagine. His ways always bring good out of bad.

As a parent, I know full well that my children don't understand the love that I have for them. Nor do they understand the way that love is sometimes manifested. I make them do a task that they might view as difficult and unpleasant because I know it is good for them. God deals with us in much the same way. There is growth, both emotional and spiritual, that comes from experiencing pain, and that is good. Although your burden may seem unbearable now, trust that God, in His wisdom, will bring good things out of it. His only Son suffered and died a humiliating and painful death, but the good that came out of that is priceless—eternal life with Him in heaven!

The Father knows what He is about. His plan is beyond our thinking. Let us go to Him in prayer with our requests and resolve ourselves to His will.

Again he went away for the second time and prayed,
"My Father, if this cannot pass unless I drink it, your will be done."

~ Matthew 26:42

Holy Thursday: Washing Their Feet

It's often difficult to understand just exactly what God is doing with our lives. Sometimes, especially when things are good, you can see, understand and accept God's plan and be grateful for it. Other times, especially when things are seemingly going wrong, His plan is a total mystery. You just keep trying to figure out what is going on. You think that God's way of doing things should be the same way you would do things. You want what is good, so shouldn't that be what God's plan is?

At the last supper, Jesus washed the feet of the apostles. When He came to Peter, Peter was flustered. He said, "You will never wash my feet." But Jesus insisted, telling him that if he did not let Him wash his feet, He would not inherit eternal life. And Peter replied, "Lord, not my feet only but also my hands and my head!" (John 13:9). This situation was similar to the day Jesus called Peter the "rock" on which He would build His Church. Moments after bestowing this honor, making Peter the first pope, Jesus sternly rebuked him. Peter did not want Jesus to suffer and be crucified. Peter's bottom line, in both circumstances, was even if he did not understand, he would still trust Jesus.

As Jesus washed the feet of the disciples, He told them to follow His example to wash one another's feet. What does that mean for us in today's society? What does that mean for you, personally? Very simply, it means that we should take the role of the servant, the humble one. How different the world would be if we all sought to serve one another instead of ourselves and our foolish pride.

For you, it means you must wash the feet of the people in your life, including the ones that are causing you grief. The person that won't let you change lanes on the freeway, or takes the parking spot you were waiting for, or the co-worker at the office who gossips about you or constantly boasts; the family member who constantly points out your faults or criticizes how you live; the ex-spouse who incessantly makes your life painful and difficult through many tactics. Yes, in all these situations, we need to serve if we want to follow Jesus. We wash their feet through refraining from using harsh language with them, refraining from being angry with them, and refraining from blaming them. We wash their feet through forgiving them and praying for them.

This is not what the world teaches us to do but in the end, "the world and its desire are passing away, but those who do the will of God live forever." (1 John 2:17). We may not understand why God does things the way He does, but let us place all our trust in Him, as Peter did, and follow Him.

For I have set you an example,
that you also should do as I have done to you.

~ John 13:15

Good Friday Reflection

"It is finished" (John 19:30).

No one can escape the finality of those words. As you contemplate this scene of Our Lord's death, imagine being there at the foot of the cross. Feel the chill of the cold wind blowing on your face. Hear the weeping of Mary Magdalene and the village women as our Blessed Mother holds the lifeless body of her innocent Son in her arms. Experience the deep pain of watching Joseph of Arimathea place His broken body in the tomb. The tomb was such an empty and cold place.

Pray: Lord Jesus, one of the last things You said before You died was, "I thirst." You thirst for souls; You thirst for my soul. I reflect on my soul in light of your words, Lord. Is it empty and cold like the tomb you were laid in? In Your great mercy and love for me, Jesus, You have provided an opportunity to soften my heart. Through the sacrament of reconciliation, You make my soul a warm and inviting place for You to live. I need your help to overcome my fear and weakness. Fill me with true contrition for my sins and a deep desire to begin again. Pour your grace down upon me in this sacrament of love.

After this, when Jesus knew that all was now finished,
he said (in order to fulfill the scripture), "I am thirsty."

~ John 19:28

Rejoice! He Is Risen!

Scripture tells us, there is a time for everything:

> For everything there is a season, and a time
> for every matter under heaven:
>> a time to be born, and a time to die;
>> a time to plant, and a time to pluck up what is planted;
>> a time to kill, and a time to heal;
>> a time to break down, and a time to build up;
>> a time to weep, and a time to laugh;
>> a time to mourn, and a time to dance;
>> a time to throw away stones, and a time to
>> gather stones together;
>> a time to embrace, and a time to refrain from embracing;
>> a time to seek, and a time to lose;
>> a time to keep, and a time to throw away;
>> a time to tear, and a time to sew;
>> a time to keep silence, and a time to speak;
>> a time to love, and a time to hate;
>> a time for war, and a time for peace. ~ Ecclesiastes 3:1-8

Today is a day to rejoice. No matter what your situation, hope lies in the very thing we celebrate today—the Resurrection of our Lord, Jesus Christ, and His triumph over sin and death.

---

*May the peace of Christ that surpasses all understanding
be yours today.*

THANKSGIVING

Thanksgiving Day Inspirations

For the gift of waking up this day,
I thank you, Lord.
For the gift of my sight and being able to speak and hear,
I thank you, Lord.
For the gift of your glorious nature and the beautiful world
I live in,
I thank you, Lord.
For a roof over my head,
I thank you, Lord.
For the gift of free will and the ability to make my own choices,
I thank you, Lord.
For the gift of my faith,
I thank you, Lord.
For the gift of knowing what it is like to love,
I thank you, Lord.
For the gift of my children and the opportunity
to be a parent to your precious souls,
I thank you, Lord.
For the gift of experiencing life as a child, brother or sister, parent,
aunt or uncle or cousin, grandmother or grandfather,
I thank you, Lord.
For the gift of my friends who love me,
I thank you, Lord.

For the gift of experiencing a little of what you suffered for me
as I carry my cross,
I thank you, Lord.
For the gift of the good things you will bring out of my suffering,
I thank you, Lord.
For the ways you will change my heart and help me become
a better person because of what's happened,
I thank you, Lord.
For the little triumphs as well as the big ones,
I thank you, Lord.
For forgiving me, for saving me, and for not forgetting about me,
I thank you, Lord.
For calling me by name into existence out of all eternity
and giving me a purpose in life,
I thank you, Lord.
For loving me with the most perfect love
anyone could ever experience,
I thank you, Lord.
For the promise of eternal life with you in heaven,
I thank you, Lord. Amen.

O Lord, our Sovereign, / how majestic is your name in all the earth!

~ Psalm 8:1

ADVENT AND CHRISTMAS

Live And Let Change

As we approach the season of Advent, we are coming to a close of the liturgical year. It's a reminder that things don't stay the same, just as it is for human beings.

Everything that lives, changes. If it doesn't change, it dies. As a Christian, you need to grow and change. You may find this difficult to accept because of your struggle with divorce. You may be suffering terribly from the pain caused by the loss of your marriage. But this change does not have to be for nothing.

St. Paul is a great example for anyone who is suffering. St. Paul's life was difficult, but his sufferings did not deter him from his mission. He was always willing to go wherever the Holy Spirit led him. He was always open to a higher purpose.

Be open to the changes that will occur because of your new state in life. Like St. Paul, if you follow the Holy Spirit wherever He leads you, your pain will be transformed into peace.

Sorrow is better than laughter, /
for by sadness of countenance the heart is made glad.

~ Ecclesiastes 7:3

Preparing Yourself For The Holidays

All the time I hear people saying, "The holidays just snuck up on me." As a divorced person, you can't let this happen. You don't want the holidays to sneak up on you. You may find yourself faced with all kinds of difficult situations, overwhelming emotions, and lots of downtime that can be conducive to pity parties. You want to prepare for these things and prepare as early as possible.

First, make a list of things to do when you know you'll have a lot of time to yourself. You know all those things you say you never have time for? Put those things on the list—cleaning out closets, reading a book, waxing your car, etc. It won't be glamorous, but you will have things to do to keep yourself occupied and busy. This is the key to avoiding the depression that accompanies these situations. And don't forget to put something that you would enjoy on there, too!

Next, think ahead to how you will handle those uncomfortable and awkward comments that come from family and friends. Personally, my rule of thumb is "charity at all costs" which means I need to look past the remark and recognize who is saying it. I know they don't like to see me in pain, and they want to help but don't really know how or quite what to say. Let them off the hook and know they are simply trying to find a way to make you feel better. Even if it doesn't make you feel better. Lastly, focus as much as you can on Christ as an infant and His glorious birth. For this, we can always give thanks because for us, it means everything; it means eternal life.

The voice of one crying out in the wilderness:
"Prepare the way of the Lord, make his paths straight."

~ Luke 3:4

Christmas Presents

Some years ago, we were going through terrible financial difficulty. Christmas was approaching, and I was in panic mode because I knew there was no money to buy gifts for the children. I did not want the children to know how bad things were, so I had to be resourceful to make Christmas special. So one day, I invented what I called "Presents." I sat down and started cutting out strips of paper. On each piece of paper I wrote down a "Present," something that each one of us could do for another to show our love. There were fun things, like giving everyone a high five or singing or reciting a tongue twister. There were chores, like cleaning the kitchen that night or folding the laundry. There were acts of charity, such as "name two reasons why you love your sister" or "give mom a big hug and kiss." I thought of as many as I could, folded up all the pieces of paper, and put them in a big fish bowl. When everyone had finished their dinner, we each drew a piece of paper from the bowl, read it, and performed the act with smiles and laughter all around! It was a HUGE HIT! These little acts of love that were done while we were carrying our cross, truly prepared us for the coming of Christ. And we still do Presents every year.

If you are finding it difficult to see the joy in this Advent season, take a small step in the direction of hope. Create your own Presents that you and your children can give to each other. I know many of you will find yourselves without your families during the holidays, but you can still bring a cup of coffee to a co-worker, give the store clerk a pleasant smile, stick a few dollars in the charitable donations bucket, or bring some baked goods to neighbors you don't know that well. Just a few suggestions on how to find simple ways to give when you feel as if you've got nothing to give.

On entering the house, they saw the child with Mary his mother; and they knelt down and paid him homage. Then, opening their treasure chests, they offered him gifts of gold, frankincense, and myrrh.

~ Matthew 2:11

Getting Through the Holidays Gracefully

Long before the holidays come along, many divorced men and women experience a feeling of dread. The thought of putting on a smiling face for relatives, or having to answer sensitive questions, or enduring well-intentioned but painful comments like, "There's someone better out there for you" can make anyone barricade themselves in their room. These things, however, often take a backseat to the fact that the real pain comes from the constant reminder that the family is no longer whole. What can you do to get through the holidays gracefully?

First, try to remember that your family doesn't like to see you suffer. They want to take away your pain, and many times their statements are rooted in the desire to "fix" the problem. Second, begin planning for the time you will have off from work or school. Volunteering is always a great way to take the focus off your sadness. Make sure you have as little time alone to feel sorry for yourself as possible. Lastly, try to remain focused on this season in our Church. If the emotions are overwhelming you, contemplate Mary and Joseph's sudden midnight trip to Bethlehem, or the fact that a stable was all that was available to them to have their Baby. Unite your suffering with Jesus, Mary and Joseph and ask them to obtain the graces you need at this time. You may be pleasantly surprised at the good things you will receive through your sincere efforts.

Take my yoke upon you, and learn from me; for I am gentle and humble in heart, and you will find rest for your souls.

~ Matthew 11:29

The Incredible Glory
Of The Little Babe In The Manger

Christ was born into the world as a tiny, helpless infant who had to rely on other people for everything! Food, clothes, shelter, education, etc. His mother bore Him in a stable without heat or a midwife in attendance. Yet this tiny baby showed humanity the strength of God that is contained within this human poverty and weakness. Thirty-three years later, He hung on the cross at Calvary, in what the world saw as complete powerlessness, but instead was the greatest triumph in salvation history.

As you approach Christmas Day, you may be feeling weak, lost and defeated, stripped of your precious things. But remember Christ's example to us of strength in weakness as the example par excellence! Open yourself to Christ, for this is when He has the room He needs to start working in your life. He needs your weakness and your trust. He will give you the strength you need.

But he said to me, "My grace is sufficient for you, for power is made perfect in weakness." So, I will boast all the more gladly of my weaknesses, so that the power of Christ may dwell in me.

~ 2 Corinthians 12:9

Your Christmas Miracle

In the years after my divorce, I had many difficult Christmases. But one year in particular, I spent a lot of time during Advent reflecting on the Holy Family, trying to glean something new from the story I had heard for so many years of my life. I tried to imagine being present in this story and see the scene exactly as it played out. I imagined Mary and Joseph as they traveled to Bethlehem, shut out in a cold stable to deliver their newborn child. I imagined fifteen-year-old Mary, nine months pregnant, and probably more uncomfortable than she'd ever been in her life, riding a donkey in the middle of the night. I was thoroughly impressed by her sacrifice. I observed the obedience of Joseph who had nearly divorced his pregnant wife and still didn't quite understand why things were happening to him the way they were but trusted and obeyed God. His simplicity deeply affected me.

Then I contemplated Christ as a newborn in the manger. I pictured the baby Jesus and looked at His little hands, knowing they would be pierced and torn one day—for me. I looked at His little newborn body and thought of the sword that would one day pierce His side, shedding blood and water for my salvation. During this time of reflection, God's grace was somehow softening my hardened and bitter heart, replacing the anger I felt toward my ex-spouse with a tiny seed of forgiveness.

As that seed began to sprout and take root, it was like scales fell off my eyes. I experienced a whole new existence. That Christmas during mass, as I received Jesus in Holy Communion, my heart was filled with His love. It didn't change my circumstances, but it changed me. Despite all I had been through, I began to experience peace in my heart and hope for good things in my future.

This Christmas may be very difficult for you, and I'm truly sorry if it is. But know that I am praying for you. My hope is that you will let go of any bitterness and anger you may be harboring so you can make room for the peace of Christ's birth. Just like the little children whom Christ tells us we must be like to go to heaven: Believe, forgive, hope.

This will be a sign for you: you will find a child
wrapped in bands of cloth and lying in a manger.

~ Luke 2:12

About the Author

Lisa Duffy is a Catholic writer with an enthusiasm for helping others carry their crosses, specifically divorced Catholics. She suffered the pain and devastation of divorce back in the early 1990s, and after years of intense struggle and spiritual growth, she remarried in the Church and has three miracle children. She now dedicates her time to helping people rebuild their lives after divorce so that they may find happy, lasting relationships.

Lisa is author of several books including *The Catholic Guide to Dating After Divorce*, creator of the parish divorce support program *Journey of Hope,* and creator of the Journey of Hope 2010 and 2011 international conferences in Atlanta, Georgia. She blogs for CatholicMatchInstitute.com, Patheos.com, and contributes to many print and online publications such as Aleteia.org. Aside from her spending time with her family, Lisa speaks at conferences, appears on television and radio, coaches one-on-one and in groups, and holds online events. She resides in South Carolina.

Thanks for reading

A Road To Healing:
Daily Reflections For Divorced Catholics

For more resources and to sign up for our newsletter, please visit our website:
www.CatholicMatchInstitute.com

HOPE & HEALING AFTER DIVORCE

"You all know that this [divorce] is a particularly painful situation. . . The Christian faith involves giving oneself to the community of the Church, a community that promises each believer that he or she will never be left alone in suffering and that calls each Catholic to reach out to others."

- Pope Benedict XVI

www.catholicmatch.com/divorce